Praise for *Monster:*

"The story of one man's painful spiritual journey from violence toward transcendence . . . A book that sheds harsh new light on the violence that erupted . . . after the Rodney G. King verdict . . . The volume attests not only to Shakur's journalistic eye for observation, but also to his novelistic skills as a storyteller, an ear for street language that is as perfectly pitched as Richard Price's, a feeling for character and status potentially as rich as Tom Wolfe's. This is a startling and galvanic book."

—Michiko Kakutani, *The New York Times Book Review*

"A first-person chronicle that exquisitely documents urban warfare in the streets of Los Angeles since 1975, providing ample glimpses of its reach into the claustrophobic prison system . . . Scott-Shakur pens this vicious treatise with relentless sincerity riddled occasionally by humorous anecdotes. . . . Scott-Shakur proves an impressively capable storyteller."

—Wanda Coleman, *Los Angeles Times Book Review*

"Is Shakur compelling? Yes . . . he voices the rage and desperation among bangers."

—Roger Chesley, *Detroit News and Free Press*

"*Monster* is an incredible, often brutal look at one man's rise from child to "ghetto star" killer to revolutionary black activist. . . . Shakur has an excellent dry wit and a fast–paced style. . . . The importance of *Monster* is that it explains the gang lifestyle; it shows us how much more there is to learn before we can begin to solve the problem." —Jeff Charles, *Houston Chronicle*

"This remarkably straight-ahead account of life as a member of an L.A. street gang lets those of us on the other side feel and know a bit of what street life is like."

—Scott Walker, *Star Tribune* (Minneapolis)

"The real force of the book comes from the angry electrifyingly violent, streetwise credibility that Scott gives his story. While it is no doubt depressing, it demonstrates the stern measures that must be taken to control our cities, and the monsters who terrorize them. . . . Anyone who wants to know why our urban areas are dangerous combat zones should read these stunning, sinister memoirs of Kody "Monster" Scott."

—Louis B. Cei, *Richmond Times-Dispatch*

"[An] electrifying life story: an angry, stunningly violent odyssey through gang warfare and prison to redemption."

—*Kirkus Reviews*

"[*Monster*] is a compelling and frightening, bizarre, yet insightful insider's look at the society that spawned gangs and the gang's violent retaliation within it. If that was [Sanyika Shakur's] goal with *Monster,* to reveal the vagaries of gang-banging and its deadly consequences, he clearly succeeds."

—Tony Cox, *Quarterly Black Review of Books*

"With an eye for detail and a straightforward writing style, Shakur depicts a myriad of brutal scenes with cool clarity."

—Steve O'Neil, *Albuquerque Journal*

"[Shakur] makes us see what we do not want to see through writing that is fresh, forceful and poetic."

—June Arney, *Virginian Pilot and Ledger Star*

"The book succeeds as the story of a man struggling to make sense of a hostile environment, and Shakur must be credited for progressing from gang-banger to messenger."

—Paul Tullis, *Might Magazine*

MONSTER

The Autobiography of an L.A. Gang Member

Sanyika Shakur, aka Monster Kody Scott

GROVE PRESS
New York

Printed in the United States of America
Published simultaneously in Canada

This is a work of nonfiction; the names of some persons involved, however, have been changed.

Library of Congress Cataloging-in-Publication

Scott, Kody, 1964–
Monster: the autobiography of an L.A. gang member/Kody Scott.
ISBN: 978-0-8021-4144-6
1. Scott, Kody, 1964– . 2. Crips (Gang). 3. Gangs—California—Los Angeles—Biography. I. Title.
HV6439.U7L774 1993 364.1'06'092—dc20 93-14948

Designed by Laura Hough

Grove Press
an imprint of Grove/Atlantic, Inc.
841 Broadway
New York, NY 10003

Distributed by Publishers Group West

www.groveatlantic.com

10 11 12 13 14 16 15 14 13 12 11

To my dearest mother, Birdie M. Scott, who had the courage to push me out in a world of which we control so little.

To my children, Keonda, Justin, and Sanyika, who have been an endless light at the end of my tunnels, and my indomitable wife, Tamu Naima Shakur, for patiently waiting for my change.

WE CARRY ON

ACKNOWLEDGMENTS

Acknowledgments are in order for those who have stood up against the tumultuous blaring of the pied pipers' propaganda and who in spite of unpopularity have gone a separate way; those who have taught me the right way to resist.

Bullet-proof love is extended to Muhammad Abdullah and the Islamic Liberation Army, the Provisional Government of the Republic of New Afrika, the Spear and Shield Collective, and all the forces involved in the New Afrikan independence movement to free the land.

Bullet-proof unity is extended to Ice Cube and Da Lench Mob, Public Enemy, X-Clan, Blackwatch, KRS-One, BDP, Paris, Operation from the Bottom, Digable Planets, Tupac Shakur, Ice-T, Kris Kross, and Bone from Athens Park Bloods.

ACKNOWLEDGMENTS

Bullet-proof appreciation is extended to Bill Broyles and Karen Jensen-Germaine from ABC Productions for their invaluable help and inspiration with my project; Léon Bing for writing about us when it was unpopular to do so; Thomas Lee Wright for his incredible eye for detail and all-around friendship; and my agent, Lydia Wills, for her never-ending determination to go forward. Teflon bullets are sent to the sellouts.

CONTENTS

PREFACE

Helicopters hover heavily above, often no higher than the treetops that dot the battlefield. Staccato vibrations of automatic gunfire crack throughout the night, drowned out only by explosions and sirens. People hustle quickly past, in a dangerous attempt to get anywhere the fighting happens to be heaviest. There is troop movement throughout the city, and in some areas the fighting is intense. The soldiers are engaged in a "civil war." A war without terms. A war fought by any means necessary, with anything at their disposal. This conflict has lasted nine years longer than Vietnam. Though the setting is not jungle per se, its atmosphere is as dangerous and mysterious as any jungle in the world.

Neither side receives funding from any government, nor

does either side claim any allegiance to any particular religion or socioeconomic system of government. There are no representatives from either faction in the United Nations, nor does either side recognize the Universal Declaration of Human Rights. Recruitment, or conscription, begins at eleven years of age.

Squads of five usually make raids into neighboring territories for preemptive strikes or retaliatory hits on enemies and targets useful to the opposition. Although both armies are predominantly made up of males, there are many females involved in the fighting. These infrastructures were built initially on robberies and extortions. Today, however, they are maintained by proceeds from major narcotics deals and distribution throughout America. Each army has a distinct territory—the boundaries of some very large areas are broken by enemy cluster camps. Each army has a flag, to which total allegiance is pledged. Each army has its own language, customs, and philosophy, and each has its own GNP.

The war has been raging on for twenty-two years. The death toll is in the thousands—wounded, uncountable, missing-in-action unthinkable. No one is keeping a tally. No one has noticed, except for those recently involved in the fighting and those indirectly drawn in by geographical location, economic status, or family association.

Other than this, the war has been kept from the world, hidden like an ugly scar across the belly of an otherwise beautiful woman. Under the guise of being a showpiece for the world where prosperity is as easily found as water in a stream, America, for all her ostensible beauty, has an ugly scar across her belly that she has tried repeatedly to suppress and keep hidden from curious onlookers. More than a few times she has almost been exposed, and this ugliness brought to light, but always another garment would quickly be thrown over the rough spot and all the turmoil and ugliness again blanketed. But not this time.

On April 29, 1992, the world witnessed the eruption of South Central Los Angeles, the concrete jungle–battlefield of the Crips and Bloods. The scar of over twenty years that had been tucked out of sight and passed off as "just another ghetto problem" burst its suture and spewed blood all across the stomach of America. People watched in amazement as "gang members," soldiers of the Crip army, pelted cars with rocks, sticks, and bottles, eventually pulling civilians from their vehicles and beating them. This was hours after they had routed a contingent of LAPD officers. Troop movement escalated, and Los Angeles was set ablaze. All this began on Florence and Normandie in South Central, the latest Third World battlefield.

I have lived in South Central Los Angeles all my life. I grew up on Florence and Normandie. That is part of my territory. I was recruited into the Crips at the ripe old age of eleven. Today I am twenty-nine years old. I am a gang expert—period. There are no other gang experts except participants. Our lives, mores, customs, and philosophies remain as mysterious and untouched as those of any "uncivilized" tribe in Afrika. I have come full circle in my twenty-nine years on this planet, sixteen of those with the Crips. I have pushed people violently out of this existence and have fathered three children. I have felt completely free and have sat in total solitary confinement in San Quentin state prison. I have shot numerous people and have been shot seven times myself. I have been in gunfights in South Central and knife fights in Folsom state prison. Today, I languish at the bottom of one of the strictest maximum-security state prisons in this country.

I propose to take my reader through the life and times of

my own chilling involvement as a gang member with the Crips. I propose to open my mind as wide as possible to allow my readers the first ever glimpse at South Central from my side of the gun, street, fence, and wall. From my initial attraction and recruitment to my first shooting and my rise to Ghetto Star (ghetto celebrity) status, right up to the South Central rebellion and the truce between the warring factions—the Crips and Bloods. Although no longer aligned with gang or criminal activity, I still draw a great deal of support from this quarter.

Come with me then, if you will, down a side street lined with stolen cars and youngsters armed with shotguns and .38 revolvers, lying in wait for the enemy, all members of a small gang. Then return with me five years later as the street is lined with luxury cars, dope dealers, and troops with AK-47 assault weapons, the gang now an army.

Let me tell you of funerals that have been overrun by enemy forces and the body stolen and "killed again" for reasons of psychological warfare. Think not that this war is some passing phase to be ironed out with a truce in five days—impossible! Sophistication has not, by any means, passed the gangs of Los Angeles. Surveillance, communication, and technology have now found their way into the military buildup of these two army factions.

It is not for glory that I write this. It is out of desperation for the survival of the youths and civilians who are directly and indirectly involved in the fighting. I will attempt to draw serious analytical conclusions designed to bring about a better, more in-depth overstanding of this malady, so as to help reach workable solutions for all concerned. As with my life, I propose to bring the reader full circle to show the reality of a city gone mad in an attempt to rank as the nation's murder capital longer than the District of Columbia and more consistently than Detroit.

Look then, if you dare, at South Central through the eyes of one of its most notorious Ghetto Stars and the architect of its most ghastly gang army—the Crips.

I

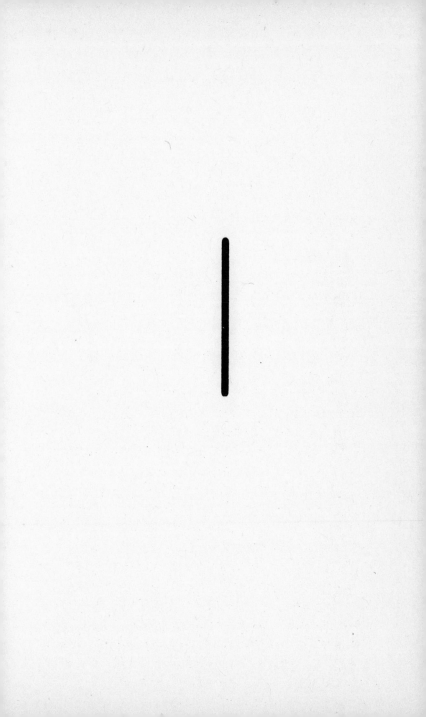

INITIATION

June 15, 1975. I proudly strolled across the waxed hardwood stage of the auditorium at the Fifty-fourth Street elementary school under the beaming stares of my mother, aunt, and Uncle Clarence. Taking my assigned place next to Joe Johnson, as we had rehearsed for a week, I felt very different, older, more "attached" than any of my fellow classmates. This feeling made me stand more erect, made me seem more important than any of my peers on stage—even Joe Johnson, who was the "king of the school."

Looking back now it's quite amusing to remember how proud I was and how superior I felt next to Joe Johnson. I first sensed my radical departure from childhood when I was suspended a month before graduation, driven home by Mr. Smotherman, the principal, and not allowed to go on the grad-class outing for flashing a gang sign on the school panorama picture.

Mr. Smotherman was appalled and accused me of destroying a perfectly good picture, not to mention that I was "starting to show signs of moral decay." Actually, half of the things Mr. Smotherman told me I didn't catch, because I wasn't listening, and besides, my mind had been made up weeks prior to my having gotten caught flashing the sign on the panorama picture. How I expected to get away with flashing on a photograph is beyond me! But, too, it points up my serious intent even then. For I was completely sold on becoming a gang member.

As our graduation activities bore on, my disinterest and annoyance at its silliness escalated. I was eager to get home to the "'hood" and to meet my "moral obligation" to my new set of friends, who made Joe Johnson look weak. After the seemingly year-long graduation my mom, aunt, and Uncle Clarence congratulated me with lunch at Bob's Big Boy. I was the second youngest in a family of six. Everyone's name began with a K: my brothers were Kevin, Kerwin, and Kershaun—the youngest; Kim and Kendis were my sisters. My father and I never got along and I couldn't overstand why he mistreated me. While returning home I sat transfixed to the side window, looking out into the streets but not seeing anything in particular, just wishing my Uncle Clarence would drive faster. Tonight was to be my initiation night, and I didn't want to be late or miss out on any activities that might occur during my first night "on duty." Bending the corner onto our block in my uncle's Monte Carlo, I sunk down in the back seat to avoid being seen in my white knit suit and tie. Peeking to make sure the coast was clear, I bolted past Moms into the house, down the hall, and into my room for a quick change.

"What's your damn problem, boy?" bellowed Moms from the hallway. "I know you don't think you going out anywhere until you have cleaned up that funky room, taken out this trash and . . . "

I never heard the rest. I was out the window and in the wind—steaming toward my destiny and the only thing in this life that has ever held my attention for any serious length of time—the streets.

Stopping once I'd gotten around the block, to collect my coolness, I met up with Tray Ball, who had accepted my membership and agreed to sponsor me in.

"What's up, cuz?" Tray Ball extends his very dark, muscular, veined hand.

"Ain't nothin'," I respond, trying to hide my utter admiration for this cat who is quickly becoming a Ghetto Star. A Ghetto Star is a neighborhood celebrity known for gangbanging, drug dealing, and so on.

"So, what's up for tonight, am I still on or what?"

"Yeah, you on."

As we walked to "the shack" in silence, I took full advantage of the stares we were getting from onlookers who couldn't seem to make the connection between me and Tray Ball, the neighborhood hoodlum. I took their looks as stares of recognition and respect.

At the shack, which was actually a backhouse behind Tray Ball's house, I met Huckabuck, who was dark, athletic, very physical, and an awesome fighter. He came to California from New York—accent included. For the most part he was quiet. Leprechaun, who we called "Lep," was there. I had known him prior to this, as he went to school with my older brother. Lep had a missing front tooth and a slight build. Fiercely loyal to

Tray Ball, Lep stood to be second in command. Then there was Fly, who dressed cool and with an air of style. Light-complexioned and handsome, he was a ladies' man, not necessarily vicious, but was gaining a reputation by the company he kept. Next was G.C., which stood for Gangster Cool. G.C. was possibly the most well-off member present, meaning he "had things." Things our parents could not afford to give us. He gangbanged in Stacy Adams shoes.

"What's your name, homeboy?" Huckabuck asked from across the room, through a cloud of marijuana smoke.

"Kody, my name is Kody."

"Kody? There's already somebody name Kody from the Nineties."

I already knew this from hearing his name. "Yeah, but my *real* name is Kody, my mother named me that."

Everyone looked at me hard and I squirmed under their stares—but I held my ground. To flinch now would possibly mean expulsion.

"What?" Huck said with disbelief. "Your mother named you Kody?"

"Yeah, no shit," I replied.

"Righteous, fuck it, then we'll back you with it. But you gotta put work in"—"put in work" means a military mission—"to hold it 'cause that's a helluva name."

Fly piped up from his relaxed posture in an armchair. "I'm gonna put some work in tonight for the set."

"We know," Lep replied, "we know."

G.C., who was dressed like a gas-station attendant in blue khakis with a matching shirt, and I started out to steal a car. All eyes were on me tonight, but I felt no nervousness, and there was no hesitation in any of my actions. This was my "rite of passage" to manhood, and I took each order as seriously as any Afrikan would in any initiation ritual from childhood to manhood.

G.C. was the "expert" car thief among the set. "Gone in Sixty Seconds" could have very well been patterned after him. He had learned his technique from Marilyn, our older homegirl who always keeps at least two stolen cars on hand. Tonight we were out to get an ordinary car, possibly a '65 Mustang or '68 Cougar—these, I learned, could be hot-wired from the engine with as little as a clothes hanger touched on the alternator and then the battery. The only drawbacks here were that the gas gauge, radio, and horn would not work and the car would only run until the alternator burned out.

Nevertheless, we found a Mustang—blue and very sturdy. G.C. worked to get the hood up and I kept point with a .38 revolver. I was instructed to fire on any light in the house and anyone attempting to stop us from getting this car. I paced in a tight to-and-fro motion, watching closely for any sign of movement from either the house, the yard, or the shrubbery flanking the house. I was the perfect sentry, for had any movement occurred or any light flashed on, I would have emptied six rounds into the area, if not the person. Actually, I had only fired a real gun once, and that was into the air.

Under the cloak of darkness I heard G.C. grunt once and then lift the hood. It took him longer to unlatch the hood than to start the car. The engine turned once, then twice, and finally it caught and roared to life.

"It's on," G.C. said, with as much pride as any brand-new father looking for the first time at his newborn child. We slapped hands in a gesture of success and jumped in. Pulling out of the driveway I noticed a light turn on in what I believed to be the kitchen. I reached for the door handle with every intent of shooting into the house, but G.C. grabbed my arm and said, "Don't sweat it, we got the car now."

On the way back to the shack, I practiced my "mad dog" stares on the occupants of the cars beside us at stoplights. I guess I wasn't too convincing, because on more than a few occasions I was laughed at, and I also got a couple of smiles in return. This was definitely an area to be worked on.

At the shack we smoked pot and drank beer and geared up for the mission—which still had not been disclosed to me. But I was confident in my ability to pull it off. I have never, ever felt as secure as I did then in the presence of these cats who were growing fonder of me, it seemed, with each successive level of drunkenness they reached.

"Cuz, you gonna be down, watch," Lep pronounced, as if telling a son in law school he would be a great lawyer. He stood over me and continued. "I remember your li'l ass used to ride dirt bikes and skateboards, actin' crazy an' shit. Now you want to be a gangster, huh? You wanna hang with real muthafuckas and tear shit up, huh?"

His tone was probing, but approving. He was talking with heated passion and the power of a general-father.

"Stand up, get your li'l ass up. How old is you now anyway?"

"Eleven, but I'll be twelve in November." Damn, I'd never thought about being too young.

At this time I stood up in front of Lep and never saw the blow to my head come from Huck. Bam! And I was on all fours, struggling for equilibrium. Kicked in the stomach, I was on my back counting stars in the blackness. Grabbed by the collar, I was made to stand again. A solid blow to my chest exploded pain in bold red letters on the blank screen that had now become my mind. Bam! Another, then another. Blows rained on me from every direction. I felt like a pinball. I knew now that if I went down again, I'd be kicked. And from the way that last kick felt I was almost certain that G.C. had kicked me with his pointed Stacy Adams.

Up until this point not a word had been spoken. I had heard about being "courted in" ("courted in" means to be accepted through a barrage of tests, usually physical, though this can include shooting people) or "jumped in," but somehow in my still-childish mind I had envisioned it to be a noble gathering, paperwork and arguments about my worth and my ability in regard to valor. In the heat of desperation I struck out, hitting Fly full in the chest, knocking him back. Then I just started swinging, with no style or finesse, just anger and the instinct to survive.

Of course, this did little to help my physical situation, but it showed the others that I had a will to live. And this in turn reflected my ability to represent the set in hand-to-hand combat. The blows stopped abruptly and the sound of breathing filled the air. My ear was bleeding, and my neck and face were deep red, but I was still standing. When I think about it now, I realize that it wasn't necessarily my strength that kept me on my feet, but the ways in which I was hit. Before I could sag or slump I was hit and lifted back up to standing.

Tray Ball came in and immediately recognized what had taken place. Looking hard at me, then at the others, he said, "It's time to handle this shit, they out there."

In a flash Lep was under the couch retrieving weapons—guns I never knew were there. Two 12-gauge shotguns, both sawed off—one a pump-action, the other a single-shot; a .410 shotgun, also a single-shot; and a .44 magnum that had no trigger guard and broke open to load. G.C. was now in possession of the .38 I had held earlier.

"Give Kody the pump." Tray Ball's voice echoed over the clanging of steel chambers opening and closing, cylinders turning, and the low hum of music in the background. "Check this out." Tray Ball spoke with the calm of a football coach. "Kody, you got eight shots, you don't come back to the car unless they all are gone."

"Righteous," I said, eager to show my worth.

"These fools have been hangin' out for four days now. Hittin' people up"—"hittin' people up" means asking where they are from, i.e., which gang are they down with—"flaggin' and disrespectin' every Crip in the world."

I sat straight-backed and hung on every word Tray Ball said.

"Tonight we gonna rock they world."

Hand slaps were passed around the room and then Lep spoke up.

"If anybody get caught for this, ride the beef, 'cause ain't no snitchin' here."

Head nods and looks of firmness were exchanged, and then the moment of truth.

We piled into the Mustang, Tray Ball driving—and without a gun. Lep sat next to Tray Ball with the old, ugly .44. Huck, directly behind Lep, held the .410 between his legs. Fly, next to him, had the sawed-off single-shot 12 gauge. I sat next to him with the pump, and G.C. was on my left with his .38. In silence we drove block after block, north into enemy territory.

"There they go!" Lep said, spotting the gathering of about fifteen people. "Damn, they deep too, look at them fools!"

I looked at my enemy and thought, "Tonight is the night and I'll never stop until I've killed them all."

After driving down another block, we stopped and got out. Each checking his weapon (mine being the most complicated), we started out on foot. To rid the world of Bloods, Brims in particular, stealthily we crept up to where the gathering had assembled to promote their set's ideology. Tray Ball sat idle in the car and was to meet us halfway after we had worked over the enemy. Hanging close to buildings, houses, and bushes, we made our way, one after the other, to within spitting distance of the Bloods. Our strategy was to just jump out and shoot, but on the way Lep made the point that the single-shots should go first. Then I would follow suit with eight shots, Lep with five shots in the .44, and G.C. with six in the .38.

Huck and Fly stepped from the shadows simultaneously and were never noticed until it was too late. Boom! Boom! Heavy bodies hitting the ground, confusion, yells of dismay, running, and then the second wave of gunfire. By my sixth shot I had advanced past the first fallen bodies and into the street in pursuit of those who had sought refuge behind cars and trees. Forgetting everything, I completely threw myself into battle.

A Blood who had seemingly gotten away tried to make one last dash from the safe area of a car to, I think, a porch. I remember raising my weapon and him looking back—for a split second it was as if we communicated on another level and I overstood who he was—then I pulled the trigger and laid him down. With one shot left I jogged back to the initial site of contact. Knowing fully that I had explicit orders not to return with any rounds in my weapon, I turned and fired on the house before which they had originally stood. Not twenty paces later,

Tray Ball sped to a stop and we all piled in, frightfully amped from the climax of battle.

Back in the shack we smoked more pot and drank more beer. I was the center of attention for my acts of aggression.

"Man, did you see this little muthafucka out there?" Fly said to Huck with an air of disbelief.

"Yeah, I saw him, I knew he was gonna be down, I knew it and—"

"Shut up, man, just shut the fuck up, 'cause he can still tell on all of us." Silence rang heavy in my ears, and I knew I had to respond to Lep's reaction.

"If I get caught, I'll ride the beef, I ain't no snitch."

Although my little statement lessened the tension, Lep's words had a most sobering effect. Tray Ball announced my full membership and congratulations were given from all. It was the proudest moment in my life. Tray Ball told me to stay after the others had left. I milled around, still high from battle, and thought of nothing else but putting in work for the set.

"Check this out," Tray Ball said. "You got potential, 'cause you eager to learn. Bangin' ain't no part-time thang, it's full-time, it's a career. It's bein' down when ain't nobody else down with you. It's gettin' caught and not tellin'. Killin' and not caring, and dyin' without fear. It's love for your set and hate for the enemy. You hear what I'm sayin'?"

"Yeah, yeah, I hear you," I said. And I had heard him and never forgot nothing he said from that point on.

Also from that point on Tray Ball became my mentor, friend, confidant, and closest comrade. He allowed me acts of aggression that made my name soar with alarming effects.

* * *

The seriousness of what I had done that evening did not dawn on me until I was alone at home that night. My heart had slowed to its normal pace and the alcohol and pot had worn off. I was left then with just myself and the awesome flashes of light that lit up my mind to reveal bodies in abnormal positions and grotesque shapes, twisting and bending in arcs that defied bone structure. The actual impact was on my return back past the bodies of the first fallen, my first real look at bodies torn to shreds. It did little to me then, because it was all about survival. But as I lay wide awake in my bed, safe, alive, I felt guilty and ashamed of myself. Upon further contemplation, I felt that they were too easy to kill. Why had they been out there? I tried every conceivable alibi within the realm of reason to justify my actions. There was none. I slept very little that night.

I've never told anyone of these feelings before.

In the neighborhood, respect was forthcoming. In 1977, when I was thirteen, while robbing a man I turned my head and was hit in the face. The man tried to run, but was tripped by Tray Ball, who then held him for me. I stomped him for twenty minutes before leaving him unconscious in an alley. Later that night, I learned that the man had lapsed into a coma and was disfigured from my stomping. The police told bystanders that the person responsible for this was a "monster." The name stuck, and I took that as a moniker over my birth name.

As Monster, however, I had to consistently be more vicious and live up to the name. Tray Ball was there for me at every level, but Tray Ball was at least four years older than I. Still, we could relate. In 1978, Tray Ball was captured for knocking a guy out in front of the police, who were questioning him about being robbed. I was left with Fly, Lep, Huck, and G.C., who seemed to have lost their will to "get busy" when Tray Ball was locked up. So I went in search of a "road dog," or best friend.

I had been seeing the name Crazy De written on walls for some time and had a pretty good idea who he was. While walking up the alley one day toward G.C.'s house, I ran into Crazy De. We formally introduced ourselves and I asked him if he wanted to kick it with us. Although he was already from the set, he kicked it with other people. A jovial cat of my age with happy eyes and a Hollywood smile, De became my road dog. He clicked right away with the others, too. I took him over to the "white apartments," where we had everybody and their parents claiming or sympathizing with our set. He loved it!

From this point on, De and I were inseparable. The set was still relatively small, and everyone knew each other. (When speaking of small here, I mean approximately seventy-five to eighty people. That's a small set. Today it's not unusual for sets to be a thousand deep.) Though there were various sides and sections, we all met up at meetings in our park, though this usually occurred only when someone had been killed or some serious infraction had been committed. I continued to see and associate with G.C., Lep, and the others—but it wasn't the same with Tray Ball missing. He was the glue that bonded us.

Besides this, I had escalated from little homie to homie, and was putting in much work and dropping many bodies. In fact, some shied away from me because I took things, they said, "too serious." But Crazy De overstood me and my thirst for a reputation—the purpose of all gang members. For I had learned early that there were three stages of reputation to go through before the title of O.G.—Original Gangster—would apply righteously:

1. You must build the reputation of your name, i.e., you as an individual;
2. You must build your name in association with your particular set, so that when your name is spoken your set is also spoken of in the same breath, for it is synonymous; and
3. You must establish yourself as a promoter of Crip or Blood, depending, of course, on which side of the color bar you live.

In 1978 I was fourteen, and still working on the first stage. But I had as much ambition, vitality, and ruthlessness to succeed as any corporate executive planning a hostile takeover—a merger was out of the question. Gangbanging in the seventies was totally different than what's going on today. The gang community on both sides was relatively small, contained in certain areas, and sustained by the few who kept the faith in their belief. Although all gang members are in the military, all gang members are not combat soldiers. Those who are stand out, and *all* fear and respect them. This is true up to this day.

By now, of course, I had acquired my own weapon—a blue steel .44 Bulldog. It was small and fit into my pocket. I kept it on me at all times.

One afternoon my little brother and a friend (both later would become fierce combat soldiers in their own right) were eating chili dogs at Art's. Frank—my brother's companion—left his chili dog wrapper on the outdoor table, and it blew to the ground. Eric, who had been hired by Art as not just a cook but a watchdog, was a hothead already and needed little provoking to act like a complete fool. He told my brother to pick up the paper. When my brother explained that it was not his paper,

Eric became angry and collared my brother and ripped his shirt. Angry and confused, my little brother went home and got my mother, older brother, and sister.

I was out on a ten-speed, patrolling the 'hood with, of course, my .44. Ironically, I was sitting on the corner of Florence and Normandie Avenue, across from Art's, when I saw my mother's car with everyone in it pull to a stop at the light. Here I was, waiting for some action, and it pulled right up—fate, I guess. My older brother signaled for me, so I followed them across the street to Art's. No one knew I was strapped. As I rode up my older brother was standing there arguing with Eric. Then my brother hit Eric in the face, and they began to fight. I immediately dismounted and rushed up on Eric's flank to get a hit in, but he was swift and struck me in the ear, knocking me back. All the while my mother was frantically shouting for us to stop, stop the fighting. Mad now, and insulted, I drew my weapon, aimed, and pulled the trigger. CLICK.

Damn, I remember thinking, *I only got three bullets*, and I didn't know where in the cylinder they were! The click stopped everything—and then everybody seemed to move at once. Eric ran toward the chili stand, my brother rushed to me. Before I could aim and fire, my brother and I were wrestling over the gun.

"Give me the gun, I'll shoot him!" my brother exclaimed.

"No, let me shoot him!" I shouted back.

In our battle for control, the gun was now pointing at my mother's chest.

CLICK.

My mother jumped, and momentarily I was paralyzed with fright. In this instant I let go of the gun and my brother turned and fired into the chili stand.

BOOM! The .44 sounded like a cannon.

CLICK: another empty chamber.

Eric had by now retrieved his shotgun and was on his way out after us. Seeing him coming, both my brother and I turned and ran. We had barely rounded the corner when the report from the shotgun echoed behind us. He chased us through several yards, firing and tearing up people's property. He fired a total of eight times, but we escaped unscathed—except for our pride. My mother, sister, and little brother also escaped unharmed, though in great fear for us, for they knew not our fate.

After meeting back at home, my mother wanted to send us all out to my uncle's house in West Covina. We protested and stayed. The next morning, however, while I'm standing at the bus stop waiting to go to school, Eric pulls up and mad dogs me. "What you lookin' at, punk?" he shouts from the car.

"You muthafucka!" I respond, though scared because he may have a gun and I couldn't get mine out the house, since after yesterday's episode Moms was searching me. There were three young ladies standing there, as well, so my pride and integrity were also involved, not to mention my reputation. I had to stand my ground.

Eric leapt from the car, circled from the front, walked up, and hit me in the mouth—*bam!* I faltered and became indecisive. But in an instant I knew I needed an equalizer, because he lifted his shirt to reveal the butt of a pistol in his waistband. I turned and bolted. Running at top speed with tears streaming down my face, I made my way back home, went right in, got my gun, and trotted back to the bus stop. I was hoping the bus hadn't come, so that the three girls who saw me get hit could watch me kill him.

Art's chili dog stand has been on Florence and Normandie since the forties, and it was still in its original decor—open and primarily wood, with big windows facing onto Florence Avenue. The bus stop was across Florence on Normandie. Turning the corner on Seventy-first at a steady trot, I was relieved to find the three girls still there, almost as if waiting for me. Passing them, I heard one say to another, "That boy is crazy!"

I was taking no chances this time; with six rounds ready I stood in the street in front of Art's on Florence Avenue. Commuter traffic was moderate, so I waited for the light to turn red. Once I saw that I could safely break back across Florence and then to a backyard, I opened fire on Art's. BOOM! BOOM! Loud baritone echoes cracked the morning stillness, as chunks of wood and shards of glass flew off of Art's with magical quickness. Cordite filled my nostrils and revenge filled my heart. BOOM, BOOM, BOOM, BOOM! Six shots I emptied into the tiny dwelling, hoping to have killed Eric, who had just opened up for business.

No such luck. I was captured the next day and given sixty days in juvenile hall, but actually only served nineteen due to overcrowding. Once out, my reputation was stronger than ever. Even Eric gave me my props, though grudgingly.

The very next week after my release for the shooting, De, myself, and two members of the Rollin' Sixties Crips (later the Sixties and my set—the Eight Trays—would become mortal enemies) were on our way to Rosecrans Skating Rink, which was where everybody who was somebody in the gang world went to further promote their name and set. Walking up Manchester Avenue westbound, we passed Pearl's Gym and Best Yet hair salon. Still within the established boundaries of my set, we came to a halt at the corner of Manchester and Gramercy Place, waiting for the light to change so we could trek on to Van Ness, where our bus was to depart. We heard two reports from what sounded like a .38. The sound came from the direction of Duke's hamburger stand, which stood on the southeast corner of Gramercy Place off of Manchester Avenue. Duke's had recently become contested territory, as the Inglewood Family Bloods had begun to frequent it regularly in hopes of establishing it as theirs. (Gangs tend to function as "states" in regard to taking or colonizing territory.)

We looked toward the sound and we saw Fly and Tracc breaking out of Duke's, running right at us across the street. Tracc had what appeared to be a big, long-barrel .38 revolver in his left hand. Without stopping, Tracc exclaimed, "Y'all bail, we just busted on some Families!" They kept running, right on past us.

We hadn't done nothing, so we kept on our way. Not a minute later, a white Camaro screeched out of Duke's parking lot. "There they go!" we heard an almost hysterical voice yell from the car. A second car, a huge orange Chrysler, came out of the parking lot, bearing down on the bumper of the Camaro—which was now heading directly for us. We scattered.

De and I darted into an adjacent alley behind Best Yet, and I don't know where Stone and Snoopy went. The chase was on. Hopping a fence in the alley, De and I hid ourselves in the dense shrubbery behind Pearl's Gym. The Camaro and the Chrysler roared up and down the alley several times as we lay in wait. The thoughts that ran through my head were hopes that the Blood who had been shot would die.

It's significant that there were no Crip-on-Crip wars raging in these times. The worst enemies were Crip and Blood sets. Today, of course, Crips are the number-one killer of Crips. In fact, Crips have killed more Crips in the last twelve years than the Bloods have killed in the entire twenty-two-year conflict. And, too, sets in the Crip and Blood communities have increased twenty-fold—so that there is literally a gang on every street. Also, there are the huge conglomerate sets spanning hundreds of city blocks at a time, extending themselves into other cities and counties. It's not at all unusual for one of these huge conglomerate sets to be policed by five separate divisions of both the LAPD and the sheriff's department. (The East Coast Crips are one such set, spanning from First Street in downtown Los Angeles to 225th Street in Harbor City.)

After an hour or so we emerged from hiding and walked east in search of Snoopy and Stone.

"Man, them fools was mad!"

"Huh?" De spoke up. "If they would have caught us, Kody, we'd have been through." De was very serious when I finally looked at him. "Why you didn't bring the gat"—gat is a generic term for gun—"anyway?"

" 'Cause of the metal detector at Rosecrans. Ever since the Families blew the door off they been really tight on security. Besides, all homies be there anyway."

We found Snoopy and Stone standing on Western Avenue and Manchester. Well aware that the Families were now out in mass looking for revenge, we devised a new strategy for getting to the skating rink. Just then the orange Chrysler hit the corner of Eighty-fifth Street, packed with occupants from the Red side. We had two choices: run into the street and try to make it across Western and further into the interior of our 'hood and possible safety, or run into the surplus store behind us and hope they wouldn't follow in view of such a big civilian crowd. We quickly chose the second option.

De broke first, with myself, Snoopy and Stone heavy on his heels. Looking back, I immediately realized that we had made a terrible decision, for the Bloods were bailing out of the huge Chrysler like beans from a bag and chasing us straight up into the store! I remember taking one last look back after I had jumped the turnstile, and I knew then that we were trapped.

The surplus kept a huge green trash can by the door that was full of axe handles of heavy oak; each Blood grabbed one as he entered. Alarmed and not knowing if this was a gang raid on his store, the manager locked the door once the last Blood had come in. I knew we'd be beaten to death.

Snoopy and Stone went one way and De and I went another. I followed De up some stairs that led to an attic supply room and further entrapment. Four Bloods followed us up, swearing to kill us for shooting their homeboy. One guy was shouting about the victim being his brother. Damn, how in the hell had we gotten into this?

Running up into the small attic area, I thought seriously about death for the first time in my life, and for the slightest second I wanted to turn and tell the Bloods, "Hey, all right, I quit. I'm only thirteen, can't we talk?" Diplomacy was as foreign as Chinese to us all, but it's a trip that when under pressure, clear thoughts seem to abound.

Stopping and crouching, temporarily having lost my tail among the rows and aisles of stocked clothing, I heard De trying to explain that it wasn't us, that they had made a mistake. "Hold it, man, it wasn't us," I heard De say in a cracking tone of sincerity and terror.

"You a muthafuckin' lie, we saw you Blood!"

Crack! "Ahh!" Crack! "All right, man, all—" Crack! "Ahh!"

Terrified, I crouched lower and closed my eyes, hoping they wouldn't kill De, who was now on the ground and silent. But the beating continued. I felt completely helpless.

"Here go another one!" Crack! "Ahh!" Across the top of my head the heavy axe handle came down. Swoosh! A miss, and in an instant I was on my feet. Crack! "Ahh!" One to the back, as I tried to get past another in the semidarkness.

"Wait, wait!"

"Fuck that wait shit, fool, you didn't wait when you shot Mike!" Crack! "Ohh." Crack! "Ahh . . . " Blackness.

When I came to I was on my stomach, handcuffed. Next to me was De. Both of us were bloody and swollen. Craning my neck to the left, I saw Snoopy and Stone. They, too, looked whipped and soiled.

"Which one of you did the shootin'?" a police officer asked from somewhere behind me.

"Him, the one in the blue overalls and sweat jacket."

That was me! "What?" I managed to say through fog and loose teeth. "Who, me?"

"Yeah, you, you little crab-ass punk!" (Crab is a disrespectful term used by Bloods against Crips—defacing the enemy.)

For the first time, I noticed her—a girl. Looking up, I brought her into focus. Never seen her in my life.

"You a lie, bitch—" I blurted out and was abruptly cut short by a police boot on the back of my neck.

"Shut up, asshole. Are you sure this is the shooter, ma'am?"

"Yes, yes I'm sure, officer. He was trying to talk to me and then found out who I was with and just pulled a gun and started shooting. I just—"

"Bitch, you lying, I don't know you, I was—Uuugh!" I was

kicked in the side by the police officer who had already smashed my face to the ground.

"One more word, dipshit, and you'll get another ass whipping."

I felt it best to remain silent. I was transported to the Seventy-seventh Street Division and booked for attempted murder.

Now I was hoping he wouldn't die. I was the only one arrested. At the station, I was asked a series of questions, of which I answered none. I was taken to Los Padrinos Juvenile Hall to await court. I was no doubt facing a camp term now, worse than juvenile hall, for the attempted murder, which I hadn't even had anything to do with. The strict code of the street held me, though, and I said not a word to anyone about who had really shot the Blood.

The Hall (juvenile hall) was another territory to conquer, just like South Central, but all the sets were now face-to-face, bunched together in units of fifty. I met Crips who I had heard about and others whose names I had seen spray-painted on walls. I fought against Bloods whose sets I had never heard of and, of course, against those who were our worst enemies.

I went to trial three months later. The gang turnout was surprising. Along with my family, at least fifteen of my homeboys came. All were in full gear (gear is gang clothes, colors and hats—actually uniforms). On the other side, the Bloods also came in force, in full gear. Tension ran thick through the courtroom as stares of hate were passed back and forth.

I was told after the first day that a shoving and shouting match had taken place in the hallway outside the courtroom. My homeboys had to serve as bodyguards for my family. On my next court date, I was released into the custody of my mother, pending trial proceedings. During my next scheduled court date, three gangs filled the court—the Crips, the Bloods, and the LAPD CRASH unit (Community Resources Against Street Hoodlums).

The atmosphere was tight with rage that ran just below the surface, and this is where I began to grasp the meaning of "low-intensity warfare." I couldn't believe how personally the Bloods were taking this. After all, their homie was shot "legally," that is, within the unspoken but generally known guidelines of gang warfare. He was fired on in a free-fire zone. In fact, this area, as I explained above, was contested. We had gotten numerous reports of Blood sightings. He just happened to be the first caught.

And now here they were, taking the war off the streets and into the courtroom, where neither of us had the experience to win. Blood after Blood testified to my shooting of their homeboy—all lying, of course. The final witness was the victim himself. He was thin and wearing cornrowed braids; his would be the testimony to seal my fate. After the prosecution asked him to convey the events of that day and time, he was asked if he saw the person who had shot him in the courtroom. Silence. And then . . .

"No, he ain't the one who shot me."

"What?" The D.A. couldn't believe his ears.

Murmurs filled the courtroom as his homies whispered their disbelief at his honesty. Snickers and taunts came from our side. I sat still and just looked at Mike, who stared back without a semblance of hate, but with a sort of remorse for having put me through this.

The judge's gavel struck wood. "Case dismissed."

I stood, still looking at Mike, who was dismounting the witness stand.

"Tell Tracc," Mike whispered as he passed me, "that I'll see him at another time."

I said nothing, turned, and fell into step with my crew.

That night I led an initiation party into Family 'hood and dropped two bodies. No one was captured.

My relationship with my mother soured continuously as I was drawn deeper and deeper into the streets and further away from home and school. My sixth-grade graduation was my first and last. Actually, it was the last time I ever seriously attended school—for academic purposes. My homeboys became my family—the older ones were father figures. Each time I shot someone, each time I put another gun on the set, each time I successfully recruited a combat soldier, I was congratulated by my older homeboys. (Every gang member is responsible for bringing guns into the gang. We used to break into neighbors' homes and steal their weapons. Now, with the influx of narcotics and overseas connections, guns are bought by the crate.) When I went home I was cursed for not emptying the trash. Trash? Didn't Mom know who I was? Apparently not.

De and I continued to campaign hard, but we couldn't transcend that first stage of reputation. Today, it's twice as hard to break through because there are so many competing factors: the Crip and Blood communities have grown to astronomical proportions since the seventies, the police have a vast array of laws and techniques to curtail the bangers' growth, and, of course, there are narcotics—everyone wants to be rich and no one wants to go to war.

On February 14, 1979, when I was fifteen, I was captured for assault and auto theft. I took a car from a man by striking him over the head. Too drunk to drive, I hit every car on the block in my attempt to flee the area. The last and final car I struck was a Cadillac. Once I slammed into the rear of the Cadillac, the bumpers must have gotten caught, because the car I was in would not go into reverse. As I exited the vehicle I was surprised to find practically the whole block chasing me. Actually, it turned out to be just the owners of the cars I had hit. I'm certain the chase closely resembled a lynch mob in pursuit, because the chasers had sticks and baseball bats and were initially all running together in a tightly held group. But as I began to accelerate out of fear and youthful energy, their group dwindled to two.

Both men were quite intent on catching me. I continued to run, however, at top speed. Falling farther and farther behind, they cursed me and swore my death upon capture. I struggled on. Luckily, I had taken the vehicle not far from my home (I lived on Sixty-ninth Street and I had taken the car on Sixty-sixth). Therefore, my run was not that far.

Rounding the corner onto my block I was elated to see that my pursuers were at least four houses behind me. I darted down the drive of our next-door neighbor and hopped the fence into our backyard. I then staggered heavily into the house and literally collapsed on my mother's bed. Pulling myself up, I began to discard my clothing, putting on fresh pants, socks, and sneakers. I deliberately omitted a shirt, so as to look as at-home as possible, just in case.

Not ten minutes later, I heard the police helicopter hovering over my house. I felt good at least to know that my mother was, as usual, at work. Five minutes after I heard the first hum of the helicopter, I heard voices coming from the front room. I quickly hid myself in my mother's closet, to no avail. I was violently pulled from the closet and promptly arrested. I later found out that it was a mentally ill cat name Theapolis who had snitched me off to my pursuers, who in turn summoned the police.

During the trial on assault and grand theft auto charges, my sister, Kendis, perjured herself to save me from a jail term, but was not convincing enough against thirteen witnesses who had originally given chase. I was subsequently convicted and sentenced to nine months in camp. (Camp is the third testing ground in a series of "tests" to register one's ability to "stand firm," the streets, of course, being the first and juvenile hall the second. With each successive level—the Hall, camp, Youth Authority, prison—comes longer, harder time. This, coupled with a greater danger of becoming a victim, pits one hard against the total warrior mentality of "Do or Die." Here, the slogan ends and reality sets in.)

Nine months later I was released from Camp Munz and dropped off in the initial stages of a war that would forever change the politics of Cripping and the internal gang relations in South Central. Although my camp term lent prestige to my name, it did little to help me break through to the desperately sought-after second level of recognition. Crazy De, I learned, was due out in December, so I just did "odd jobs"—wrote on walls, i.e., advertised; collected guns; and maintained visibility.

It was during my stay in camp that my younger brother chose to follow me into banging and ally himself with the Eight Trays. Seventy-nine was the year of the Li'l's, that is, the year of the third generation of Eight Tray gangsters. All those who were of the second resurrection—beginning in 1975 and ending in 1977—acquired little homies bearing their names. For example, there was Li'l Monster, Li'l Crazy De, Li'l Spike, etc. In a nine-month period, the set doubled.

Meanwhile, the war between us and the Rollin' Sixties was beginning to heat up. The first casualty was on their side. Tyrone, the brother of an O.G. Sixty, was gunned down during a routine fistfight by a new recruit calling himself Dog. The O.G. whose brother had been killed wanted us to produce the shooter before a full-scale war broke out. The shooter, who few of us knew, as he was new, immediately went into hiding. We thus could not produce him and our relationship with the Sixties soured dramatically.

Up until that point only one of our homies had been killed, and his death was attributed to the Inglewood Families. Threats of revenge grew loud, as did rumors of an imminent war. In the midst of these warnings, our homeboy Lucky was ambushed on his porch and shot six times in the face. Witnesses reported seeing "a man in a brown jogging suit flee the area immediately after shots rang out." The night Lucky was murdered, Mumpy, a member of the Sixties, was seen at Rosecrans Skating Rink in a brown jogging suit. It had been further noted that Mumpy had been heard telling Lucky that "since one of my homeboys died, one of yours gotta die." A fight had ensued and had subsequently been broken up by members of both sides.

After Lucky's death tension ran high in our 'hood. We

wanted the shooters to fall under the weight of our wrath. A meeting of both sets was called by the O.G.s, in an all-out last effort to curtail a war, which would no doubt have grave consequences. The most damaging thing that we all held in mind was that we all knew where one another stayed—not more than six months before we had been the best of friends. The meeting was a dismal failure. It erupted into an all-out gang fight reminiscent of the old gang "rumbles." Diplomatic ties were thus broken, and war was ceremoniously declared. Another casualty quickly accrued to their side, as their homeboy Pimp was ambushed and killed. Several others were wounded.

At about that time, De was released. I relayed to him the drastic chain of events of recent times, and we both chose to give one hundred percent to the war effort. And perhaps, we concurred, this was the issue to carry us both over into the second realm of recognition on our climb to O.G. status.

In retaliation for Pimp's death—which the Sixties without a doubt attributed to us—our homie Tit Tit was shot, and while he lay in the street, mortally wounded, the gunmen came back around the corner in a white van. Before we could retrieve Tit Tit, they ran his head over and continued on. The occupants in the van had also shot two other people before shooting and killing Tit Tit, though both were civilians. This was the second homie to die in a matter of months. Shit was getting major.

Although we had been engaged in a war with the Families, it had always, somehow, been contained to fistfights and flesh wounds, with the exception of Shannon—who, we contend to this day, died at the hands of the Families. This escalation was new and actually quite alarming, for Crips tend to display a vicious knack for violence against other Crips—as will be duly noted in following chapters. Seemingly every Crip set erupted in savage wars, one against the other, culminating into the Beirut-type atmosphere in South Central today.

The news-catching items of violence to date are a result of clashes between Crips and Crips and not, as the media suggests, "Red and Blue," "Crip and Blood." Once bodies began to drop, people who were less than serious about banging began to fall by the wayside. Excuses of having to "be home by dark" and to "go out of town" abounded. The set thus dwindled to, I would learn, fighting shape.

De and I held fast and "seized the time." China, a very pretty but slightly plump homegirl, became my steady girl. She and I would often dress alike to further prompt our union.

China lent me her eight-track tape player. One afternoon, as De and I were walking with China's radio, we drew fire from a passing car—no doubt Sixties. Unscathed but very angry, De and I climbed from the bushes.

"Check this out." De spoke with barely controlled anger. "Kody, we gotta put a stop to these muthafuckas shootin' at us and shit."

Looking at me hard in search of some signs of overstanding and compliance, I said, "You right, homie, I'm wit' it."

"You serious?" De gave me a sinister smile. "All right then," he continued, "let's make a pact right now to never stop until we have killed all of our enemies. This means wherever we catch 'em, it's on!"

"All right, I'm serious, De," I said as I pledged my life to the Sixties' total destruction, or mine—whichever came first.

With that, I spun and threw China's radio high into the air as an all-out gesture of total abandonment. The radio seemed to tumble in slow motion, twisting and twirling as my gang life up until that time flashed in vivid episodes across my mental screen.

From graduation to this—blam! The radio hit the ground, shattered into a hundred pieces, and the screen in my mind went blank.

There was De with his hand extended. I reached, grabbed, and shook it with vigor. From that point on the medium of exchange in my life has been gunfire.

2

BOYS TO MEN

Trying hard not to come across too thuggish in front of China's grandparents, I sat stiff-backed, pretending to be interested in what Ben, China's ostensibly aristocratic grandfather, who drove an RTD bus, was saying.

"You youngsters don't have any incentive, no drive. You are always looking for someone to put something in your hands."

China, sighing loudly, nudged my leg and shot me a stare of "I've heard this a million times." She was eager to get back outside. We had only come indoors to retrieve China's coat but had gotten caught in one of Dot—China's liberal grandmother—and Ben's discussions on youth. Now night had fallen.

China's well-kept house sat smack in the middle of the

block on Eightieth Street, our newest possession in our latest recruitment drive. I would imagine that our aggressive conquering of territory in those days, and still today, resembled Hitler's sweep through Europe.

The apartment complex on the left end of the block off of Normandie Avenue became our base for this block. We have since referred to it as the "blue apartments." We had "lost" the "white apartments" on Sixty-fifth Street to Bloods while I was a prisoner in youth camp. The battle, I'm told, was fierce, but not worth the price. Although we suffered no fatalities, our wounded and MIA list grew steadily. Besides this, the Brims, whom the battle was with, had called in reinforcements from the Rollin' Twenties Bloods. The white apartments thus passed to the Reds and new ground was sought.

Eightieth Street was just one street out of many that fell under our jurisdiction. The mechanics involved in taking a street, or territory, is not unlike any attempt, I would assume, on behalf of early Euro-American settlers. Send in a scout, have him meet the "natives," test their hostility level, military capabilities, needs, likes, and dislikes. Once a military presence is established, in come the "citizens"—in this case, gang members. Those who are not persuaded by our lofty presence *will* be persuaded by our military might. All who are of fighting age become conscripts. The set expands, and so does our territory. Sometimes there is resistance, but most of the time our efforts are successful. China's younger brother was one of our first recruits from Eightieth. Recommended by China and sponsored by me, he became Li'l G.C.

"Listen now, Kody," Ben continued in a deep baritone, pronouncing every syllable of every word. "You have got to stop pussyfooting around with your life. We are quickly becoming a technological country, and computers are going to overtake manual labor. What that means is—"

A shot rang out, cutting Ben's monologue short. For an instant I thought he himself had been hit; he was belly down on the floor. Another shot resounded, this time a shotgun blast.

Jumping to my feet I headed to the front door, opened it, and ran out onto the porch. My heart was pumping, but my adrenaline was urging me on. Looking first to the right, toward the blue apartments, and then to the left, in the direction of Halldale, I spotted a burgundy Cutlass creeping down the street, a shotgun barrel in the passenger's hand barely visible through the open window.

Jumping the Creeping Charlie plants on the porch, which grew in huge flower pots, I darted into the street. Pulling out my chrome .25 automatic, recently put on the set by a new recruit, I began firing at the car. The car sped away. I kept firing at its rear as it turned left on Normandie Avenue.

I turned and bolted toward Halldale to assess the damage of their ride-by. Once I reached that corner I heard Dee Dee, Butchy's sister, hollering. At first I couldn't make out just what she was saying in the midst of the escalating confusion. Civilians had come out of their homes, and homeboys were starting to gather in front of China's house. Then it dawned on me.

"Monster, here they come, they comin' back . . . "

Damn, I was out of shells! No sooner had I turned to run and take cover, thinking I'd be shot in the back, then a black-and-white police car hit the corner and all but ran into the shooters' car. The police pulled their weapons and ordered the occupants out of the car and face down in the street. We all gathered to identify our enemies—not to help the police, but for our own intelligence.

There were three occupants, a .38 service revolver, and a pump shotgun, sawed off at the barrel for a spraying effect and sawed off at the stock for stealth and close combat. One shooter we knew—Bank Robber; the other two were obviously new recruits, probably putting in work for the first time. They were members of the Rollin' Sixties. My response went virtually unnoticed by the police, though I saw two holes in the passenger door. No one inside was hit. The shooters were taken away amid death threats and shouts of revenge. In the absence of the police, the car was promptly torn up and set ablaze. Ten minutes later the impound came and scooped up the remains.

On my trek by China's house on my way to the blue apartments I encountered Dot and Ben on their front lawn.

"Kody." Dot started in on me first. "You don't be runnin' *toward* no gunfire, you run *from* it. You could have been killed!"

"Yes, ma'am," I replied, grateful that they hadn't seen me firing on the car. Apparently Dot had dived for cover as well, joining Ben on the floor. "I just thought that one of my friends had been hurt."

"Well, goddammit, you are not Superman, boy," Ben said. "You could not have possibly helped anyone in such a crisis." He pronounced crisis like Nixon speaking on the energy crisis.

"You're right, Ben, I lost my head," I replied and put one foot in front of the other, trying to exit the conversation and get to the blue apartments to mount a retaliation.

"Where you going now?" Dot retorted with genuine concern. "Ain't nothin' but police out here."

"To the apartments to check on my little brother," I lied and kept on stepping.

At the apartments I was congratulated by the homies for a proper response, but I shook their flattery off. Shit, I wanted to know how, after I had alerted everyone to enemy presence, the shooters were still able to make it off the block and come back around to shoot again? Heads dropped and gestures of dismay abounded. I looked on in disgust, thinking then that I was the only serious one in this.

For the past five years I had gotten up every morning and ironed my gear with thoughts of nothing else but doing propaganda for the set. I did this with all the zeal of a religious fanatic.

Until I was nine years old we had lived on Hillcrest Drive in the Crenshaw district. This is a moderate middle-class neighborhood of block after block of sparse lawns, well-paved streets and shady trees. My mother and stepfather had lived there since 1965. This neighborhood is now Rollin' Sixties 'hood. Up until 1980 my mother still shopped at Buddah Market on Slauson Avenue, owned and operated by Orientals.

In the summer of 1980 my mother asked me to accompany her to Buddah Market to shop. I refused with vigor, but my resistance was in vain. Mom didn't overstand the complexity of our conflicts with other gangs. We are trying to kill each other. Up till then she always took my spiel about our seriousness as melodramatic exaggeration.

I went to Buddah Market with her that day—and I weighed two pounds extra. I had a Browning 9 millimeter with fourteen shots. It was an unusually bright afternoon, and I recall feeling light and almost happy, content actually. Riding up Slauson past Crenshaw I remember tensing and cringing as I read line after line of their graffiti on walls and buildings. Amusing myself, I jokingly asked Mom to pull over so I could cross them out. In return I got a "you damn fool" look. Then

I noticed Mom's face cloud over with what I took to be utter helplessness. Ironically, I never gave stopping an inkling of a thought. This was my career, my "calling," as church folks say when someone does one thing real well.

We traveled further west past West Boulevard, passing our old street. We both looked to the right briefly. Turning into Buddah Market's parking lot, I tightened my belt and gave my appearance the once-over. G-down (short for "gangster down," or dressed in gang attire) in my gear, I had on blue khaki pants, white canvas All-Stars, and a blue sweatshirt, with my hair in braids. Brownies—brown garden gloves worn by gang members for fighting and shooting—hung halfway out of my right back pocket, and a blue flag hung out my left. Crips wear their left ear pierced and their flag in the left back pocket. Bloods are on the right.

"Why don't you tuck in that old rag," Mom blurted out while she gave herself the once-over.

"It's not a rag, Mom, it's a *flag,*" I said, wishing she would for once see my seriousness here.

This was not some awkward stage of my life. This was a job to me, and I was employed full-time, putting in as much overtime as possible. Life from that vantage point seemed to be one big test of show and prove, pick and stick.

Mom went through her usual greetings with the Orientals. They had known each other for years.

I was on point. Not only was *I* in jeopardy, but with me I had Mom, who I was sure would try to talk an enemy into doing an about-face. Fat fucking chance of that happening, I remember thinking.

"You remember my son Kody, don't you?"

"Yes, yes," I heard the Oriental woman saying amid other comments such as "he's so big, so strong looking." After a few other exchanges we started down an aisle. Canned goods, no interest here.

"Mom, I'm going over to the cereal section," I said and stepped quickly so she couldn't call me back.

Turning the corner at the end of the aisle, I felt relieved to be alone, both for my safety and Mom's. I had every intention of going to the cereal section when I was distracted by a nice-looking young lady in produce. I made a beeline for the vegetables, and that's when I saw him. Damn! Enemy! Enemy! My adrenaline alarm was going off. Sonic booms of heartbeat filled my ears. My throat got tight and my movements became automatic. We both reached for our waistbands simultaneously. The young lady had still not looked up from her inspection of the vegetables, yet the tranquil surroundings of an otherwise routine shopping trip were about to explode around her.

I managed the drop and drew first. He was still drawing his weapon. Shit, had this been "Baretta," or "Barnaby Jones," he would have thrown his hands up and surrendered. Not bothering to aim, I fired.

BOOM!

Confusion and chaos swept the aisle like buckshot, screams following in quick succession. Damn, I'd missed!

I fired again and hit him in the torso. The bullet knocked him back, and his weapon discharged into the air. He had what sounded like a .22, a small-caliber weapon. Folks now knew that two weapons were involved—one loud, my 9 millimeter, and one not, his .22. I shot at him three more times to create an atmosphere of intensity, then turned and went in search of my mother. Since my last encounter with the ride-by shooters, where I had emptied my clip and was left vulnerable, I had learned to keep "exit" or "safety" shells.

Running aimlessly about, frantically looking for Mom, I totally forgot I had the gun in my hand. I tucked it while jogging down the household appliance aisle. Not finding her there, I panicked, remembering how I had been locked in the surplus store. I made my way then to the door and there, among the other scared-to-death shoppers, I found Mom. She was grief stricken and with her nerves in shambles; I grabbed her arm and ushered her away from the crowd.

"Boy, was that you?" she said, hoping against hope that it wasn't. "Kody, *what* happened?"

I made no attempt to explain. My sole intent was a timely escape. We drove in silence, block after block. We never even looked at each other.

Back across Western Avenue I began to breathe better as I finally reflected on what I had done. Fuck him, he was going to shoot me. I justified my shooting of him with self-defense. This thing was very dangerous; we all knew one another. It's like the CIA and the FBI going to war. There's no escaping once sighted.

I thought for sure I'd be captured for this one. After all, the Oriental knew me, and folks had seen me with the strap (gun). However, my arrest was not forthcoming.

After getting out of camp in 1979, I met Tamu through my brother Kerwin and sister Kendis, who all worked together at the Thirty-second Street Market. Tamu was a looker, tall and graceful with a smile that shouted for attention; I was naturally attracted. However, she was older than I. In fact, we had nothing in common. She was tall, I was short. She had a job, I was an armed robber. She liked jazz, I liked funk. She had a car, I had a bicycle. She was drug and alcohol free, I smoked pot and PCP and drank beer. We clicked immediately.

Today she'll say she didn't chase me, but in actuality she did. Once she and I began to go steady, she'd let me drop her off at work and keep the car until she got off. Her shift was from 3:00 P.M. till 11:00 P.M. My attraction was not just physical, but to the fact that she was not of my world. She was a civilian. To me, that was most appealing. She was not with me because of my reputation or clout, but for me as an individual. So when I went around her I would present myself as Kody, without the Monster persona. I'd take my shades off, tuck my flag, and not let her know when I was strapped. I also would douse myself with some of the expensive cologne Mom had bought me. Later, Tamu told me that I had been using too much but that at the time she didn't want to embarrass me, for she saw that I was trying to impress her.

I would take Tamu up to the market and kiss her goodbye, drive to the corner, make sure she was inside the store and out of view, then reach for the glove compartment. I'd open it, pull out my flag, put on my murder-ones (dark shades, also called Locs or Locos), button the top button on my shirt, put my strap in my lap, and drive on to the 'hood. I did so many ride-bys, drive-ups, drive-throughs, and chase-aways in her car that it's a wonder she didn't either go to jail or get shot. I guess everyone assumed the car was stolen. Then, too, we left few witnesses.

Tamu and I continued to date up until the time she told me she was pregnant.

"Pregnant?" I asked in disbelief.

"Yes, pregnant," she replied matter-of-factly.

I felt so young at that moment, just a baby myself. I panicked. Anything but a child. Things had gotten too serious, out of hand. I began to dodge Tamu.

"Tell her I ain't here," I would tell family members when she called or came by.

Mom, however, adored her, and they would sit for hours and talk. Often I'd come in from a hard day of campaigning, shotgun slung over my shoulder, and Tamu and Mom would be in the front room talking. I'd acknowledge them with a nod, then head on down the hall to my room and fall out in a dead sleep. I began not to care if she saw me as Monster or not. I tried to push her away with the raw reality of who I was. She wasn't budging. Besides, Mom hated China for reasons I never knew—perhaps because she saw that she and I were on the same path, whereas Tamu could be a positive influence in my life.

I wasn't by any means ready to have a child, though. To me that meant settling down, another obligation. I already had pledged my allegiance to the set, so I was in a rough spot. I had to pick either Tamu and my unborn child or my career in the set. This ate away at me for several months. Sure I liked Tamu, but not enough to forfeit my stature in the set. All I had worked so hard to build would be left to dangle in the wind, unfinished. Enemies, I thought, would overrun the 'hood if no one rallied the troops. Then, too, I felt an obligation to Tamu. She hadn't got pregnant alone. Besides, the child would be a totally innocent party in this matter and deserved a fair chance.

In those months of consternation I shot more than a few civilians as my concentration was continually broken with zigzag thoughts of my future. On July 28, 1980, I got a call from the hospital.

"I'm in labor," I heard Tamu's voice squeak over the phone. "Are you coming here?"

"Yeah, yeah, sure I'm comin'," I responded as all my confusion and indecisiveness boiled up and over the brink of comprehension.

I got my coat out of the closet in a complete daze, not knowing exactly what to do. I reached under my pillow and took hold of my 9 millimeter, checking the clip—fourteen shots. I was past the days of half-loaded weapons. Shit had escalated to the point where individuals were being sought for extermination. I, of course, was on at least three sets' "most wanted" lists. Walls told the story. In fact, enemies spray-painted my name on walls in death threats more often than I did to advertise.

Wearing my fresh Pendleton shirt, beige khakis, and biscuits (old-men comfort shoes, the first shoe officially dubbed a "Crip shoe"), I threw on my black bomber jacket and stepped out into the warm summer night. I walked up Sixty-ninth Street to Western Avenue and took a car at gunpoint. Still in a state of indecision, I drove toward the hospital.

I intentionally drove through Sixties 'hood. Actually, I was hoping to see one of them before I had made it through, and what luck did I have. There was Bank Robber, slippin' (not paying attention, not being vigilant) hard on a side street. I continued past him and turned at the next corner, parked, and waited. He would walk right to me.

Sitting in the car alone, waiting to push yet another enemy out of this existence, I reflected deeply about my place in this world, about things that were totally outside the grasp of my comprehension. Thoughts abounded I never knew I could conjure up. In retrospect, I can honestly say that in those moments before Bank Robber got to the car, I felt free. Free, I guess, because I had made a decision about my future.

"Hey," I called out to Robber, leaning over to the passenger side, "got a light?"

"Yeah," he replied, reaching into his pants pocket for a match or lighter. I never found out which.

I guess he felt insecure, because he dipped his head down to window level to see who was asking for a light.

"Say your prayers, muthafucka."

Before he could mount a response I blasted him thrice in the chest, started the car, and drove home to watch "Benny Hill." Bangin' was my life. That was my decision.

The next day I woke up feeling good. I got a call from China and we talked briefly about my decision. She had been totally bent out of shape by the fact that I had gotten a civilian pregnant. She felt disrespected, as she thought she was all I needed in a woman—lover, comrade, shooter, driver, etc. She didn't overstand.

I have always been intensely private, or at least I've always wanted a side of me to remain private. Being with Tamu in her world afforded me this opportunity. It was an escape to a peaceful enclave for a couple of hours. The places she took me, bangers didn't frequent.

This was before the influx of narcotics, primarily crack. We were all of the same economic status—broke. Now, with so many "ghetto rich" homeboys from every set, no place is beyond the grasp of bangers. I needed those escapes to maintain sanity.

Often I felt that I was carrying the weight of the whole set on my shoulders.

On a chilly October night in 1980, about twenty homeboys were assembled in front of the blue apartments on Eightieth Street when a '64 Chevy came barreling down the street with its occupants hanging out holding guns—long-barreled shotguns. Instinctively, we took cover. Instead of shooting, they just hollered their set—Sixties—disrespected ours, and kept on going.

Though I didn't know it at the time, simultaneously, four blocks away on Eighty-fourth Street, Twinky and his girlfriend were arguing. April wanted to go home that night instead of spending the night again. Twinky had no problem with that, but it was almost midnight. April insisted on being walked to the bus stop. Twinky gave in. Taking his .25 automatic along, they made their way to the nearest bus stop, at Eighty-third and Western. April lived on Sixty-second and Harvard in Blood 'hood. Once at the bus stop, they stood and talked about different things concerning the set. April was China's road dog, and a homegirl, too.

Suddenly Twinky spotted the Chevy, which we had identified as Pretty Boy's car. He pulled out his weapon to fire on the car, but April grabbed his hand, saying he should let them go on, they weren't bothering anybody, and that they probably hadn't even seen them. Twinky put away his strap.

Not three minutes later, the Sixties crept up from behind and fired one round from the long-barreled shotgun, striking Twinky in his upper left side below the armpit—basically a heart shot. Twinky, in shock, ran across the street and collapsed.

The shooters sped away. Twinky's mother and younger brother, Jr. Ball—also a homeboy—were retrieved. It's been reported that in his last moments Twinky said repeatedly, "Mama, I'm gonna be good, I ain't gonna bang no more Mama, I'm gonna be good."

He died soon after with buckshot in his heart. Twinky was fourteen years old. At approximately 3:00 the next morning I was awakened by a call from Twinky's mother. I still did not know of his death.

"Kody," she said in an icy voice unfamiliar to me, "they killed my baby last night, they killed my James last night."

Then she started screaming frantically. "Who?" I managed to say through her screams.

"The motherfuckin' Sixties! Come over here *right* now, Kody, *right* now!"

I dressed quickly, strapped down, and rode my bicycle the twenty-four blocks to her house without so much as a care about security or the wind-chill factor. I had not put Twinky on the set, but I dug him. He was a stalwart soldier and would have been a Ghetto Star.

On Thanksgiving, 1979, he, another homie—Li'l Doc—and I were walking down the street. I was strapped with a .22 revolver and Li'l Doc had a .44. No sooner had I handed the gun to Twinky than the police rolled up on us. Twinky was captured with the strap; Doc and I ran. He had just gotten out of camp, and now he'd been murdered.

Grieving, I made my way up their drive and knocked at the door. It was opened by Jr. Ball with a fixed expression of grief and anxiety on his face. Stepping inside, I could feel the tension. In the living room I saw four guns on the coffee table—two shotguns and two revolvers. I looked from the guns to Twinky's mother, her face a mask of steel, eyes burning like hellfire. Doc came in after me. Once both of us were seated, Twinky's mother got to her feet and walked around to us.

"Those guns belonged to James," she said, picking up one revolver and then another. "He would want you to have them. He would also want you to use them. You were his homeboys, his friends, and because of this I have called you two over here to tell you personally . . . I don't want to ever see you again if you can't kill them motherfuckers that killed my boy! You bring me newspapers, you make the news, but you better do something to avenge my son's death!"

I just sat and looked up at her with total admiration. Damn, she was down.

"But first," she continued, "I want you two to come to April's house with me."

She grabbed her car keys and we both followed her out to her car. Once inside the car she explained that Jr. Ball had been unnerved by Twinky's death and had, that night, abdicated his oath to the 'hood. He could not be relied on for a retaliatory strike.

In front of April's house we sat momentarily, then Twinky's mother got out . . . with a revolver. Standing wide-legged on April's grass, she opened fire, emptying six rounds into her house. I thought about doing likewise, but I felt she needed to do that alone.

Back in the car she said she honestly felt that April had set Twinky up to be ambushed and that, she added, we should kick April off the set. I told her I'd talk to China about it.

Rumors about April's survival and Twinky's death spread. "Why hadn't April been shot?" and "Why did she instruct him not to shoot?" Rumors and ill feelings intensified when April went into hiding. Not long after that she was specifically targeted and a hit was put on her.

We made the 5:00 P.M. news that day and the day after. On our third night we found the Sixties 'hood empty. Weaving our way through the streets we found it hard to believe that they had knuckled under. Not a soul was in sight. We drove down Third Avenue by the Fifty-ninth Street school, where they hung, circled the school once, then pulled to a stop and sat idle, peering into the darkness of the school yard. The Sixties had yet to procure a park and were using the Fifty-ninth Street school as a meeting place.

"Hit the corner once more," Frogg said from the passenger seat, a .357 magnum sitting firmly in his lap. Li'l G.C. sat on edge behind me. He had a .22 Remington rifle with eighteen shots.

Starting off around Third Avenue again we picked up a tail. Keeping my head straight, so as not to seem panicky in case it was the police, I surveyed the front grille and lights. No, it wasn't a police car. The police, at least the Seventy-seventh Street Division in our 'hood, were driving Furys. This car behind us was a Chevy, a '66 Impala.

Keeping my head straight I spoke softly to Frogg. "Cuz, you know why we can't find these fools?"

"Why?" Frogg answered.

" 'Cause these muthafuckas is behind us!"

"Don't look back," Frogg mumbled and adjusted his rearview mirror. "Just keep straight, keep straight. Now speed up a little and turn left on Fifth Avenue." Frogg was instructing me like a driving instructor. "At the first driveway, bust a U-turn."

Speeding up to Fifth Avenue past Fourth, I thought about the danger of clocking (continuously, nonstop, as in time) these cats three days in a row. Perhaps we had put too much on it. No doubt, they were out on patrol and were possibly heavily armed in hopes of finding some intruders, just our fuckin' luck. Frogg was fresh out of prison and already on the campaign trail. He loved the set intensely.

Turning left on Fifth Avenue I made another hard left into the first driveway. No sooner had I backed out and come to a rolling stop at the corner of Fifty-ninth and Fifth, than the other car slowly bent the corner in front of us. Had they been good military tacticians they would have stopped in front of us and prevented our forward motion, while simultaneously having their shooters try to take out the driver to leave the occupants stranded and on foot to be hunted and killed. But no, this was not their tactic. They drove slowly around, coming alongside us, but facing the opposite direction.

As they inched closer and closer I said to Frogg, "Shoot, shoot these muthafuckas, man!"

"Hold on, hold on," he said. Both of us were sitting still in the front seats like we didn't have a care in the world. "A little more, a little . . . "

BOOM, BOOM!

Frogg was leaning right over me, shooting into their faces. Powder and cordite flew into my face from the gun's cylinders.

Pac, pac, pac, pac I heard from behind my head. Li'l G.C. was shooting with the .22.

Caught by surprise, their driver panicked, punched the accelerator, and hit a light pole, which fell across the hood and roof of the car. We sped away down Fifth Avenue to Slauson and made a right. When we got to Second Avenue we turned back into their 'hood, heading toward our set. I saw two of their little homies on bicycles and ran one over. Well, actually not *over,* but I hit him and he flew a few yards—about twenty. He didn't get up before we had gotten off the block.

I felt nothing but a sense of duty. I had been to five funerals in the previous two years and had been steeled by seeing people whom I had laughed and joked with, played and eaten with, dead in a casket. Revenge was my every thought. Only when I had put work in could I feel good that day; otherwise I couldn't sleep. Work does not always constitute shooting someone, though this is the ultimate. Anything from wallbangin' (writing your set name on a wall, advertising) to spitting on someone to fighting—it's all work. And I was a hard worker.

3

THE WAR

In the fall of 1980 the war between the Eight Trays and the Rollin' Sixties was in full swing. Five casualties had accrued on our side, eight had fallen on their side. Even though people die every day in South Central and by most any means, it was the timing and the viciousness of these killings that made the gang community stop and take notice. Escalation was the order of the day. Entire streets were turned into armed camps to be used as liberated territory, where safe "meeting and mounting up" could be carried out with not so much as a worry about enemy gunfire. ("Meeting" means a gang gathering to choose a riding party or group of shooters to invade enemy territory. "Mounting up" means starting out on the mission.)

This particular war is of the utmost importance; it was this very conflict that changed the politics of gang relations in South Central—a significant factor in the development of the critical climate that prevails throughout the region today.

Once the Eight Trays had really fallen out and our intent at the Rollin' Sixties' destruction was obvious, the entire Crip community split and began to side with one set or the other. We became, in effect, superpowers, not unlike the former Soviet Union and United States. Sets whom we'd had small skirmishes with or who favored the Sixties over us sided with them. Also included were their natural allies—other Neighborhood sets. "Neighborhood" or "N-hood" is the name of a loosely knit group of sets throughout Los Angeles, including Lynwood, West Covina, and Compton. The Neighborhood Crips as a whole make up a large part of the Crip community, quite possibly comparable to the expansive republics spread throughout the Union of Soviet Socialist Republics. They are like Soviet republics, but not necessarily united, as each is of a different culture, with a diversity of customs and philosophical beliefs. The Neighborhoods had only ever been loosely associated; however, with the brutal escalation of the war, they became a united front against us and our allies.

Sets began to predict the winners, a virtually impossible deed as our war, like most gang wars, was not fought for territory or any specific goal other than the destruction of individuals, of human beings. The idea was to drop enough bodies, cause enough terror and suffering so that they'd come to their senses and realize that we were the wrong set to fuck with. Their goal, I'm sure, was the same. "Points" were scored when individuals with prestige were hit. The aggression displayed in 1980 was unprecedented. We set a decibel level in violence that still causes some to cringe today.

What most folks miserably fail to realize is that our wars are no less complicated than world wars, or wars fought to either suppress or liberate a country. The difference is not legality, but cause. Some causes are righteous and in accord with human nature, while others are reactionary and repressive. Gang wars fall somewhere in between. I can quite easily justify the retaliation on enemies for killing one of my comrades. But simultaneously I will condemn the murdering of noncombatants.

Retribution is a natural reaction. It's easy to persuade the general public of your "righteousness" when you control major media. But those of us who control nothing are in the precarious position of having someone guess what our position is. This leaves quite a large gap for misinformation. Who fired the first shot? Who knows?! But, too, who cares, when one of theirs is lying in a pool of blood with his brains blown out. This question becomes weightless in the aftermath of a shooting where someone has died. Thus the goal becomes the elimination of the shooter or as many of his comrades as possible. This inevitably leads to war—a full-scale mobilization of as many troops as needed to achieve the desired effect: funerals.

It was in this season that I was captured for murder. This particular incident began in my 'hood. I had taken my li'l brother's ten-speed out this day, as I was only venturing around the block to Shadow's house. Time seemed to fly by, and before I knew it night had fallen, and I was left in the dangerous position of having to get back home. This task would indeed be most trying as our 'hood was now being clocked by not just the Sixties but their allies and our new enemies. Night was the killing time.

Dreading my upcoming journey and cursing myself for not having brought a strap, I mounted the bike and started out. Peddling fast toward the dark side street of Halldale, I noticed four occupants in what appeared to be a blue T-bird; they were parked on the left-hand side of the street facing me. I slowed to a precautionary coast and strained my eyes to survey the situation I was riding into. Upon further observation I realized that the T-bird belonged to my homeboy Sleepy. This meant the others had to be homies, as well. A sigh of relief fell over me and I picked my pace up again.

But then I noticed hand gestures coming from Sleepy's car. Thinking they were joking with me and clowning, I flipped them off as I approached the front of the car. Unbeknownst to me, they were trying to warn me of the imminent danger. For they had seen the carload of shooters bend the corner with their lights off moments after I rolled out of Shadow's driveway into the street. They sat motionless and waited for me to be cut down.

I never saw the car until it was parallel with me and I was staring down the barrels of five weapons under the unfriendly faces of my enemies. Fortunately, they wanted to see who they were killing—they wanted some points—and this gave me an edge.

"Look, look," exclaimed an overly excited voice from within the car, "it's Monster Kody!"

"Shoot that nigga, shoot him!" another faceless voice shouted.

Too late. By now I had reached the front of Sleepy's car and was diving behind it in an attempt at survival. Before I hit the ground the shooting began. Sitting parallel with Sleepy's car, they proceeded to riddle the car with bullets. I lay in the dirt and hoped they wouldn't have the heart to exit their car and see if I were hit or dead. It seemed like five minutes before the shooting stopped. I knew for sure the homies inside the car were dead.

I waited until I heard the shooters' car screech away before I began to move, or even think about coming from behind Sleepy's car. This had been a close call. Death, it seemed, was stalking me. My brushes with it were becoming more frequent and increasingly more serious. Had they used the shoot-first-ask-who-later policy, I would have been killed.

From the sound of their weaponry they had some heavy calibers. I distinctly remembered seeing an M-1 carbine and some big handguns. I later found out the identity of the shooters, as well.

Getting up slowly so as not to be tricked into the screeching-tire trick—where a soldier would be waiting with a weapon when I emerged—I began to hear rustling in the car and was awestruck to find that everyone was still alive. Sleepy was sitting in the driver's seat. Next to him sat Big Lynn, who stood six feet, three inches tall and weighed in at a hefty 340 pounds. Her arms measured twenty-two inches around. We often used her as a disciplinary board for unruly homegirls and, to be perfectly frank, some homeboys. Behind Big Lynn was Gangster Brown, and to his left sat his younger brother, Fatty.

They had been sitting there for some time, slipping bad, smoking PCP. When they saw me dive behind the car, they slid down in their seats. Miraculously, no one was killed, though all had suffered buckshot strafing and glass cuts from the shattering windows.

They pulled themselves from the wreckage—and that's exactly what it was. It's amazing how in a matter of seconds a car of such expense can be reduced to a hunk of Swiss metal, absolutely useless. Standing there in the street surveying the damage, Sleepy could not believe what he saw. We counted twenty-eight bullet holes in the body of the car, not including the individual buckshot dents. Fatty had taken a large-caliber shot right through the bib of his hat. Everyone was bleeding on the arms and neck; areas not covered by clothing were bloody. What held them from falling into shock was the PCP. Even after the shooting, they were not in total control of their faculties.

I was not on PCP and was visibly shaken. I had no sedative. By now my nerves were all but shot. Combat was starting to take its toll on me. It seemed as though I was viewing a body every other month, or having brains and blood splattered all over me. Death, or the fear of death, became my constant companion. But still my dedication, my patriotism, was strong; the *can't stop, won't stop* mentality had taken control of my being.

Trying to stir Sleepy into a retaliatory mood proved fruitless. He and the others were too intoxicated to mount any serious defense and seemed unconcerned about anything but their wounds and Sleepy's car. This goes back to what I have already explained about military personnel and combat soldiers. Although all of the victims in this case were in the military, none were actual combat soldiers. When struck, they had no immediate inclination to strike back. Often they'd relay the assault to the combat division, and a counterattack would then be carried out. Combat troops, on the other hand, would have assembled, mounted, and been en route to a designated spot before the smell of cordite cleared the air. Rapid deployment brought instant recognition to those involved as a serious group of cats bent on upholding their prestige.

Disgusted at their lack of concern, I mounted the bike and continued my journey home. When I turned onto my block and had gone about four houses, a purple Duster sped toward me and fired one shot. Either the driver or the shooter—or perhaps both—were inexperienced in the technique of doing a drive-by, because I didn't even feel the closeness of the bullet. My forward motion and their speed in the opposite direction had obviously thrown the shooter's aim off. He probably aimed directly at me—a moving target—causing his shot to go somewhere behind me, no doubt into one of the houses I was passing. The car kept straight but picked up speed, probably thinking they had actually done something. My pace had been momentarily broken, but I never dismounted my bike.

When I got to my house my sister was standing out front. Though she had heard the shot, she had not known what had happened. Surprisingly, she was not accosted and asked to identify herself. Had the shooters found out that she was my sister, she would have been shot or kidnapped. Though our war had not yet reached the level of kidnapping and executing family members, it was being talked about as an inevitable consequence in our headlong escalation.

This, too, pointed up the inexperience of these shooters. If they were on Sixty-ninth Street, that meant they knew I lived there, and their intentions were to try to catch me or one of my homies coming from or going to my house. My combat mentality was still at its peak from the brush with death around the corner, so when I got to where my sister was standing I yelled at her to "take her ass in the house," and that "didn't she know there was a goddamn war going on out here?" She stared for a moment then ran inside.

Putting up Li'l Monster's bike, I had a thousand thoughts

running through my head. Once in my room I sat down on the end of my bed to devise a plan in the midst of this latest attack. Usually we'd respond right away, but tonight there seemed to be a lull in our communication—the drums weren't beating. I phoned Sidewinder in an attempt to consolidate a riding party of able soldiers and was shocked at what I heard. The very same car that shot up Sleepy's car had also rode on Sidewinder and some other homies up in the Eighties 'hood; their initial attack had taken place on Seventy-first Street. But this wasn't the shocker, for it was common for one car to make a full sweep of an entire neighborhood. The surprising news was that in their attempt to shoot one of our homies, they had shot and critically wounded a member of the Inglewood Family Bloods, who had been creeping into our 'hood to shoot Sidewinder and the homies. The shooter car met a righteous resistance in the Eighties and didn't get the chance to do any damage, although shots were exchanged. When asked what they did with the Blood, Sidewinder responded, "We sent him to his Maker."

Now I was depressed. It seemed then that we were in totally occupied territory. Hanging up the phone I lay back on my bed and looked over at the empty bed beside mine. My younger brother, Li'l Monster, had been captured for an armed robbery along with Li'l Harv and a woman named Speedy—a close associate of the 'hood and a firm supporter of the criminal class. He had been given six months in camp. I wished he was there because he'd be down to launch an attack from right here. But Bro was not there and Crazy De was still in the Hall. Shit. I felt trapped. I had to do *something.*

I retrieved my double-barrel from beneath the dresser and checked it for munition. Then I went out and got back on Bro's bike. Holding the shotgun—which had been sawed off for stealth—across the handlebars, I peddled west toward the borderline that separated our 'hood from the Sixties.

Wearing my combat black I crossed Western Avenue and entered their 'hood on the left flank, in what today we call the first parallel. I made my way cautiously up Sixty-ninth Street to Horace Mann Junior High School. Rumor had it that they had been using Horace Mann as a meeting place, for they had still failed to procure a park for their meeting and mounting place.

I circumvented the school on its left side, which was on Seventy-first. There I parked my bike and traveled on foot. I hopped the school fence with the shotgun in my waistband, landing on the other side with a thud. When I got to the lunch area I was disappointed to find no one there. Had they been at the school, this is where they would be found, because the lunch area was covered with a roof.

Moving now on instinct, I continued through the lunch area and out to the makeshift bungalows, which had been constructed to allow school to continue while the administration building was being renovated. I began to hear music in the distance. The closer I came to the north side of the school, the louder the music got. "Finally," I said to myself, "someone to shoot."

Creeping slowly toward the area I believed the music—and now loud talking—was coming from, I kept a vigilant eye out for sentries or stragglers who might announce my presence and blow my surprise attack. And, of course, the very real possibility existed that if I did not strike swiftly, causing much damage and confusion, they could mount a response and trap me in the school. I had brought only two shells, both 00. At each corner I crouched and peeked from a low position—combat training I had learned from old war movies. But as I negotiated each corner I found no one there. Where were they? Then a terrifying thought occurred to me—the roof. These muthafuckas were on the roof. This gave them a vantage point far superior to my ground-level position.

But the sound disproved my theory: it was an even-level sound and not, as I had surmised, an above-level sound. My second thought was confirmed as I made my way around the next set of bungalows. They were not even in the schoolyard, but outside its gate, parked on Sixty-eighth Street, talking as they played the car radio, beer bottles on the hood and roof of the car. Luckily for me, they were on my side of the street, for had they been on the other side I would not have been able to maximize my damage.

Not only did I have to shoot through the fence, but my targets were in the street. This put about seventeen feet between us. I had 00 buckshot, which would compensate for the distance; but my weapon was sawed off. This meant that my shot would be more of a spray than a solid impact.

Realizing that my transportation was clear across the school, I debated whether I should expend one or both barrels. Expend one and use one to secure my escape, or pull both triggers at once, using the tremendous sound as a diversionary tactic and hoping to realize my intent, which was a funeral or two.

Making my decision, I stepped to the gate, stuck the barrels through and shouted, "Gangsta!"

BLOOM, BLOOM!

I let loose one and then the other in rapid succession, then turned and ran back through the bungalows and the lunch area and finally reached the fence on Seventy-first. Stopping to put the shotgun in my waistband, I saw a car bend the corner. I held the shotgun out instead and ducked behind a trash bin to let the car pass. It was occupied by two older civilians. When I got back up and shoved the gun in my waistband, I jumped. "Ahhh!" The barrels were still hot and burned my private parts. Holding the gun in my hands, I scaled the fence.

I ran back to where I had left the bike and, goddamn, someone had stolen it! Now I began to panic, because Western Avenue, the first parallel, was over a block away. Surely, I thought, the survivors would be in the vehicle looking for their assailants—and they'd be armed. Besides, I had no shells.

I turned on my heels and trotted down Seventy-first, trying to stay as close as possible to the lawns in case I had to run through a yard. Once I got to the first parallel I felt better, but no safer. The barrels had cooled down enough now to put the gun in my waistband, so I hid the weapon. Finally I made my way down our driveway and into the house.

I reloaded the shotgun and laid it against the stereo speaker. I then turned on the TV and watched the "Benny Hill Show." I felt much better.

Then next night, while Gangster Brown and I were traversing to a party in the 'hood, an undercover car pulled to a stop beside us. Both police officers exited the car and approached us.

"Monster, what's up?" said the first officer, with a fake appearance of friendship.

"Nothing," I said with as much deceiving concern as I could muster. Actually, nothing but hostility exists between us and them, but some officers try to put on a jovial show of cosmetic concern to woo the naive banger into a trusting relationship with them.

"Listen," the officer continued, "auto detail wants to talk to you about a stolen car. Now I know that ain't your style and I told them that, but you need to come on down to the station and iron it out."

My instincts said run, but I didn't.

I said, "Man, you know I don't be stealing no cars, that's bullshit!"

"Yeah, we know, but it's best if you clear this up now." His partner had now joined in on the "friendly persuasion."

I looked at Brown to see what he thought.

"Don't worry, Brown," the first officer said. "We'll bring Monster right back to the party."

Still Brown said nothing. By now I was being handcuffed. I told Brown that I'd see him later and to hold down the party until I got back. He said he would. After we drove off, the jovial facade vanished.

"Monster Kody," the driver said, as if weighing the poundage of my name. "You are in big trouble."

Damn. I felt claustrophobic, trapped and helpless.

"You cannot keep going around killing people and leaving witnesses." He was shooting stares at me through the rearview mirror as he spoke. "Now we got you. You done fucked up this time. Yep, got an eyewitness who saw you plain as day.

"But listen," he continued. "What's been eating away at me is this . . . Was that you driving that burgundy Grand Prix that shot Lip Dog from Brim, which we chased and lost?" His eyes held mine for a moment.

"Naw, man, that wasn't me."

"Oh, you can tell us, we don't give a fuck one way or the other. I just wanted to compliment you on your driving." Now he broke a faint smile. "Oh, incidentally, Lip Dog survived those four holes you put in his chest."

"I told you, man, that wasn't me."

"Well listen, Ace Rat said he saw you kill his homeboy D.C. last night." He was speaking now in a matter-of-fact tone. "We wouldn't even bother with it if he hadn't positively I.D.'d you.

"But," he continued, "Ace Rat ain't gonna be no good witness no way. Hell, he shot his own brother today." With that he winked in the rearview mirror.

Now I was really wondering just what was going on. How had anyone seen me under the cover of darkness? Or, better yet, *had* anyone actually seen me? And if so, why hadn't there been mention of the others who had been shot? I distinctly remembered counting five people out there. From seventeen feet with a sawed-off, everyone was getting sprayed. Besides, they had been standing in a tight circle, and I had used 00 buckshot. Surely I'd also have some assault charges and perhaps attempted murder, as well. But this went unmentioned during our ride to the station. At the station, I found out more.

According to the homicide detectives handling the case, myself, Sidewinder, who had been captured, and an unidentified driver caught several Sixties on the corner of Sixty-seventh and Van Ness and opened fire with a 9 millimeter and a .22 rifle. I supposedly had possession of the .22 and had allegedly shot Delta Thomas, a.k.a. D.C., several times. He was said to have run half a block and then expired. Sidewinder had supposedly supplied cover fire. I had been positively identified as the murderer of Delta Thomas.

Of course I knew I had not shot D.C., but how could I explain that I had been at another site, possibly killing other Sixties? I had no alibi as to my whereabouts that night. I made no statement at the station other than, "I want to speak to my attorney."

I was asked a series of questions ranging from how old I was (most of the policemen couldn't believe I was sixteen) to what my body count was. I shook them off with ignorant stares and shoulder hunches.

Later, after what seemed like hours in the cooling tank—a deliberately chilled holding cell designed to keep its occupant freezing and uncomfortable—I was transported to Los Padrinos Juvenile Hall. There I was strip searched, made to shower, dressed in jail clothes, and escorted to the box. The box is actually solitary confinement, where those being held for murder one are sent for seven days. I was not sweating the case in the least. In fact, once I was put in my room I went directly to sleep.

But when I awoke the next morning I felt the strain of being captured. Now I'm quite used to being trapped behind a heavy metal door or a barrage of bars. Even behind Pelican Bay's 8,200 holes—a metal slab over the entire front of my cell with multiple holes drilled in it—I can function quite normally. But back in those days, before my prison-life conditioning, I had a hard time coping with cell living.

In those days my writing and reading were bad. I couldn't compose a decent letter or even read a whole comic book. I began to think about my schooling and my relationship with my mother, which had deteriorated to a series of staring matches, when we could even stand to be in each other's company for any length of time. I felt she didn't overstand my generation. She, on the other hand, said I was a no-good hoodlum. Our clashes were frequent.

On my second day in solitary she came to see me. I strode out into the dayroom visiting area and sat next to her. For a few seconds she said nothing. Then she looked straight into my eyes with the most puzzling look and spoke through quivering lips.

"Kody, *what* has happened to you? *What is wrong?*"

And for the first time in a while I started to shed tears and could not speak. Raising my head to look her honestly in the eyes, I said, *"I don't know,"* and meant it.

My life was totally consumed by all aspects of gang life. I had turned my bedroom into a virtual command post, launching attacks from my house with escalating frequency. My clothes, walk, talk, and attitude all reflected my love for and allegiance to my set. Nobody was more important than my homeboys—nobody. In fact, the only reason my little brother and I stayed close is because he joined the set. Anybody else I had nothing in common with. My transformation was subtle. I guess this is why most parents can't nip it in the bud. How?

I was six years old when the Crips were started. No one anticipated its sweep. The youth of South Central were being gobbled up by an alien power threatening to attach itself to a multitude of other problems already plaguing them. An almost "enemy" subculture had arisen, and no one knew from where it came. No one took its conception seriously. But slowly it crept, saturating entire households, city blocks, neighborhoods, and eventually the nation-state of California.

Today, no school, library, institution, business, detention center, or church is exempt from being touched in some way by the gang activity in South Central. Per year, the gangs in South

Central recruit more people than the four branches of the U.S. Armed Forces do. Crack dealers employ more people in South Central than AT&T, IBM, and Xerox combined. And South Central is under more aerial surveillance than Belfast, Ireland. Everyone is armed, frustrated, suppressed, and on the brink of explosion.

I had no adequate answer then for Mom about what was happening to me. Actually, I wasn't fully aware of the gang's strong gravitational pull. I knew, for instance, that the total lawlessness was alluring, and that the sense of importance, self-worth, and raw power was exciting, stimulating, and intoxicating beyond any other high on this planet. But still I could not explain what had happened to pull me in so far that *nothing* outside of my set mattered.

In the years since, I have battled with my intellect to find an adequate answer to that question. Not to justify my participation, but to see what makes others tick. I have always been a thinker, not necessarily academically, but more on a psychological level. I have always been interested in how people think, what causes any particular thought, and so on. Action and reaction has always held my attention.

After Mom left I felt extremely bad and a bit torn. I was restless, and the day seemed to drag on forever. On my third day in Los Padrinos, my name was called for release. When I got up front to the administration building I found out that my case had been rejected for prosecution by the District Attorney's office.

Mom was there to pick me up. On our way home she tried to make me commit to stop banging and get back in school. I told her I *was* in school, and to this she angrily retorted, "To learn, dammit, to learn!"

The fact is, I was being bused to an all-American (white) school in Woodland Hills: El Camino Real High. With some promises from Mom and some stern commitments from my probation officer, I was able to get in right out of juvenile camp. I went to school every day, but I never attended classes. Academics just couldn't hold my attention. The only reason I went at all was because of the long trip from South Central to the San Fernando Valley, during which I was able to take in some awesome sights. Any relief from the drab grayness of the city was welcome, so I went along for the ride.

Once there, I'd get with the others who had no interest in academia and we'd stand around and pose in all of our cool South Centralness. The punk movement was in full swing at that time, and the Valley punk rockers initially mistook us—the eight of us who were steeped in the subculture of banging—for punk rockers because of our dress code. Perhaps they thought we were their New Afrikan counterparts from the city. We dressed almost alike, but it was only coincidence—we had never seen or heard of punk rockers before coming out to the Valley. A couple of us thought that they were Crips. We circled one another in an attempt to distinguish authenticity, then finally made a pact and began to hang out together.

But eventually I had to stop going to school there altogether, because the Sixties discovered the bus route, which ran through their 'hood. One day they stood and taunted the bus, and the next day they shot it up. By the third day I was not on that bus anymore.

Now, as if all other attempts would be useless, Mom gave up trying to persuade me.

I mad dogged every occupant of every car that came next to us, giving everyone a deliberately evil stare. I had perfected this look and no one except another serious soldier could hold my stare. I now overstand the look. It's not *how* you stare at someone, but *what* you've been through that others can see in your eyes and that tells them you're the wrong one to fuck with. Some refer to this as the thousand-yard stare.

Once I had gotten home, showered, and geared up, my shaken mentality of the day before vanished, as I was back "in country"—in the war zone—and conditions dictated that I think in accord with my present situation. I called around to notify the homies of my release and my continued support of and participation in the war, which had just escalated to another level.

Ckrizs's sister had been kidnapped by the Sixties from the L.A. County Jail after she had gone to visit him: She was a civilian with no ties to gang activity other than her blood relation with Ckrizs. So now kidnapping had been added to the list of tactics used to terrorize the other side into withdrawal. Back in 1980, unlike today, there were no "high rollers," or "ballers," substantially anchored in any particular 'hood ("high roller" is Crip terminology for a ghetto-rich drug dealer; "baller" is the equivalent in Blood language). So the kidnapping had nothing whatsoever to do with ransom. This was a straight, ruthless move designed to strike terror in us. But, of course, it didn't work.

A meeting was held for a select few who, it was determined, could pull themselves a notch above the latest terrorist attack and commit an even more hideous act to show the Sixties that two can play this game. Only our target would be not a civilian but one of their troopers.

We plotted and planned most of the night trying to decide on which act would most grab their attention. We pondered castration, blinding, sticking a shotgun up the victim's rectum and pulling the trigger, and cutting off his ears. The latter, we felt, would be most significant. After all, killing him would be too easy, too final. No, we wanted him to live, to be a walking reminder of our seriousness.

After deciding our course of action and selecting those to carry it out, we sat and waited to hear the fate of Ckrizs's sister. Finally, after three days of suspense, she was found in one of the Sixties' school yards. She had been raped repeatedly, stabbed numerous times, and left for dead. Fortunately, she lived. That very night our selected crew was sent out to complete its first, but not last, extra-vicious act of warfare.

Combing the streets of the Sixties 'hood in a desperate attempt to find one of their shooters, the crew drove block after block, stopping civilians to ask the whereabouts of such notables as Peddie Wac, Poochie, Keitarock, Mumbles, or Snoop Dog—their elite crew of shooters. Finding none of them around, they settled for an up-and-coming Ghetto Star. They seized him, beat him into submission, and chopped off both his arms at the elbow with machetes. One arm was taken, and one arm was discarded down the street.

Later that night we partied and had a good time. The arm that was taken was brought to the meeting as proof of completion. There were no further kidnappings and our war plodded on in an "ordinary" fashion after this. During the ensuing investigation, the police department's frustration arose not as a result of the act per se, but from their inability to find the victim's other limb. We learned from this that there was a deterrent to certain acts. We had quite possibly laid down a rule then that certain things just wouldn't be tolerated.

4

AMBUSH

By now, with the wars raging out of control and my paranoia peaking, I had ceased to recognize people—that is to say, gang members—by name. Gang members became recognizable as streets or sets. Further recognition fell into "enemy" or "friend" categories, which of course meant kill or let live. I forgot individual names, but I never failed to link a face with a set. With the exception of my particular homeboys and our immediate allies, I had no interest in storing names in my memory bank. I tried to store more crucial data, such as the addresses of enemy homes, the phone numbers of women belonging to enemy sets, and troop movements of potential danger.

I believe that I survived those chaotic times because I took my existence seriously. Since the time Tray Ball had first told me that banging was a full-time occupation, I have striven for professionalism. But banging falls short of the level of organization of, say, an institution that was formally founded on the premise of being structured, so there is no compartmentalization. No individual has a specific duty assigned to him, where his efficiency can be monitored by a superior. Therefore, the serious banger often finds himself handling several "jobs" in the course of his career. For years I found my position in the set to be manifold. At any given time I was the minister of information, which included such responsibilities as writing on walls, declaring who we were and who we wanted to kill, and verbalizing our intent at gangland supremacy on street corners, on buses, in school yards, and at parties; minister of defense, which entailed organizing and overseeing general troop movement and maintaining a highly visible, militarily able contingency of soldiers who, at a moment's notice, could be relied upon for rapid deployment anywhere in the city; teacher of war tactics, which, I guess, would fall under the heading of instructor; and combat soldier and on-the-job trainer.

All participants are obligated to represent their allegiance to their respective sets everywhere they go. You are taught from recruitment that your set is something to be proud of. Each set actually functions like the different divisions of, say, the U.S. Army. For instance, one who is in the Army may belong to the First Infantry Division, 196th Infantry Brigade, Second Battalion, Delta Company. A member of a gang might belong to the West Side Crips, Eight Tray Gangsters, North Side Eighty-third Street, or West Side Harvard Park Brims, Sixty-second Street. My point here is the complexity of both organizations. There is the Crip Army and the Blood Army. Each has various divisions or chapters. These are noted by streets and initials or abbreviations. Sets use abbreviations much like everyone else: Eight Tray Gangsters would simply be abbreviated to ETG.

As of late, sets—which are the equivalent of a company in military jargon—have started to use individual colors, outside of the universally worn red and blue, to denote their particular chapters. Most notable is the purple flag of the Grape Street Watts Crips and the all-black flags of the Compton Santana Block Crips. Of equal importance is the green flag of the San Diego Lincoln Park Pirus, Skyline Pirus, and 5–9 Brims of the Bloods.

With each new generation of Crip and Blood bangers comes a more complex system, which is now reaching institutional proportions. It is precisely because of this type of participation in the development and expansion of these groups' mores, customs, and philosophies that gangbanging will never be stopped from without. The notion of the "war on gangs" being successful is as realistic as the People's Republic of China telling Americans to stop being American. When gang members stop their wars and find that there is no longer a need for their sets to exist, banging will cease. But until then, all attempts by law enforcement to seriously curtail its forward motion will be in vain.

As November 1980 came to a close, several developments were on the horizon. We had forged an alliance with the Playboy Gangsters who, as we duly noted, were situated behind the Sixties. Their 'hood was far west, out of the chaotic labyrinth of South Central. This gave us an escape place to plot and plan, rest and retreat.

At this time we'd also seriously pondered the possible

unification of all gangster sets, to roll back the united front of the city-wide neighborhood threat. And we were in desperate need of weapons. The Sixties had just hit an army surplus and secured hundreds of semiautomatic rifles and handguns, which they were putting to use nightly. Arms proliferation was definitely an issue. An arms race is what came out of this situation. And because there is no ceiling on numbers, or checks and balances, the proliferation continues to date.

Our goal was to wait until New Year's Eve, when the entire community would be openly armed and celebrating, and run a truck through the wall of the Western Surplus and secure as many guns and munitions as possible. This was a good plan, we thought, as who would supply security for a store on New Year's Eve?

It was also during this time that Crazy De and I took the "split-side" proposal to Sidewinder for possible approval. Sidewinder was the closest our set came to having a leader. He was the only one who lived on Eighty-third Street and was solely responsible for the set's break with Tookie's regime that involved the entire west side of Los Angeles. Tookie is the founder of the West Side Crips. Before there were any divisions by street, there was one big Crip army. Sidewinder, in effect, won liberation of the set, which was then simply called Original Gangster Crips (OGC). This is where the term "O.G." originated, from Sidewinder's usage of it to denote our break and thus our independence from Tookie's West Side Crips (WSC).

So, as I explained above, with each generation comes new, more advanced ideals about the continuation of Crips in general and of one's set in particular, as shown here with Sidewinder's idea of an individual set on Eighty-third Street. While remaining in conjunction with West Side Crips, the set would not necessarily be controlled by them. Its conception was to promote autonomy.

All attempts at new ideas are not successful. Sets fail, much like businesses. Much work goes into establishing a set. With the success of a set comes universal recognition. Sidewinder reached Ghetto Star status by this act alone, but he still was active in all of our wars and still lends his experience to the set's ascent today.

Our proposal, our contribution, was based on war strategy. For it seemed like every time we'd neutralize one Sixty, two would be recruited. They have always had great success with recruitment. I would honestly say that today the Rollin' Sixties have the third largest set in South Central, following the East Coast Crips and then the Hoover Crips. We took notice of this threat early on and tried time and again to reduce their population by any means necessary, all to no avail. So our last resort was the psychological approach. Make them believe we were bigger than they thought—deceive them.

What blew me away later on, while I was a prisoner in San Quentin, was when I read Sun Tzu's *Art of War* and he said "War is deception." We had figured as much long before we knew who Sun Tzu or Mao Tse-tung even were.

Our deceptive tactic was this: We would seem to divide the entire 'hood up into sides—North, South, East, and West—thus making the Sixties believe we were so huge that we had to break the 'hood up into subdivisions. It was our belief that they'd fall into confusion, trying to find the sides they most wanted to attack. We also believed they'd feel enveloped by a larger, more entrenched enemy than they had originally anticipated.

But when I explained this to Sidewinder, he rejected it out

of hand, citing some abstract notion that this was, in effect, breaking up the 'hood. This was straight hypocrisy on his behalf, because earlier that same year he had concocted some off-the-wall idea about turning the whole set into a new gang, calling it "West Coast Gangster Trays" (WCG3s). Crazy De and I backed him on it and supported his idea, even though it was immensely unpopular amongst other O.G.s. He had even suggested we change the color of our flag.

Despite his adamant disapproval, De and I went forward with our plans. Ironically, the same O.G.s who had disagreed with Sidewinder's idea about the WCG3s backed our development of subdividing the set. Initially, we had four sides, but the East Side fell off the following year when its staunchest members were captured for murder. We began right away on our campaign to inform the Sixties and the entire gang community about our latest development. We went about this task with a vengeance, writing on walls, turning out parties ("turning out" means to disrupt with violence) and at schools—most anywhere we felt like shouting our presence out.

This campaign was actually carried out by no more than four dedicated soldiers: Crazy De, Legs Diamond, Tray Stone, and myself. What started out as a tactic began to produce serious strategic results. Just as we had anticipated, confusion as to who was who set in over in the Sixties 'hood, and we were able to make some stunning strikes in the midst of their indecisiveness. In the meantime, our idea was gaining momentum in our 'hood. Others began to campaign for their respective sides, though all in unity with the original idea of deception.

In mid-December I broke into a house and secured two more weapons—another double-barrel and a Browning 9 millimeter. It was also around this time that we began to put serious dents in the Rollin' Sixties' offensive capabilities. On a cold, gloomy night, the Sixties tried to drop some of our West Side soldiers and were cut down. On the South Side a similar situation befell one of their units when one of their shooters hung out of the back window of a rolling car in an attempt to shoot some homies and was instead blasted back into the car with a full charge from a shotgun. The car sped away with the would-be shooter—turned victim—screaming in sheer agony.

Morale was picking up, and our level of recruitment also went up. One of the most damaging things we did to our own set during this time was to call meetings where we'd whip our troops and kick certain people off the set, taking for granted we'd always be strong. When we later found ourselves at meetings with as few as thirty-five soldiers in attendance, we began to regret our earlier acts of irresponsibility in regard to the treatment of troops.

I shot two people in December, but neither died. One I caught at McDonald's on Florence and Crenshaw, and the other I shot on Tenth Avenue and Hyde Park. Both I sprayed with buckshot. I liked to see the buckshot eat away their clothing, almost like piranha fish.

By this time my name and courageous exploits were ringing with alarming regularity in most 'hoods in the gang community. Crazy De was right beside me. We had finally broken through to the second stage of recognition. De, however, had been captured for a murder and was in juvenile hall awaiting trial. I was doing a solo while fashioning Li'l Monster, who had gotten released from camp by this time, Li'l Harv, Li'l Crazy De, Joker, and Li'l Spike into an awesome young fighting machine. They had begun to put in work on a constant basis, really getting a kick out of the whole thing.

We all were waiting for New Year's, not necessarily to usher in the new year, but to hit the Western Surplus and procure the much-needed, desperately sought-after guns and munitions. We had grand ideas about launching a final offensive on the Sixties—our own little Tet offensive.

December 31, 1980, was an ordinary day, overcast and a bit chilly. Putting on my gear I took extra care to dress warmly enough so as not to have to come back home for a coat. We had all agreed to meet at the blue apartments on Eightieth, which in accord with our subdivision of the 'hood was now the South Side. At approximately 4:00 P.M. I left my house on Sixty-ninth Street, which was in the North Side. I was dressed in white Chuck Taylor Converse All-Star tennis shoes with black and white shoestrings, heavily starched 501 Levis, a blue sweatshirt under an XXL blue penitentiary shirt, and a thick Pendleton jacket. I had cornrowed my hair to the back, and over this I wore a blue flag in bandana fashion.

Feeling very confident, I walked through the 'hood, up through the Seventies to the South Side. Of course I had the Browning 9 millimeter in my waistband. I reached the South Side without incident. Upon entering the apartment complex I found China, Li'l Spike, Stone, and Spooney kicking back drinking Night Train wine and smoking pot.

As we began to talk, Li'l Crazy De and Joker pulled up on ten-speeds. Joe Joe, who we had been considering giving the name Baby Monster, also came up. It didn't take long for the pot and cheap wine to start having its mind-altering effects on me. Never much of a drinker, I felt the alcohol hit me first. My equilibrium was shot.

By now it was dusk, and I was brandishing my 9 millimeter with abandon. I instructed Joker and Li'l Crazy De to go to my house and retrieve the double-barrel. I called from one of our supporter's homes to let Li'l Monster know that the homies were coming after the strap.

By the time they returned I was even more intoxicated. Seizing the shotgun, I instructed everyone to come out into the street. Once all had assembled out in front of the apartments, I moved under the street lamp and shot it out. Glass fragments rained all over my head and shoulders.

As I stepped onto the curb to shake the shards of glass out of my hair and clothing, my peripheral vision caught a black-and-white police car hitting the corner. Spinning with surprising quickness, as I was quite drunk, I tossed the shotgun to Joe Joe and told him to "break." But he was not aware of the police car and ran right into it. He was immediately apprehended. Remembering the 9 millimeter in my waistband, I broke through the apartment complex and discarded my weapon. I then made my way up to Peaches's house for refuge.

Watching the goings-on from the window, I painfully observed the police finding and confiscating my 9 millimeter. "Shit," I thought, "two damn weapons lost at once." I consoled myself by keeping in mind our planned mission for midnight—the surplus.

Once the coast had cleared I made my way back out front. Joe Joe had been captured and taken, along with the guns. Standing around now unarmed, I felt naked and longed for the comfort of my gun. I had simply to go back down to the North to retrieve another gun, but I was reluctant to walk or ride anywhere unarmed. So we just hung around Peaches's apartment and listened to music.

Darkness finally descended on the city. In front of the blue apartments it was especially dark, because I had neutralized the light. A car bent the corner off of Normandie and onto Eightieth with a precautionary pace that could have been misconstrued as a "shooter's coast." We shrunk back further into the camouflage of darkness in an attempt to conceal ourselves and avoid drawing unfriendly fire.

The car came to a California stop in front of the apartments. I was able to discern three occupants, all in the front seat. From their silhouettes it appeared that all three were female. This was still no less dangerous, for we had been using women drivers for missions as of late and this was not a patented tactic. Someone with a rifle, shotgun, or hand weapon could quite easily be lying down in the back seat waiting for the women, who seemed innocent enough, to lure an unsuspecting victim to within shooting range for execution. We watched and waited. After a couple of minutes of them trying to distinguish who we were and us trying to differentiate them as friend or foe, someone among us made their I.D.

"That's Pam, Yolanda, and Kim," whispered a voice through the darkness.

Pam was currently going with Li'l Hunchy. (This was the first Li'l Hunchy. He has since been replaced by a more righteous soldier.) She had, however, in the past dated a member of the Rollin' Sixties. Shaky and elusive is the best description I can offer for her relationship with the set. Her sisters' dealings with our 'hood fell even shorter than this. But she was Li'l Hunchy's girl now, and those were her sisters.

I had met all three in a previous exchange about the escalated developments of the war. Their position in this matter was neither pro nor con in respect to us. In reference to the Sixties, they had taken the Fifth. I had never trusted them and had always kept my dealings with them to a minimum. Fence sitters disgusted me. Hell, I would have felt better if they had just come out and said they were pro-Sixties, which did not necessarily mean they were anti-us. But their ambiguity threw me off.

I sallied forth from my seclusion in calculated steps. I walked on the balls of my feet so that in case a shooter did materialize from the back seat, I'd be ready to retreat and would hopefully escape with minimal damage. When I got close enough for them to identify me Kim rolled down the passenger-side window. She leaned out with both hands open in a "I'm unarmed" gesture, and urged me to the car.

"Hi, Monster," she said in a squeaky voice. "How you doing?"

"I'm fine," I said, not biting. "What's up?" I was clearly suspicious now.

"Oh," she began, "we're on our way up to the surplus and wanted you to come with us." Her tone had suddenly turned pleading.

"Why you want me to go with you?" I asked. Something wasn't right here. But my rational thinking was being impaired by the earlier consumption of alcohol.

" 'Cause you aren't going to let no one bother us," she responded.

During this exchange I began to think of the advantages of going to the surplus with them. I could survey the site for our midnight raid, then have them transport me down to the North to secure another weapon and bring me safely back to Eightieth. Hmmm. The notion was quite appealing.

"Awright," I said after debating it. "I'll go with y'all."

"Oh," Kim continued. "Where is Diautri?" This was Crazy De's given name.

"De is in jail," I said, and then added guardedly, "Why?"

"No real reason, just asking. I know that's your best friend, just thought he'd be with you."

"Naw," I said as I climbed into the back seat, "De is in jail for murdering Sissies." (Sissies is a derogatory term for Sixties.)

In response to this I got silence. I made a mental note to sit directly in the middle of the back seat so as to monitor the driver's eye movement. And in case we were ambushed I would be in the center and not by the door or the back window—an easy target. I tried never to make it easy for someone to destroy me. When we got to the corner of Eightieth and Halldale, I saw Li'l Hunchy rounding the corner on foot.

"Stop," I instructed Pam. "Stop and pick up Li'l Hunchy." I would feel better with another homie with me. Besides, it was his girlfriend who was driving.

"No," Pam said with staunch conviction, "we don't need him with us."

Now my suspicion was really mounting. Why didn't she want her boyfriend with us?

"Well, if he can't go, let me out," I said.

She pulled to the curb and I motioned Li'l Hunchy over and into the car. I made another note to inform him of Pam's unusual behavior once we were alone.

Now, the surplus had two parking lots. One was primarily for customers and was situated in front of the store on Western

Avenue. This parking lot was illuminated by a multitude of lights, not just in the lot but off the main street. Further illumination came from passing vehicles. The second lot, in contrast, was dark, barely lit by a small bulb that hung off the roof of the surplus. This parking lot was behind the store, on Eighty-fifth Street. Although this lot was for employees, it was also utilized as an overflow lot for customers. It was in this second, dark parking lot that Pam parked.

"Why you parking back here?" I protested, my security alarm going off.

"Look, Monster, this is my mother's car and I can park anywhere I want," Pam said in an almost hostile voice.

I decided to hold my tongue at this point because had I responded with what I was thinking there would have been an explosion in the car. My main objective was to survey the surplus for weak and strong points and retrieve another weapon from the North. Although I was in my 'hood, I felt very uncomfortable without a gun. This uneasiness perhaps would be equivalent to a businessperson leaving home without any credit cards. A weapon in South Central is a part of your attire, a dress code. "This gun goes with these pants and this shirt," or "I can put this weapon here with this outfit and still be chic." So my plan was to get my weapon for one, and also to check the site where we could get still more weapons.

Once the car was still I exited quickly, to get a bearing on the dark parking lot. I also wanted to avoid a clash with Pam. Li'l Hunchy followed suit. The girls, however, busied themselves with what I believed to be purses and jackets. Not wanting to be in their company, Hunchy and I started out around the side of the building on Eighty-fifth Street. I walked next to the building and Li'l Hunchy took the other track by the street.

Realizing suddenly that the girls were nowhere behind us, I stopped and gave a small shout.

"Y'all better hurry up." I waited a second, got no response, and turned to walk away.

As if out of thin air, three men had materialized in front of us. Wary now, because I was unarmed, I continued walking toward the three that were coming toward us. I put on my mask (a mask is an extended version of a mad-dog stare; it's one's combat face) and prepared for a possible confrontation. Taking in the attire of the three, I noticed no unusual bulges that would indicate they were strapped. And by their facial appearances they looked to be older, perhaps in their late twenties or early thirties. One had a full beard, another had a mustache. The third was clean-shaven. All three, I remember, were quite earnest, stern-looking cats. Their masks, if they were wearing any at all, were a bit more convincing than mine.

Li'l Hunchy felt the tension as well, for when I glanced over at him he looked nauseated. There was no sign of Pam, Yolanda, or Kim. The atmosphere quickly deteriorated to a kind of *High Noon* showdown—them walking toward us and us walking toward them. All the while our eyes were locked onto one another, trying to get an edge, if there was one to get at all. The closer we came to one another the thicker the tension became. My security alarm was screaming in my ear: "PROBLEM—DANGER—PROBLEM—DANGER!" But what could I do? Break and run? Although I have retreated in the past, as a tactic, I was not about to run now in the face of potential danger. They might not even be enemies, or they might not be armed, in which case we could handle the hand-to-hand combat. Three against two were winnable odds.

And then, the moment of truth.

"Ain't you Monster Kody?" the mustached one said. He seemed to be the one in charge.

Looking directly at him in my best confrontational stare—a combination of annoyance and insanity—I spoke through gritted teeth. "Yeah, I'm Monster Kody, Eight Tray Gangsters, what's up?"

Without another word he swung into motion, reaching into his coat for his weapon. To my immediate left I saw another movement, this one equally disturbing: Li'l Hunchy had broke and left me.

Turning quickly on my assailants, I was just in time to see the first muzzle flash and hear the resounding BOOM of his gun. Hit in the stomach first, I was knocked up and against the surplus wall with such force that shock and surprise overrode any pain. Once he saw that the wall kept me up on my feet and that the first shot was not fatal, he stepped in close to shoot me in the chest. My instinct shouted, "SURVIVAL!" I tried a desperate rush toward the gun.

BOOM!

Another shot. This time in my left hand, which had come within inches of the gun. The shot would have been a heart shot had my hand not been extended in an attempt to grab the weapon.

All the while the other two assailants were looking on approvingly, almost as if watching a movie. But I had had enough and decided to try an escape. Turning in the direction of Western Avenue I tried to run, but in midstride—

BOOM!

I was shot again in the back. This shot, like the first, had a devastating impact, and I was slammed to the ground.

Dazed, I struggled to get back to my feet. On one knee

now, I was kicked in the side by the shooter, knocking me back down on my back. As they stood over me, aiming down, I had no other defense but to raise my legs in an attempt to avoid being shot in the torso.

BOOM, BOOM, BOOM! And then—

CLICK, CLICK, CLICK.

"Damn," I remember wishing, "I hope they haven't invented a seven-shot."

Silence rained down like the deafening crash of cymbals; then I heard the sounds of running feet.

Lying there, looking up at the sky, I was swarmed by a million thoughts. My first one was sort of comical: He shot me like I be shooting people. And then the seriousness sank in as I saw a line of blood trickling down the sidewalk. My life was draining into the gutter, and I thought of all the things I had never done but wanted to do. I thought—for the first time—about my daughter, Keonda. She'd never know me. My thoughts were purely civilian. Payback was not even an issue. My thoughts gravitated toward things I had never done, people I'd never see again. And then I began to see, as if on a TV screen, everybody I had ever known in my sixteen years on this planet. Hundreds of people paraded past my inner vision, and they were as clear as day. Peacefully I lay there and watched the show. In that time, there on the sidewalk, I began to know what "rest in peace" meant. For until that moment I had lived only in war. Now the war was over. I settled back and waited to die.

And I'll be damned if someone didn't interrupt my peaceful fadeaway.

Li'l Hunchy had run around the whole block and come back to help me. A little too late.

Leaning over me he said, "What happened?"

I couldn't believe this dude. With all the strength I had I said, "Muthafucka, I'm shot!"

Seizing me by the collar, he dragged me around to the front of the store, where someone else helped him get me inside. Now confusion hit in full swing. From within the gathering crowd I heard voices.

"Isn't that Monster Kody?" And, "Ooh, it's gonna be some shit now!"

Some girl who I didn't even know was sitting on my legs crying and saying, "Calm down, calm down!" though I had not so much as moved since I'd been half-dragged, half-carried into the damn store.

In an attempt to console me, Li'l Hunchy said that I would be fine, that I had "only" been shot in the leg and the hand. These were my visible wounds, but I was burning elsewhere.

"I'm shot in the stomach and in the back, too," I managed to say.

"No, no, you ain't, I can see the holes."

He was telling me where *I* was shot!

Meanwhile, this girl I didn't know was wailing away, crying out of control about me calming down—and she was more hysterical than anyone in the store.

My breath was getting short and my anger was growing. Trying to get someone to unbutton the top button on my coat was the hardest task. Each time I'd point to my neck for help, signaling for someone to unbutton my collar, Li'l Hunchy would pipe up.

"You ain't shot in the neck, only in your hand and left leg."

I was steadily losing breath.

"Calm down, calm down!" this goddamn girl was constantly yelling.

Turning my neck and looking around to possibly secure some sane help, I saw an elderly man come forth out of the crowd.

"Cut his shoes off, cut his shoes off of him."

Oh, shit, I thought, it's these fools that are going to kill me, not my wounds.

Finally, the ambulance arrived.

Before I was carted off I managed to tell the hysterical stranger, "Bitch, if I live, I'm gonna kick your ass!"

Astounded, she finally calmed down. Amazing.

In the ambulance I lost consciousness.

When I came to, I was in tremendous pain, in ICU. Three days had elapsed, although I didn't yet know that. A tube ran up my nose and down into my stomach; I had one IV tube in my arm and another tube in my penis; stitches extended from my hairline to my solar plexus; there was a cast on my left hand and three huge bullet holes in my left leg. The pain was almost unbearable.

A nurse came in and administered a shot, which took me up and away.

The next time I came to I was in another room. The nurse said my condition was stable. She gave me another shot. Weak, very skinny, and dehydrated, I drifted off again.

5

CAN'T STOP, WON'T STOP

I walked to the driver's side window and demanded his wallet, at which time he smiled with a baneful sneer, drew a pistol, and fired one round into my chest.

BOOM!

The sound reverberated again and again, echoing away in my unconscious mind.

My own screaming woke me from my fitful sleep. Sitting up in the hospital bed, I struggled for clarity. Was it just a dream? I felt my chest for blood, a hole, anything that could prove or, for that matter, disprove my fearful thought of being shot again. I *had* been dreaming—having a nightmare would be more accurate. But my dreams, or those I could recollect, have always been punctuated with gunfire. Gunfire directed at me, coming from me, or in my general vicinity. And never have I shrunk from the presence of such lethal violence.

Being chased by Randy's huge donut is quite another matter, one to which I could not attach any sort of logic whatsoever. That *scared* me. For years that damn donut chased me around in my dreams. I was so deathly afraid of those donut dreams that once I had started banging I often contemplated destroying the huge plastic replica on Normandie and Century. Even today I loathe the sight of it. My screams alerted the on-duty nurse, not to mention scaring the daylights out of my roommate, who was also a gunshot victim. In minutes I was being attended by a nice-looking Chicano nurse who, as it turned out, had seen such postshooting behavior many times. She explained that it was quite normal and expected. My main concern at first was to make sure I had just been dreaming, and then my pride stepped in and I inquired about the tone and sound of my screaming. "Was I really *screaming* or was I just shouting? Was it *loud*, or what?"

Against my worst fears of damaged masculinity, or what I perceived to be such, she confirmed that yes, it was a scream and it was very loud. Perhaps she felt she had been too literal for my young ego, as I'm certain she saw me slump into a mournfully sagging posture. She fell heavily into a spiel about my nightmares being "normal," "natural," and "a result of the terrifying experience I had been through." All that was fine and sounded good, but could she please go down to South Central and explain that to my homies? Or, better yet, my enemies, who would just love to hear of me having nightmares. This line of thinking caused me for the first time to question my roommate's origins and set affiliation. For if he belonged to the wrong set this could be very harmful to my reputation and perhaps make it all the more difficult to continue my ascent through the ranks. Monster Kody having nightmares? Unthinkable.

Shortly after the nurse's departure and before the morphine she'd administered took me under, I questioned my roommate. He was a hapless civilian, fresh out of the backwoods of a small town in Georgia, whose people lived in a highly active part of Los Angeles. He had been sprayed with buckshot from a passing vehicle. The possibility that he was a civilian had never crossed my mind, perhaps because I always tried not to shoot civilians, unless of course the bangers outnumbered them in a gathering. Should we get some flack for that later on, we could always claim "association." We were hard-driven for results, for confirmed body counts of combatants. From what my roommate said, he was simply standing in the front yard when a passing car unloaded some buckshot into him. After he told me of this and his immediate plans to depart for "back home," he repeated over and over in a strong southern drawl, "Damnedest thang . . . damnedest thang."

He was totally taken aback by L.A.'s madness. But to me it all seemed quite normal. "Normal" like the nurse had explained my nightmares were normal. It was "natural" for me to retaliate against anybody as a "result of the terrifying experience I had been through," just like the nurse had explained. Of course I twisted her explanation of my psychosis into a perverted alibi for my continued behavior. I rationalized my actions continually, and with each successive level of consciousness I reached, my rationalization became less convincing to me. Questions were often left to hang in the balance because my conscience simply refused to process them due to such illogical reasoning. So I'd avoided questioning myself about my ongoing radical behavior. I'd deadened my conscience with PCP, alcohol, and friends, who themselves had done likewise. I dozed off under the soothing waves of the morphine, wondering how it must be to live a civilian life.

I just couldn't imagine living the life of a "hook," those seemingly spineless nerds who were always victims of someone's ridicule or physical violence, who never responded to an affront of any type. I had, while in primary school, been victimized by cats during their ascent to "king of the school." My milk money was taken. My lips were busted two or three times. Not because I decided to defend my dime or my honor, but because my assailant simply whacked me. Early on I saw and felt both sides of the game being played where I lived. It was during my time in elementary school that I chose to never be a victim again, if I could help it. There was no gray area, no middle ground. You banged or held strong association with the gang, or else you were a victim, period. To stress this when we made appearances at high schools, we'd often jump on hooks and take their money, leather jackets, hats, and such.

What's contradictory here, and is one of the irrational questions I battled with in my later years, is why are hooks victims of our physical wrath but unfair game in our lethal violence? The answer seems to be that hooks seldom, if ever, shoot back. Other bangers—whom I'm convinced, like me, have been victimized at some point in their lives and refused to let it continue—respond with the same violence they receive, if not something more lethal. Because of this, they must be smashed. Hooks are easy pickings for most anyone. But bangers know that there is no glory in killing a hook. In fact, it's frowned upon in most areas. To me, however, to be unconnected meant to be a victim. And I couldn't imagine that.

* * *

The next time I surfaced from my morphine-induced drift, I was in tremendous pain. Everywhere and all at once pain pounced on me with mind-wracking weight. My stomach, which had been surgically cut open to remove some shredded intestines, was now closed with sutures and staples. Since the surgery was so recent the cut skin had not yet started to heal, and in between the staples the openings looked pus-filled. The sutures were so tight that I could barely move without feeling tied down. My stomach resembled railroad tracks that in some areas had been blown apart by saboteurs. The sight of this alone caused lumps in my throat. To the left and slightly below my navel was where the bullet had entered. There was just a hole there, uncovered and open. I could see pink inside. My pain in this area came from under my navel and around the staples. The tube in my nose, which ran down into my stomach, was attached to a pumplike machine next to my bed. Looking at it caused pain. It was extracting green slime from my stomach and storing it in a clear jar. The nurse called it poison. I couldn't comprehend that and just assumed I had been hit with poison bullets. The catheter in my maleness ran from under the covers over the side of the bed and into what, I don't know. I never looked. This was also very painful. My left hand had been broken by the impact of the second shot and was in a cast. It, too, throbbed with pain.

I had taken three hits in the left leg, two side by side in the meatiest part of my front thigh, and one up a bit higher near my hip, almost on my butt. Like my stomach wound these, too, had been left open and exposed. I had also been hit in the upper back. I assumed this hole was also left open. From every hole, or its surrounding area, I had pain.

Looking from my stomach to the catheter to the open wounds and then to the pumping machine, I just couldn't put it all together. My thoughts ran at lightning speed in an attempt to answer some of the questions now being submitted for clarification. I was seriously dehydrated. My lips were cracked and dry. I reached out for the nurse's aid button hanging next to my bed, but my stomach pain was too intense, and I fell back in a heap. Frustration rose up like an evil serpent from a murky river, snatched me, and drew me under. It was then that I began to realize the impact of my being wounded and all the mental strain that I had actually been under.

I lay prone for what seemed like a day or two, trying to piece together what had taken place in my life over the past five years. Damn, had it actually been five years? Yes, five years had elapsed since my joining up with the set. Although it seemed like a long time, it had gone very quickly. At the same time, the seriousness of my chosen path had made me age with double rapidity. At sixteen I felt twenty-four. Life meant very little to me. I felt that my purpose on earth was to bang. My mind-set was narrowed by the conditions and circumstances prevailing around me. Certainly I had little respect for life when practically all my life I had seen people assaulted, maimed, and blown away at very young ages, and no one seemed to care. I recognized early that where I lived, we grew and died in dog years. Actually, some dogs outlived us. Where I lived, stepping on someone's shoe was a capital offense punishable by death. This was not just in a few isolated instances, or as a result of one or two hotheads, but a recognized given for the crime of disrespect. Regardless of the condition of the shoes, the underlying factor that usually got you killed was the principle. The principle is respect, a linchpin critical to relations between all people, but magnified by thirty in the ghettos and slums across America.

I had no idea of peace and tranquility. From my earliest recollections there has been struggle, strife, and the ubiquity of violence. This ranged from the economic destitution of my family to the domestic violence between my parents, from the raging gang wars to the omnipresent occupational police force in hot pursuit. Peace to me was a fleeting illusion only to be seen on TV programs like "The Brady Bunch." I've never been at peace, and nothing has ever been stable. Everything in my life has been subject to drastic change or subtle movement, without so much as a hint or forewarning. I've always felt like a temporary guest everywhere I've been, all of my life, and, truly, I've never been comfortable. Motion has been my closest companion, from room to room, house to house, street to street, neighborhood to neighborhood, school to school, jail to jail, cell to cell—from one man-made hell to another. So I didn't care one way or another about living or dying—and I cared less than that about killing someone.

The set was my clearest vision of stability. Although changes took place *in* the hood, the hood itself *never* changed. To ensure that it didn't, we vowed to kill all who set out to eliminate it. This obsession has been evidenced by our carriage in warfare. The ultimate stability, however, was death—the final rest, the only lasting peace. Though never verbally stated, death was looked upon as a sort of reward, a badge of honor, especially if one died in some heroic capacity for the hood. The supreme sacrifice was to "take a bullet for a homie." The set functioned as a religion. Nothing held a light to the power of the set. If you died on the trigger you surely were smiled upon by the Crip God. On my homie Lucky's tombstone it simply says: "My baby Brother taking a rest." He was fourteen when he was murdered, but he had lived so hard through so much that he needed a rest. We all learned quite early through experience that it was sometimes better to rest in peace than to continue to live in war.

In Vietnam when a soldier was wounded badly enough he was sent home. Home was a place where there was peace. No real danger of the 'Cong existed stateside. The war was ten thousand miles away. In contrast, our war is where we live. Where do we go when we've been wounded bad, or when our minds have been reduced to mincemeat by years, not months, of constant combat? If Vietnam vets suffer from post-traumatic stress syndrome, then I contend that gang members who are combat soldiers are subject to the same mind-bend as are veterans of foreign wars.

For us there is no retreat to a place ten thousand miles away, where one can receive psychiatric attention with full benefits from the Veterans Administration. No, our problems are left to compound, and our traumatic stress thickens, as does our abnormal behavior caused by the original malady gone unchecked. Is there any wonder our condition continues to worsen?

Talking with any gang member one will quickly pick up on the high praise and respect given when, in the course of conversation, a dead homie is mentioned. Usually before or right after the name of the deceased is spoken, "rest in peace" will be communicated in a very respectful tone.

Being wounded, on the other hand, can be taken two ways. In some cases, cats who've been wounded simply drop out of sight and use their injuries as an excuse to say "enough," which, of course, still leaves the set in the position of having to respond to the attack. *All* strikes against the set have to be answered in a timely and appropriate manner; otherwise the set's prestige wanes and eventually it collapses under the weight of the ridicule and military hegemony. But sometimes the wounded party utilizes their affliction to reaffirm their commitment to the 'hood. In so doing, they automatically climb another notch up the ladder toward that desired status of O.G.

Li'l Crazy De, for instance, has been shot thirteen separate times and is still committed to the 'hood. In the tenth unsuccessful attempt on his life he lost his left eye and a piece of his scalp. He is loved by few, hated by many, but respected by all. His legend is like that of the notorious gangster Legs Diamond, who had been shot repeatedly and survived. My wounding, however, fell deep within this second category, though there really was no need to reaffirm my commitment, for it went without saying that I'd be back. But the Sixties were certain that I had died. In fact, their premature celebration is what drew the set's attention to them as the possible shooters. We were at war with so many sets that it was hard to pin my shooting on any one 'hood, so the homies responded by hitting every 'hood we didn't get along with and a few that we did, just to be sure. The violence level rose dramatically in the days following my shooting—so much, in fact, that two officers from CRASH had come to the hospital with pleas for me to somehow stop it. When I'd gestured helplessly with my palms turned up they'd resorted to threats of conspiracy and accessory charges. I couldn't possibly help them.

When I finally reached my call button, I was surprised to find that I was being attended by an Afrikan nurse. She hurried about the room, checking on my general state, and then informed me that I was to be moved to yet another room, on the ninth floor. She was very talkative and witty, perhaps in her mid- to late thirties, and buxom. I pegged her as a stalwart Christian who was a third-generation immigrant from the National Territory (that is, the rest of the United States). She was very dark and very shiny and her name was Eloise. When she spoke she lit up the room with a radiant smile generated by sparkling white teeth.

"Now what happened to you?" she asked, hands planted on both sides of her shapely hips.

"I'm in pain," I responded. "Can you give me a shot?"

"Fo' what, so you can turn into a junkie?" she shot back.

"No, so I can stop hurtin'."

"Baby, you been gettin' twenty-eight grams of morphine every four hours for three days now. I think it's time you slowed down."

"What? Three days! What is the date today?"

"Today is," she said, looking at the watch on her fat wrist, "January third, nineteen eighty-one."

I had no sense of time and just couldn't believe that three days had elapsed since I had been shot.

"Now, what happened to you?" she asked again.

"I was shot."

"Shit, boy, I can *see* that. But *what happened?*" She asked in a voice of genuine concern, so I felt compelled to tell her.

"Gangbangin'. I was shot by other gang members." This sounded awkward to me, trying to explain it to her.

"And who shot you?"

Damn, I thought, was she some kind of detective or what, asking me all those questions.

"Don't know, maybe some Sixties, but I really don't know."

"And where you from, the Eighties?" she asked, but somehow she already knew.

"Yep, how you know?" Now I was getting very uncomfortable.

"I know 'bout that war y'all got going on over there. My son is involved in that shit," she said with disgust.

"Who is your son and where is he from?"

"Now don't you worry about that."

"Is he from my set, one of my homies?" I asked anxiously.

"I ain't got nothin' to say 'bout it no mo'. It's a damn shame how y'all do each other over some concrete no one owns."

Oh shit, I thought, here comes one of those sermons about how we are fighting for nothing and that we are all black people. Save it, lady. But she didn't say anything else, so I asked her why I was being moved. Because it was requested by the authorities, she said. I didn't give it a second thought, but I did ask if she'd still be my nurse, to which she replied she would.

"Now can I please have my shot?" I asked pleadingly.

"Yes, yes, chile, you can have yo' dope," she answered, and mumbled something unintelligible under her breath as she strode out of the room.

My roommate was gone, but I never asked after him. For what? He was a civilian. I got my shot and started drifting again. When I came to I had been moved to another room, a single-occupant room. The pain was not as intense, but I was even more dehydrated. Apparently another day had passed.

"Good morning, Mr. Scott." An American, Dr. Blakewell, spoke to me over an aluminum clipboard as he jotted down some notes.

"Wha's up?" I said through parched lips. "When can I go home?"

"Well," he spoke in measured tones, "we have to keep you

here a bit longer so as to monitor your development. You've had a difficult operation, but you seem to be faring well. Perhaps you'll be ready for discharge in a couple of weeks."

He lifted up my hospital gown and felt around my stomach.

"How's the medication?"

"Awright, I guess."

"Well, we are going to stop giving you shots and give you codeine fours. These will work just as well," he said, humming now as he continued to write more notes.

"Yeah, well check this out, Doc, can I get one last shot of what you been givin' me?"

"No, Mr. Scott, I don't think it's necessary. Your pain should not be that intense now."

"How you gonna tell *me* 'bout pain, muthafucka?" I blew up and surprised the shit out of Dr. Blakewell. "I'm in pain *now,*" I continued, "all over, man, so what you talkin' 'bout?"

"Yes, of course there is pain, Mr. Scott, simply due to the severity of the wounds and the extent of your operation. However, we must not allow you to become dependent on the pain medicine. Do you understand?"

I simply said, "Aw, man, save that shit."

Dr. Blakewell left my room red as a beet.

When my nurse, Eloise, came to work that afternoon I was glad to see her. We had begun to develop a healthy rapport and her wit, in the face of my condition, was appreciated. Not long after she came in and we joked a bit about me shouting at Dr. Blakewell—which she got a tremendous kick out of—she brought me a telephone and informed me that I had a caller who asked for me by my full name. Perhaps it was Li'l Monster or

China. I knew it wouldn't be Tamu, because she had left the year before and gone to Texas.

I elevated myself up with the remote that controlled my bed and prepared to have a good talk. Gathering the phone from Eloise I held it to my chest, insinuating that I wanted privacy, and waited for her to leave the room. If this was anyone from the 'hood our conversation would definitely be about combat and, in this light, I could trust no one, especially a civilian. Once she left I cleared my throat and spoke into the receiver.

"Hello."

Silence.

"Hello."

And then, "You ain't dead yet, tramp?!"

Stunned, I said nothing. After a few seconds of thought fueled my anger I exploded into the phone.

"Naw, punk muthafucka, yo' homies got scared and couldn't finish the job. Bitch-made Sissies!"

I got no response to this.

"Hello? Hello?"

The caller had hung up. Mad, nervous, and irritated, I sat there and fumed. The nerve of them muthafuckas, I thought, calling to verify my status. My head was spinning. When Eloise came in I snapped at her. She demanded an apology, for she is that type of strong sister, so I gave her one. After all, she was not the cause of my anger, and even if her son was in the enemy camp, she had not told him who I was. I explained to her that I needed to make a call and could she please excuse me. She readily complied and exited the room.

Still, I couldn't come to grips with the chutzpah of my foes. Clearly they had wanted to quash the debate once and for all. Was I dead or not? The rumors ran hot and cold. Of course, this was also a scare tactic, one that was truly wasted on me. I phoned Li'l Monster, let the phone ring sixteen times, but got no answer. I knew my mother and older brother, Kerwin, would be at work. I hung up, a bit frustrated, and called Li'l Crazy De. When I reached him, he explained the latest developments.

Upon hearing of my shooting, the others had aborted the surplus mission. Li'l Hunchy, who was with me and had run when the shooting started, was questioned at length about the circumstances surrounding the ambush. No one had any idea that he had run out on me. He told everyone that the shooters had specifically wanted me. Li'l Monster, taking the call to colors, went in search of a crew of elite shooters, troops steeled in the ways of urban guerrilla warfare. That night they did nothing but plan. Several units were organized in the hours following my shooting, but just six individuals were selected by Li'l Monster to roll with him: Li'l G.C., Rattone, Al Capone, Li'l Capone, Slim, and Killer Rob. Others were organized to hit various targets, but this crew was specifically assigned to the Sixties. Search and destroy was the mission.

At dusk on January 1, 1981, a van was commandeered by one of the selected soldiers to be used in the execution of the upcoming mission. Earlier in the day Li'l Monster had acquired two shotguns from an older supporter who had been informed of the shooting and wanted to give assistance in the way of arms. His offer was acknowledged and the weapons were secured: a double-barrel over and under, a 12 gauge, and a 20-gauge pump that shot six times. Because the mission was search and destroy, the weapons were not sawed off. Also in stock were an 8 millimeter Mauser that had ten rounds and looked like a Daniel Boone gun, a six-inch .357 magnum, an eight-inch .44 magnum, and a .38 Long. The driver was to be unarmed. Gathering at their respective launch sites, the crew began to fall out when darkness came. The order of the night was "body count."

According to Li'l Crazy De, wasn't no one on the streets but police and fools, the police not giving a fuck and the fools doomed by their own ignorance. How many fell that first night? And from what sets did they come? No one knew the actual count, except the recipient set and the parents who had to bury their children. And that's what we all were, children. Children gone wild in a concrete jungle of poverty and rage. Armed and dangerous, prowling the concrete jungle in search of ourselves, we were children who had grown up quickly in a city that cared too little about its young. Males, females, dogs, and cats were all targets. Curfew was declared in enemy sets: dusk to dawn. Anyone caught out after dark and before dawn would be shot. The Tet had begun.

The first night was pretty much catch and clobber. The second night was a bit more complicated, as word traveled fast around the colony. The third night, I'm told, was harder still, as troops literally had to go house to house in search of "suspects." It was in this climate that the officers from CRASH had come to see me. But prior to talking with Li'l De I had had no idea of the scope of the retribution and, for sure, I had not conspired with anyone to make it happen. Could I stop it? Perhaps, but why? "Fuck 'em" was pretty much my attitude then. And why was CRASH concerned about stopping the violence? They had been helping us kill ourselves, so why were they so interested? It is my contention that they simply wanted to go on record as having tried to stop the killings. Shit, if they wanted to stop the killings, they would have begun by outlawing the choke hold!

After being briefed by Li'l De about the Tet, I informed him that Li'l Hunchy had run out on me. He asked what I wanted to have happen to Li'l Hunchy. I said simply that he should not be allowed to run out on anyone else. That made the set look awfully bad. Li'l De gave me his word that he'd handle it. Putting the phone in its cradle I lay back and smiled inwardly, feeling extremely proud of the set. The mighty Eight Trays . . .

By my fifth day in the hospital, I had grown quite accustomed to the comings and goings of the orderlies. I had learned, for instance, that the Chicano woman who had attended me first was the mother of the candy striper who now cleaned my room and who was a gang member from Eighteenth Street. She and I chatted twice. But still I had no visitors, and I had not talked with Li'l Monster. On the afternoon of January 4, as I lay back in my bed thinking, I noticed three people standing in my doorway. At first glance, I took them to be ordinary people who were just passing through looking, as I used to, into anyone's hospital room. But these people looked familiar—in no friendly way. Their look was menacing, and I'll be damned if it didn't hit me like a ton of bricks. It's them! The same three who had ambushed me! The mustache, the beard, and the clean-shaven one stood erect and alert at my door. No doubt it was also them who had called my room. What to do? With an I.V. in my right arm, a catheter in my penis, a tube in my nose, stitches in my stomach, a cast on my left hand, dehydrated and weak, I knew I didn't have a chance.

As slowly and as inconspicuously as possible I reached for my nurse's call button, hoping that Eloise was on duty. My assailants seemed indecisive and fidgety, looking around and, I guess, waiting for the proper moment to make their move. I figured they'd probably stab or suffocate me so as not to make much noise. I pressed my call button several times, hoping to irritate someone, anyone, and have them rush to my room. This, I thought, would persuade my assailants to leave. All the while I was acting as if I was heavily sedated, so much so that I couldn't tell that I was being sized up. Damn, any other nurse would have responded by now. Just my damn luck. I began to despair and settle for the final rest. Of course, I told myself, I was going to resist. I would swing as much as I could with the cast, kick with my right leg, and bite, if I could. But I was sure I'd lose, and I resigned myself to that end. Just then, as in a Hollywood movie, where the star never gets killed, in rushed Eloise, past the three and to my bedside.

"What's wrong, baby?" she asked, concerned that something was bothering me medically.

"Listen," I began in a low voice, "see those three people at the—"

"I can't hear you," she said.

"Shhh, listen, *listen,"* I said, trying to control my voice. "See those three dudes at the door? *Don't look, don't look!"*

"What about 'em, baby?"

"They come to kill me!"

"Oh, there you go dramatizing, you need to—"

"Look," I said, grabbing Eloise by the collar and yanking her down face-to-face with me, "they come to *kill* me, now goddammit, do something!" I was speaking low through clenched teeth. For sure she now saw, perhaps for the first time, my thousand-yard stare.

Her eyes grew wide when it registered that I was for real. Even when I let go of her collar she remained in my face.

"Go, *now,* and handle that," I told her and, as if hypnotized, she slowly rose to an erect position and strode back toward the door. I watched her through half-closed eyes, hoping they wouldn't kill both of us. She stopped in their presence and traded words with them. They were out of my earshot. I saw Eloise gesture toward the hallway to the left, turn, and do the same thing toward the right. I had no idea what she was doing. Whatever it was, it worked, and my assailants moved into the hallway and eventually out of my sight. She, too, left my sight, but only for an instant. When I saw her round the corner again and come into the room she had the telephone with her and was moving rather quickly.

"What did you tell 'em?" I asked excitedly.

Thrusting the phone at me she said, "Don't worry 'bout that, you better call your people, 'cause they comin' back."

Not knowing how much time I had before they'd be back, I hastily dialed Li'l Monster's number. It rung once, twice, three times and . . . damn, I'd dialed the wrong number. On my second attempt I hit pay dirt.

"Bro, what's up?" I said quickly into the receiver.

"What's up?!" Bro shot back and stammered on, "Man, we been tearin' shit—"

"No, wait, listen. They up here!"

"Who?"

"The Sixties, man. The Sixties!"

"We on our way!"

The connection was broken. I rang for Eloise and she came right away. I explained to her the seriousness of my foes and that it was probably the same three who had originally shot me. I also turned down her offer to get the police. No, we'd handle this ourselves. She looked skeptical, but gave me her word that she wouldn't call the police. The longest twenty minutes of my life were spent waiting for Li'l Bro and reinforcements.

Finally, I saw Li'l Bro bend the corner, followed by Li'l Spike, Joker, Li'l Crazy De, Stone, China, Bam, and Spooney, the latter three being homegirls. They surrounded my bed so that nothing else was visible but them; then weapons began to materialize from under their heavy clothing. They had mostly hand weapons, a few buck knives, and Li'l Spike had a sawed-off single-shot. Li'l Monster had been out of camp for about nine months and was working in earnest toward his required second level. He displayed all the traits of promise. From under his shirt he produced a .25 automatic, and China came out with a box of bullets.

"This is for you, Bro," he said, handing me the strap and box of bullets.

"Righteous." I went on to explain the situation and gave a description of all three. Li'l Spike and Joker went in search of them, while the others stayed to talk. Bro said that he had come to see me while I was in ICU, but I had no recollection of him ever being there. He said he could not stand to see me in such a state. We looked at each other for a long moment, and I could see that he was hurt and wanted to communicate his emotions, but neither of us knew how to do it. So we settled for the unspoken medium of love, each hoping the other would somehow catch the vibes of sincerity.

Crazy De had been in an altercation with some Sixties in the Hall, China told me. No homies had been captured or shot since the Tet had begun, and the set was enjoying tremendous coverage by the media. Li'l Spike and Joker returned with Eloise hot on their heels.

"No sign of them fools," Li'l Spike said with frustration. "Besides," he said, pointing his thumb at Eloise, "we got sweated by homelady here."

"You damn right you got sweated. But tell him what you was doin'. Go on, tell him," she said loudly.

Neither Joker nor Li'l Spike said a thing, so I asked them what was up.

Joker spoke up first. "Aw, cuz, she bent the corner and caught a muthafucka strikin' up the 'hood."

"Gangwritin', in *my* hospital. Uhh-uhh, not here you don't."

"You don't own this goddamn hospital, woman, who the—"

"Stall her out, Bam, she down wit' us," I said sharply to the homegirl, who was widely known for her belligerence.

"But she—"

"Stall her out," I repeated, forcefully.

"Kody, visitin' time is 'bout over anyway." Eloise was now shooting daggers at Bam, who was returning her stares point for point.

"Awright, but let us get three mo' minutes, huh?"

"Yeah, yeah, but no mo' writin', y'all hear?" she said, looking from one hard face to another.

No one replied. She finally gave a small sigh and left the room. I began to instruct the crew about my plans once I was released. All seemed quite happy to know that I was recovering well, Li'l Bro and China especially. Not to say that there was any less affection from the others, but China and Li'l Monster knew me more intimately, so our link was stronger.

Soon thereafter the crew began to leave. The set sign was thrown in a salute by each homie, and China gave me a kiss on the cheek, promising she'd be back the following day. Bro milled around and waited for the last homie to file out. After a minute he looked at me, then dropped his head. When he raised it again we both had tears in our eyes. I had been touched—wounded—and although it was never verbally communicated, I was Li'l Bro's hero, the closest thing he had to total invincibility. Everything I did, he did. And now, with my being wounded, he knew that there was someone out there that was stronger, more determined than me. The vast weight of this fell heavy on his shoulders and it became incumbent upon him to destroy that person and "save the world"—our set. At fourteen, that's a heavy load.

"It's gonna be all right, it's gonna be all right," is all I could say.

To which Bro replied, "Yeah, 'cause I'm gonna make it right. Watch."

We hugged briefly, as much as my stitches would allow, and then Bro left without looking back. It was times like this that I hated my life. Perhaps this was due to my not knowing answers to certain questions or being able to present my emotions on an intelligible level. Being ignorant is, to me, the equivalent of being dead.

I checked my strap to make sure it was loaded and put it under my pillow. If they came back now it would not be in their interest. Against my better judgment, I dozed off.

Time flew by, and daily I became stronger. China was coming to visit every day and even brought a radio, although only after I had sworn on the set—which was much more religious than swearing to God—not to destroy it like the last one. I got no more calls or unexpected visits, and on January 14th I was discharged. This was the only time my mother came to the hospital, which didn't bother me too much then. We had grown very far apart, so I'd never expected her to come, anyway. But she had to come on my discharge day because I was still sixteen and she had to sign the release form. Our mutual greetings were lukewarm. We talked little on the way out of the hospital. I was rolled out in a wheelchair pushed by Mom. Over my knees was a blanket, and underneath it the weapon, my hand fully on the grip.

In the car we both made small talk. The days were past where Mom sought to talk me out of bangin', but still she was firmly set against it. Little did I know that Mom was under as much strain as I was. This is universally true of every mother who has a child in a gang. But usually communication has long been broken with that parent, who the child looks upon as a familiar intruder trying once again to offset stability. In this light, anything proposed by the parent—whether positive or not—is rejected. The intruding parent becomes enemylike in thought, and is to be avoided. Nothing is to alter the set's existence. For a youth with no other hope in a system that excludes them, the gang becomes their corporation, college, religion, and life. It is in this reality that gang members go to the extreme with tattoos. I now have "Eight Trays" written across my neck and "Crips" on my chest. Ever see George Bush with "Republican" on his chest or "Capitalist" on his neck?

The moment I got home the phone began ringing off the hook.

"Yes, I'm all right."

"No, I didn't get my dick blown off."

"No, I wasn't shot in the head."

The calls went on like this all day. When night fell, I hit

the streets on Li'l Monster's bike. Li'l Tray Ball rode with me and carried the weapon. We weaved our way through the 'hood, stopping here and there to explain blurry details to concerned citizens of the 'hood and a few parents who were looked upon as "friendlies." When we had circumvented a good portion of the 'hood, we doubled back toward the north. It had gotten chilly, and because of my stay in the hospital I was unaccustomed to being out in such weather. My open wounds made my trek in such weather all the more dangerous. When we reached the house, Mom was standing out on the front lawn accompanied by a host of homegirls. Kesha, Judy Brown, China, Bam, Prena, and Big Lynn were all there. Before I came to a halt I knew something wasn't right. Everyone looked grief-stricken. Mom began in on me right away.

"Kody, where you been?"

"Just ridin' in the 'hood, what's up?" I asked in a nonchalant tone.

"You are not supposed to be out in such weather with those open wounds. You know what the doctor told you." Her voice was almost a whimper.

"Aw, Mom, I was just ridin' around. Anyway, I got my jacket on," I retorted.

"But honey, you could catch pneumonia out here. Please come in the house."

"Awright, but just let me kick it a minute out here," I said defiantly, not about to be talked down by Mom in front of the homies.

"No," Mom said with new force. "Come in here now."

"Mom, you trippin', I'll be in there in a minute."

"Monster," Kesha spoke up, "you should just go on in the house."

"Wait, wait, hold it, hold it," I responded with both hands up, one palm showing and a cast on the other.

"Naw, Monster, you hold it. Yo' mama only tryin' to tell you what's right." This was Big Lynn.

Knowing her prowess I eased closer toward Li'l Tray Ball, who was armed. If she made an attempt at physically persuading me into the house I was going to bust a cap in her ass.

"Check this out, I'm only right here in the yard. I'm comin' in in a minute, okay?" Now I was looking for some support from the homegirls. I got none. Mom had apparently wooed them before I rode up.

"Kody, please come in the house." Mom was so overwhelming that even Li'l Tray Ball was now urging me to comply.

"Homie, you should go on in the pad."

I laid down the bike and stalked off toward the house, arguing about Mom being of another generation and not overstanding me. This, of course, was a genuine cop-out. For it was I who had lost touch with reality. I had encapsulated my block of reality into a tamper-proof world that made every other point of view absurd. This was especially so if I felt the other point of view was threatening to my livelihood.

Once in the house I went to my room, shut the door, and sat on the bed. Li'l Monster was out campaigning, so I began sorting through our "oldie" collection. Actually, the records belonged to Li'l Monster, who was, and still is, an ardent oldie fan. I dug out something fitting and placed it on the turntable. "I'm Still Here" by the Larks came screaming over the stereo, and I fell back on my bed and let the lyrics seep in. The refrain, "I'm still here," kept lifting me up. It held a special meaning to me after being shot six times. "I'm still here." I undressed and dozed off with the refrain still resounding in my ear, though the record had long been off.

I got up the following morning and pulled on some fresh Ben Davis jeans, a sweatshirt, and croaker sacks—shoes made from burlap. I gathered up Mom's car keys to go to the store for some cereal. When I began rolling out of the driveway I found I was blocked by an unmarked police car. Two American detectives got out and approached the driver's side of the car, so I got out. One of them asked if I was Kody Scott. I replied that I was. The other then produced a piece of paper from the inner pocket of his suit coat. He explained that they had apprehended the guy who shot me. When I asked who that was, he said Pretty Boy. I knew who Pretty Boy was. He and I used to be friends, until the start of the conflict. He, like Crazy De and me, was fiercely loyal to his 'hood and had on many occasions shot or shot at our homies. This was widely known. In fact, after his involvement in Twinky's death, he was elevated to Threat Level Two and put on our Most Wanted list. I knew he hadn't shot me, but to try and explain this to these two would be futile. The paper the officer handed me was a subpoena to appear in court as a witness to Pretty Boy's shooting me. I took the paper and threw it into the car and they left.

I made my way to the store and back without further incident. When I returned, I found my mother and my niece, Tamara, in the front garden cleaning out weeds. I spoke to them briefly and then went into the house to enjoy a big bowl of cereal, as I was quite hungry. My mom's house is a moderate three-bedroom mid-sixties dwelling with two huge picture windows on either side of the front door. When the drapes are open one can see clear into the house. We had a nice front lawn and a huge rubber tree out in the yard that gave us great shade in the summer and camouflaged military launches at night. Right in front of the porch was a beautiful garden that Mom took great pride in keeping up. It was in this garden that she and Tamara now worked as Li'l Monster and I sat staring out of the picture window eating raisin bran. As I lifted a spoonful of cereal to my mouth a car drove past at a slow observer's pace. I stopped in midmotion and let the face of the staring occupant sink in. Enemy Sixty!

"Sixties!" I shouted to Li'l Bro, who had already recognized them and was heading down the hallway toward our room and the cache of weapons now stored there. Once we had seized two weapons—both long-barrel shotguns—we made it back to the front room just in time to see the vehicle turn up into a driveway and begin to come back our way. Perhaps their intent was to shoot into the house, shoot Mom, or simply undertake a reconnaissance mission. Whatever it was, we had no intention of letting them leave this block. As they began approaching us, going westbound—the driver closest to the house—we burst through the door and leapt over Mom and Tamara and ran at top speed toward the car, weapons leveled. When Mom recognized what was happening she shouted for Tamara to go in the backyard. Before the driver could mount a response we were within killing distance of them.

Leveling the barrel to the driver's head, I shouted, "This is Eighty-third Street, muthafucka!" and pulled the trigger.

The gun was on safety.

If there is a God, He was between me and that driver because the driver, for sure, was dead that morning. Ducking down into the seat and swerving sharply to the right, he punched the accelerator, jumped the curb, and ran down Mrs. Bucks's fence.

Mom said nothing as we retreated past her and back into the house. We ate the rest of our cereal with guns in one hand, spoons in the other. It was this particular incident that rang the bells in Mom's head that said, "Hey, this thing is serious." No sooner had we finished our cereal, not ten minutes after the incident, than a black-and-white patrol car came to a halt in front of our house. Bending down so as not to be seen by the police, we darted down the hallway to stash the straps. We both discarded our clothes and donned bathrobes to shake a description, in case someone had seen us in action earlier. We then heard talking up front.

"Is Kody Scott your son?" one of the policemen asked my mom.

"Yes, Kody is my son, why?"

"Well, ma'am, we have a warrant for his arrest for murder and six counts of attempted murder."

"Oh," Mom began with a slight chuckle, "you must be mistaken. Kody was just released from the hospital two days ago. He could not have possibly killed anyone."

"Well, we have several eye witnesses who say it was in fact Monst— I mean Kody who they saw." His voice sounded no-nonsense.

"Well," Mom said, trying another angle, "can you call the station to make sure it's Kody you want?"

"Ma'am, we are sure who we want. Now is Kody here?"

"Yes, he's here. Kody!" Mom called out after me.

After hearing as much as I needed to I began to get dressed. Me and Li'l Bro hugged and said our good-byes. I stepped forward and allowed the police—henceforth soldier-cops—to take me in.

At the station I got the details. Some Brims had said that while they were shooting dice in their park, Harvard Park, I had stepped out of the shadows with, of all things, a double-barrel and blasted them. This was supposed to have happened the same night that I was released from the hospital.

Once again I found myself in solitary confinement at Los Padrinos Juvenile Hall. But this time I was in bad physical condition from the shooting and the operation. I also had the cast on my arm with the 'hood struck up all over it, along with the names of some homies. After my standard week in the box I was transferred to unit C-D. In Los Padrinos the housing units are designated by alphabet. I had pretty much been in them all. When I got to C-D I met up with Queek from Eight Tray Hoover. He and I were the only Crips in the entire unit. All of the New Afrikans were Bloods, and the Chicanos and the Americans were strongly supporting them.

There were approximately twenty-five people in the dayroom. At least thirteen were New Afrikans and the rest Chicano or American. There were twenty plastic chairs on metal frames welded together in rows of five. These were situated in front of an old black-and-white television. Queek and I sat there, primarily because to sit any other place would be foolish. We also wanted to stipulate the distinction between us and them, Crips and Bloods. Most of the Bloods were Pirus from Compton. Every so often, as if on cue, one of the Pirus would leap to his feet and shout, "All the 'Rus in the house say ho!" at which time everyone—except Queek and me—would jump to their feet fanatically shouting "Hoooo!" This went on throughout the night at hour intervals, but no one approached Queek or me personally.

The next day while Queek and I sat on our bench—our meager territory—and talked, we drew some pretty mean stares from the chair section. Once, in the course of conversation, I said "cuz" to Queek and the whole dayroom fell abruptly silent. Even the characters on television seemed to pause and look over at us. No one moved, no one said a thing. And then, as if he were an ambassador to the U.N., Bayboo from Miller Gangster Bloods cleared his throat and started walking over toward us. He was a viciously ugly person with a huge jug head, which was covered with small braids in no fixed pattern. His complexion was dark, but not that shiny smooth darkness like Marcus Garvey or Cicely Tyson. It was a flat darkness, broken in spots by chicken-pox marks that had become infected from scratching. His eyes held no light, no humor, no remorse. His eyes each had black rings around them and they were sunk deeply into their sockets. His lips and nose were uncut Afrikan from the continent. I would guess he weighed 170 pounds then, quite muscular with a broad chest. He stopped in front of me.

"What did you say?" he asked, looking down on me with total ugliness.

I looked at Queek for some sign of mutual liability, but my stare went unacknowledged. I stood up so he would not have the advantage of a downswing.

"I said cuz to my homeboy," I replied. Murmurs from the chair section began to grow louder.

"You must not know where you at, Blood. This is our unit and we don't allow no punk-ass crabs over here. I should knock you out, boy."

Far from being a fool, I took a step backward out of his firing range.

"And what you think I'm gonna be doin' while you knockin' me out?" I shot back, hoping I hadn't made him too mad, because for sure I was in no physical shape to fight anybody, especially him.

"Wha . . . " he started, and made a quick step in my direction. I took one step back and a brother whom I hadn't even noticed came between us, but facing Bayboo.

"Man, stall dude out. You see he all fucked up, cast and shit," the brother said to Bayboo.

"Fuck that fool, he don't know where he at or somethin'."

"I know where I'm at," I managed to say.

The staff was becoming suspicious, as the dayroom had grown too quiet. Shit, everything was fine as long as there were Pirus shouts every hour, I guess. But the quiet was out of order.

"You," a Chicano staff member said, pointing at me. "Come on in here." He gestured at his office. When I went in and sat down he asked what the problem was. I told him that there was no problem, but he wasn't buying it.

"Oh, I see, you a Crip. And," he continued, turning his head to read the graffiti on my cast, "you are from ETG, Eight Tray Gangster, huh?"

"Yeah, that's where I'm from."

"Well then, that explains it. You are starting confusion in my unit," he said matter-of-factly.

"Man, I ain't startin' nothin' in yo' unit," I tried to explain.

At this, he opened a desk drawer and brought out a red marker.

"Paint your cast, 'cause the gang graffiti is a problem," he said, pushing the marker toward me.

"I ain't coloring my cast dead"—a disrespectful term for red. "You must be crazy."

"Oh, well, we'll see about that."

He reached for the phone, dialed, and talked with someone. Five minutes later a New Afrikan man came in.

"What's happening?" he said.

The Chicano cat explained as best he could, which wasn't too good. When he had finished, the brother simply asked, "You a Crip?"

"Yep."

"Are you a real Crip?"

"Yep."

"Here, then, paint your cast blue," he said, handing me a blue marker.

Perhaps this was a ploy and he thought I wouldn't do it because of my situation. Well, I did. I broke open that marker and painted my cast Crip blue. The brother just stared. The Chicano was visibly upset. I went back out into the dayroom and had no further problems that night.

The next morning I went to court and got arraigned on murder and attempted murder charges. Because of the serious nature of the crime, I was being tried as an adult. This meant I would face the same time as any adult would for the case. Sixty years to life was the maximum penalty. Also because of their decision to try me as an adult, I had to stay in East Lake Juvenile Hall, also known as Central. Los Padrinos did not house juveniles who were being tried as adults. This was cool with me because Crazy De and other homies were at Central. I've always preferred it over L.P. anyway.

I was put in unit E-F. Central, like L.P., designates their units by alphabet. E-F and G-H were where all the hard-core bangers were housed. In E-F we had staff from South Central who treated us like family. There was Brother Blackburn, who let Crazy De use his radio so we could go into the unit library and jam. He also let us go into the unit office and lift weights. There was Brother Doc, who gave us phone calls all the time. He let us stay back from school and just kick it. He also tried to flirt with our mothers during visiting hours. There was Stewart, Heron, and Cryer, but our favorite cat was Brother Gains. He was a strong brother with a genuine concern for people of color. He was the source of all power in unit E-F.

De and I were on the same side, E side. Central was packed with future Ghetto Stars from both sides of the color bar and varying divisions therein. It was also packed with soon-to-be-dead gang members. Many who were there in 1981 have since been gunned down in street battles. Others were sent to prison and killed there. Few, very few, have lived since then in any prolonged state of peace.

Who became Ghetto Stars? There was Devil from Shot Gun Crips, Fish from Outlaw Twenty Bloods, Fat Rat from Five Deuce Hoover, Roscoe—a Samoan—from Park Village Compton Crips, Taco from Grape Street Watts, Macc from Eleven Deuce Hoover, and Kan from Black P. Stone Bloods. Each is of the highest level of banger. Even if any of them do not subscribe to banging today, their mark is firmly planted in their respective 'hoods.

Sundays in juvenile hall were perhaps the most exciting day of the week. Not only was it visiting day, but it was church day. No religious strings whatsoever were attached to church. On the contrary, church was a place to see the girl prisoners, and to see all your homies who were in different units. Chicanos and Americans went to the Catholic service, and New Afrikans went to the Protestant service. This was to be my first church service and, seemingly, everyone knew I had been shot, though all sorts of rumors had muddied the waters about my well-being. I readied myself for my first appearance the night before by "pressing" my county khaki pants with soap and laying them under my mattress. I had procured a fresh baby-blue sweatshirt that had a Central juvenile hall emblem on the front. I carefully cut the left sleeve off at the elbow to fit my cast. This, too, I slid under the mattress for pressing. My hair had been freshly corn-rowed, and I had some new bubble-gum tennis shoes. The next morning I got dressed with all the enthusiasm of a student on the first day of school.

Unit E-F was the last to arrive at church that morning. With all the other units already seated and situated so the staff could halfway keep an eye on them, we came through the door. Juvenile hall policy dictates that all unit movement be conducted in columns of two and in silence. De and I headed up our unit. When we came through the chapel doors all heads turned to catch our entry. Standing in the doorway briefly, De and I scanned the pews like lords looking upon their subjects.

"There he go, that's Monster Kody in the cast," said a faceless voice.

"Damn, cuz got a *blue* cast," said another.

After being told by the staff where to sit, we moved in and took our seats. De pointed out friend and foe. Because we weren't allowed to talk or communicate to each other, our hatred and happiness were transmitted by stares and quick hand gestures. Only when the preacher began the service did the whispers cease.

I was the talk of the hall. Later in the week I met Sam from Shot Gun—the Shot Guns had recently killed a Rollin' Sixty—

who was going with a female from the Sixties named Goldie. I had never met her. He said he had heard about me being shot from her. He then went to his room and brought back a letter for me to read. It was from Goldie. It was really a paltry little letter that ended with, "Oh, yeah, my homies killed that tramp Monster Kody last night." My heart skipped a beat when I read that. It was one thing to hear someone say it. Words spoken could be shaken off with a laugh or some other move that didn't make the effect of what's said last too long. They were just words in the air. But seeing it written was another thing. Unlike threat legends of *getting* killed spray painted on walls, this was written in the past tense, as in *already happened.* It was a bit eerie. I quickly folded up the letter and gave it back to Sam. I didn't comment on what she wrote, but I did store her name for future reference.

When I woke the next morning I was in terrible pain. My stomach was in knots. No sooner had I gained consciousness than I started vomiting. I tried to eat, but I could not keep any food down. This went on most of the day. De said that I should go to the nurse, but I declined. The next morning I was vomiting blood and the whites of my eyes had turned yellow. That evening I turned myself in to the nurse who, in turn, alerted the doctor. One look at me and he called for an ambulance. I was rushed back to the U.S.C. Medical Center—also known as General Hospital—and operated on immediately. When I woke up the next day I was in the same old pain of three weeks ago, the same tubes running here and there, the same machine next to my bed. My stomach once again looked like twisted and torn railroad tracks. The only difference now was that I was chained to the bed by my ankle. Two days went past and I got a visit from my mom. We talked a bit, but when I showed her my stomach, she left.

Two weeks later I was transported back to Central. When I got there the place was in an uproar. Staff members were running here and there, obviously stressing. I quickly learned that a friend of mine had escaped. Q-Tip from Geer Gang had broken out. I was happy for him. This was Valentine's Day, 1981.

I was placed in the infirmary until my stitches were removed. On that day, February 21, I walked around the corner from the infirmary to the connecting unit R and R—Receiving and Release—to exchange the hospital gown I had been wearing for facility clothing. Coming in were Li'l Monster, Rattone, and Killer Rob. All three looked haggard and distraught.

"What's up," I asked Li'l Bro with a light hug.

"Aw, man, we think Li'l Capone snitched about the murders," he said in a very tired voice. They were still dressed in street clothes. Bro had on one of my Pendletons.

"Y'all in here for murder?" I asked, looking from one to the next.

"Yep," Rattone replied.

"I think he told 'bout some shit you did, too," Killer Rob said, "'cause the police was askin' me 'bout some bodies left in the Sixties." Killer was speaking as if he were simply saying "Yo, man, your shoe is untied." Murders were that commonplace.

"Yeah, well, dude don't know shit 'bout me 'cause I wouldn't steal a hat wit fool," I spoke up, trying to put a good face on this dreary news.

"Scott," a staff member called out, so both Li'l Monster and I went to the desk. He was referring to Bro, so that he could be dressed in, but since we were both Scott and we both needed to be dressed in, he let us go together. Stepping into the next room, we rapped about family, Mom, and our neighbors.

When I took off my gown Bro said, "Damn, they fucked you up," and broke into tears. Through sobs and sniffs he said that he had never seen me that skinny.

"We'll get 'em," I said.

"That's right," Bro replied.

We talked some more and then I was sent to my unit. Because Bro, Killer, and Rattone had murders, they had to go to solitary for a week. When their seven days were up only Rattone and Li'l Monster remained. Killer had been transferred to the county jail because he'd turned eighteen while in solitary. Also captured were Li'l G.C., Al Capone, and Li'l Capone. Slim had gotten away.

Bro was put in unit M-N, across the field. Mom came the following week to see us both. The week after that I tore my cast off in the shower and began lifting weights.

When I went to court for a preliminary hearing, I was transferred to the county jail to be housed in the notorious juvenile tank. To this day, I still don't know why I was sent to the county jail. I hadn't even gotten into a fight yet. But this was par for the course for my entire life. It only served to irritate me further by allowing me no stability. I was a bit uncertain about L.A. County after hearing so much over the wire, especially because of my weakened physical condition. Fighting now would be quite a task.

It took an entire evening for me to be processed into L.A. County. I arrived in 3100, the juvenile tank, after midnight.

Now, I'm told, the juvenile tank is located in the old hall of the Justice Building, but in 1981 it was still in the new jail.

All the lights were out when I came on the tier, and there was no noise, no sound. With an almost terrifying clang, my cage was opened and I was told by the deputy to step in. Once locked behind the steel bars, I surveyed my surroundings. There were two tiers consisting of Able row and Charlie row. Each tier had twenty-six cages on it. Each cage was single occupancy, very small, very dirty, and very cold. There was a toilet and sink in each cage, as well as a light that the soldier-cop controlled. There was a rickety desk that hung halfway off the wall with no stool. I didn't remember seeing anyone awake or moving in any of the seven cages I passed to get to mine. I was number eight. This was a ploy, but I knew nothing of it then.

"Blood, where you from?" a voice shouted from the back of the lower tier—Able row. Its sharpness startled me momentarily, but my instincts overrode any delay in responding.

"North Side Eight Tray Gangster Crip."

"Aw, Blood," said another voice from the opposite direction. "We got one."

And then, as if from the adjacent cage to my right, number nine:

"We gon' kill yo' muthafuckin' ass in the mo'nin', crab."

"Fuck you slob-ass muthafuckas, this is ET muthafuckin' G, fool."

"We'll see 'bout that in the mo'nin'. Let the gates be the bell."

Another fine mess I had gotten myself into. Shit. I had no idea of how I'd get out of this one. Amazingly, I never once thought of rankin' out, pleading, or otherwise backing down. Even in the face of insurmountable odds I would rather die fighting than live as a coward. I made my bed and lay there staring at the roaches gathering on the desk top. I dozed off, but I don't know when.

I was awakened by the heavy sound of moving metal, cages being opened and closed. I quickly got up and put on my tennys and stood ready. Able row was being let out first. Looking down over the tier I saw a crowd gathering along the wall. Most faces were staring up into mine, though no teeth were being shown. No happiness lived here.

I didn't know any face down in the crowd and none, I guess, knew me. No one said anything to me, nor did I say a word to them. They began to file out to what I guessed to be the chow hall. Charlie row was next. "Let the gates be the bell" was fresh in my mind. My neighbor to the right had said that last night. So it was best, I thought, to tie into him immediately.

"Charlie row watch your gates, gates opening," the soldier-cop called down the tier.

With some effort the cage door began to slide open. When there was enough room to squeeze out I made it through and was on the tier in what I reasonably thought to be Blood 'hood. But when my neighbor in cage nine came out it was a familiar face: Bennose from 107 Hoover. Ben recognized me and broke into a wide grin. But still I was tense. Next I saw Levi from 107 Hoover, then Popa and Perry—who I didn't know, but had seen on the news—from Harlem Crip. Taco from Grape was there, too. It had all been a test to register my commitment level when in dire straits. I passed with flying colors.

They had already known that I was coming, perhaps long before I did. The grapevine could be very efficient at times, and at other times it failed miserably. I found out quickly that above and beyond unit E-F and G-H in Central juvenile hall, this was where they housed the "worst of the worst." I fell in step and was right at home. Both Able row and Charlie row were Crips. There were Chicanos housed there, as well. No Americans could survive on Able or Charlie row, nor could any Blood. Later I fixed it where Sixties were excluded, too. Bloods, Americans—there were very few—and victims lived on Baker and Denver rows, or P.C., Protective Custody.

The "slob game," as it came to be known—played on me to test my courage—was also used to uncover and weed out real Bloods. Because every American put into the tank was severely beaten or in some cases raped, the entire populace of American soldier-cops despised the juveniles of Able and Charlie rows with a vengeance. Often we'd get beat for the most trivial things. And, of course, there was inter-rivalry.

When I got there, Cyco Mike from Main Street Crips was supposedly in charge. He was a tyrant, taking food and other things from people, especially those on Able row, without so much as a word in return. He was a big, dark-complexioned cat with long hair. He, like the rest of us, had a murder charge. From day one he sensed my potential to threaten his tyrannical rule. It wasn't leadership he was providing. He had gotten his position not by popular support but by brute strength. On his team he had Green Eyes from Venice Sho-line Crips, Eric from Nine-Deuce Hoover, his homies Killer Rob and Cisco from Main Street, and Handbone, who was also from Venice Sho-line. They were all on Able row. The other Crips on Able row were simply cannon fodder. The rumble between Cyco Mike and me was inevitable. All the while I kept lifting weights and training for that day.

* * *

"When two totalitarian powers make war on each other, the anger and hatred that arise can be appeased only by the death of one or the other. More than this, such killing is profoundly satisfying. Anger and hatred are 'fulfilled' in destruction insofar as such emotions know satiety. The more lives the soldier succeeds in accounting for, the prouder he is likely to feel. To his people he is a genuine hero and to himself, as well. For him, war is in no sense a game or a dirty mess. It is a mission, a holy cause, his chance to prove himself and gain a supreme purpose in living. His hatred of the enemy makes this soldier feel supremely real, and in combat his hatred finds its only appropriate appeasement."

J. Glenn Gray

The juvenile tank has got to be the most blatant exercise the state has ever devised for corrupting, institutionalizing, and creating recidivism in youths. At the behest of a judge or on the recommendation of the probation officer or district attorney, these youths can be whisked from a structured program monitored by a civilian staff—who attempt to counsel the captured youths by developing a healthy, human rapport with them and their parents—and dropped into a prisonlike setting with not so much as an inkling of counseling or adult support or the benefit of any meaningful, structured program to aid them in correcting whatever problems they may have. Removing them from a program designed for immature, unsophisticated youths and hurling them into a highly competitive, one hundred percent criminal population and setting—where the only adults are the very same police deputies responsible for their initial capture—is clearly a way to breed a criminal generation.

Probation officers and deputy district attorneys ultimately decide who will be tried as an adult. This decision is based on what the P.O. and D.A. call "maturity of the circumstances surrounding the crime." This, of course, is euphemistic and, when examined from my side of the bars, means "If you're New Afrikan or Chicano and have a murder charge, regardless of the circumstances, you are mature enough to be treated as an adult."

It went without saying that most any American youth captured for murder would never be tried as an adult. His crime was surely not "mature enough" to warrant such harsh treatment, even if the hard evidence surrounding the case clearly illustrated that. For example: a shotgun shell had been secured to a rat trap by a U-nail and deliberately left in Mrs. Goldberg's mailbox. When she opened the box to retrieve her morning mail a wire was tripped, letting loose the swing arm of the trap, which in turn hit the primer of the low-base, high-charge .12 gauge shell, killing Mrs. Goldberg instantly. Or, while dropping hits of acid at a social gathering, a group of friends uncovered an intruder from another planet who had somehow broken their circle and was surreptitiously plotting to execute the town fathers or, more important, the connection. So, based on a Ouija board identification of the intruder, he is sacrificed and eaten. Sophisticated? Mature? Premeditated? Of course not. "This," the P.O. and D.A. will explain to the judge, "was a simple case of a good child destructively influenced by the violence of television." Or, deeper still, "a victim of the drug plague, simply needing a psychiatric evaluation. But," the D.A. would continue, "to try this young person—our very future—as an adult would be tantamount to treason!"

But the juvenile tank is filled to capacity with New Afrikan and Chicano youth, who more often than not have been charged in an alleged crime against one of their own. A New Afrikan youth in jail, charged for murdering another New Afrikan in most any form—sophisticated or not, and usually it's not—will be tried as an adult and given the stiffest sentence possible, which, without fail, will be life.

I found myself behind bars for the first time at age sixteen. Not a door, not a window, but bars. Since then I have had an indelible scar on my mind stamped "criminal." All my years of watching TV told me that righteous criminals went to jail behind bars. Wasn't Al Capone put behind bars? The Onion Field killers, Charles Manson, and Sirhan Sirhan? So by environment alone I came to look upon myself as a stone-cold criminal and nothing else. Not then overstanding the political machinations involved with me being housed in such a place, I simply assumed that my reputation had preceded me and a more secure setting was needed to hold me.

Without a doubt, I was engaged in criminality. But my activity gravitated around a survival instinct: kill or be killed. Conditions dictated that I evolve or perish. I was engaged in a war with an equal opponent. I did not start this cycle, nor did I conspire to create conditions so that this type of self-murder would take place. My participation came as second nature. To be in a gang in South Central when I joined—and it is still the case today—is the equivalent of growing up in Grosse Pointe, Michigan, and going to college: everyone does it. Those who don't aren't part of the fraternity. And as with everything from a union to a tennis club, it's better to be in than out.

So it goes that the American youths tried as adults—an insignificant number, not enough for a percentage—stayed in juvenile hall. The few that trickled into our wardom had simply been thrown away by the system. Because of our youth and political immaturity we would vent our anger, frustration, and hatred of the system—whatever that was—on them. It was totally beyond our overstanding that they were just like us: castaways condemned to an existence outside of the system. Potential allies were torn to shreds like bloody meat in a shark tank. Not one walked out, and few live today unscarred.

We stayed locked in our paltry little cages most of the day. For an hour a day we'd all be let out into the dayroom—a huge room, unobserved save for a small portion that was manned by a lookout. We watched them attempt to watch us. The demarcation was set: us and them—that is, the soldier-cops. Unlike the staff in the hall, who posed little or no threat, the deputies were outright racist dogs who always wanted a confrontation with us. We thought that as we were juveniles, they could not beat us. How naive the young mind can be. Levi was the first to be beaten. I can't recall the circumstances surrounding the altercation, but it was awfully messy. They beat him bad. Blood was everywhere. The more they beat him the more frantic they became, every one of them Americans, with the exception of one Negro. It blew my mind to hear the American deputies calling Levi "dirty nigger" and "nappy-headed motherfucker" while the Negro deputy held him for his cohorts. Even Levi looked to the Negro for some sort of explanation to this contradiction. None was given. That was heavy to me. Little did I know that the load would get heavier.

It was in Los Angeles County Jail that I learned that Americans have a thing for attacking our private parts during a scuffle. Every incident I've been involved in or witnessed, the private parts of the beatee would be viciously attacked without missing a beat, as if some personal grudge existed between them and our dicks. Later on I learned that it did. We nursed Levi back to health and began to avoid direct confrontations with the deputies. We'd fuck them in other ways.

Charlie row had coalesced the strong into a united front and violently purged the weak. Able row, which was now Cyco Mike's territory, was also being formed into a front; however, he worked through force and violence. Most of those with him felt physically intimidated by his size and prowess. Our unity on Charlie row came as a result of a common enemy: Cyco Mike. He had little idea that we were plotting his overthrow. We were taken to the roof thrice weekly and allowed to lift weights. Both tiers went together, so we on Charlie row feigned affection for Mike in his presence and continued to prepare for his destruction in private.

Mike had, at one time or another in the course of his climb to the top, talked bad to, beat up on, or taken something from almost everyone there. What's striking here is that when our generation picked up the gun, we began to use our hands less and less, so more than a few gunfighters amongst us had no ability to down Mike physically. Most folks talked behind Mike's back. When we said anything about him it was in questioning his strong and weak points, who would really go down with him on Able row, and who were just hostages.

I myself was only beginning to gain my weight back. I trained with the weights like a mad Russian. The second operation had really set me back, and since I was only out of the hospital three days before being captured, I hadn't had the proper nutrients to supplement my diet to stimulate growth. I had to suffice with jail food—ugh! Nothing was less healthful.

The Los Angeles County juvenile tank was not all humdrum, tension, and war. We had some good times as a captured family, making light of our dismal situation. Next to 3100—the module we were housed in—was 3300. On Able and Charlie rows of module 3300 there were queens and a few studs. On Baker and Denver rows were snitches classified as K-9s. The queens used to shine our shoes, braid our hair, and, if one wished, do a few other things. We had never seen queens and were awestruck by them, just as much as they were with being so close to throbbing, young, naive juveniles. One afternoon, Chicken Swoop from Long Beach Insane persuaded a queen named Silky to come over to our tier gate. Once Silky had come close enough to our gate, High Tower and Wino from Grape Street Watts grabbed him and wrestled him to the ground. They subdued him and hustled him down the tier to an open cell. After having their way with Silky, who had long ago ceased to resist, they let him go. With the excitement seemingly over for the day, we all fell into a somber sleep. But late in the night we were awakened by Chicken Swoop's loud screaming.

"Ahh! Ahhh!"

"What's wrong, cuz?"

"Ahh! Ahhh!"

"Who is that?" a disgruntled voice asked.

"Cuz, that's Swoop. Somethin' wrong wit' him," someone answered.

"I wish he'd shut the fuck up," said yet another voice, through the cold and darkness.

"What's wrong, Swoop?" asked Green Eyes from Venice Sho-Line.

"Cuz," Swoop began, "my dick is green."

"Yo' what?"

"My dick, muthafucka, my dick!"

And just then from down on the other end of the tier came another scream.

"Ahhh!"

"Who is that?" someone asked.

"Aw, shit!" High Tower stammered. "My dick green, too!"

The whole tank was awake now and out came the comedians. No one got any more sleep that night. We stayed up and clowned all night and into the next afternoon, right up until the medical crew came and hauled Swoop, High Tower, and Wino out of there. Later that afternoon a lieutenant came and gave us a sex talk about men who have somehow been twisted into thinking they are women and that we were all queers. He ended his sermon by calling us the sickest youngsters he had met in a while.

Light moments such as this tended to ease some of the stress that we were under. Once eight or nine of us were in a cell just telling war stories and joking around when someone claimed he could ejaculate faster than anyone else in the cell. Well, this was cause for a showdown. Within seconds everyone had their dick in their hand and was pumpin' away. The self-proclaimed champ did not blow off first and was clowned as just wanting to see our dicks. We threatened to urinate on him.

Our rule was simple: the sets that were there first and remained firm were "in." This meant that any set that came in that any of the "in" sets didn't get along with, no set got along with. They had to go—violently. This was even true of the Chicano sets.

When I was shipped to County, Li'l Monster was still in the Hall. Shyster was basically running the Rollin' Sixties in Central, and I thought he might try to do something to my li'l brother to get some points. Li'l Monster was in there for killing Shyster's homies, and Shyster was there for killing one of our homies. Since Shyster was being tried as an adult, he faced the very real possibility of coming to the juvenile tank. So I wrote him a letter saying basically that should one finger be laid on Li'l Monster in my absence it would be brought to bear on him when he arrived at County. I told him of our structure there and for authenticity I had everyone sign it. Li'l Monster went unmolested his entire stay.

In early March one of Popa and Perry's homies from Harlem Thirties was killed by some Brims at Manuel Arts High School. True to tradition, the alleged killers were tried as adults and rushed to the juvenile tank. They went directly to Baker and Denver rows P.C. We plotted and planned on a way to get over to their cell and kill them. In April our chance came. Ironically, Popa, Perry, Insane, myself, and both the Brims were taken to court together. We knew that as juveniles we'd all be put in the same court holding cell and then, as planned, we'd beat the two Bloods to death. The juveniles who were being tried as adults but kept in the Hall were also to be housed in this same holding cell awaiting court.

Our shackles were removed, and we filed into the cell on the basement floor of the Criminal Courts building in downtown Los Angeles. The county jail juveniles always arrived approximately thirty minutes before those from the Hall, so even though we were all in the small cell, we didn't pounce on the two Bloods, who by now knew we were getting ready to jump. We wanted to wait until the others arrived, so no one would be coming by for at least two more hours. When the door opened for the others from the Hall to enter, I was removing the braids from my hair. If the t[illegible] Bloods were going to make a dash for it, now was the time. We expected them to, but not a quip was heard from either. This meant one of two things: the Bloods were not afraid of us, as we had anticipated and surely had always believed, or they were naive enough to think that we were not going to smash them. I was relieved that they had not gone to the soldier-cops. I guess I felt a bit of respect for them, as well, because to stay in a ten-by-twenty-foot cell with four members of the opposition who had been charged with killing took a certain amount of courage. I also felt sorry for them. The ignorant bastards had no idea of how we planned to mistreat them.

Two juveniles from Central entered the tank. Both were New Afrikans and both were Rollin' Sixties. I didn't know either by face, nor did they recognize me. Popa eased over to me and whispered that the light-complexioned one was T-Bone. The other one he just knew as one of their homies. T-Bone's name carried a little weight in his 'hood. A second-level member who had shot a few people, he had recently been shot five times by the Black P. Stone Bloods. He had a slight build, short hair, and a fixed frown. When his eyes swept the cell they telegraphed contempt. He wore a black hair net down over his forehead like a sweater cap. Reaching into his pocket, he pulled out a half-smoked cigarette, fumbled in his other pocket, and retrieved a match. He struck the match on the concrete floor, lit his cigarette, and sat back coolly on the bench. His homie stood across from him near the entrance. Because I didn't know who he was, I worried little about him. I walked over to T-Bone, who was concentrating on his hard-core stare, and stood before him. I had completely forgotten about the Bloods.

"Where you from?" I asked, already knowing but wanting to hear him say it.

"Rollin' Sixties," he responded proudly.

"Get up, homeboy. We gotta get 'em up."

"Fo' what?" he asked, visibly disturbed.

" 'Cause I'm Monster Kody from Gangsta."

"Wait, man, hold it. We ain't even gotta trip that."

"Naw, I don't wanna hear that shit, fool. Yo' punk-ass homies blasted me up, killed my homeboys Twinky, Roach, and Tit Tit. Now you wanna talk that 'hold it' shit? Get yo' bitch ass up!"

I stepped back so he could get up, but still he wouldn't move. The half cigarette was now a butt, and he was nervously sucking on it through clenched fingertips. I walked back up to him and put my left foot up on the bench next to him. He would not look me in the eyes.

"Who killed my homeboy Twinky?" I asked, figuring to pump this lame muthafucka for all the information I could before I downed him.

"I don't know."

"Oh yeah?" I began. "Who killed my homeboy Roach?"

"I don't know," he responded, looking straight ahead. I think he began to ease a bit under questioning, believing this would be my only intrusion.

"Who shot me?"

"Look, I ain't supposed to tell you who shot yo' homeboys," he said, as if he were reminding me of some set rules of warfare agreed upon by both countries in Geneva. This taking of the Fifth would perhaps have been admissible in some American court of law, but in our circle it was not acceptable.

"Muthafucka," I exploded, "I'll tell you who shot *yo'* homeboys!"

"Who killed Zinc?" he asked.

"I killed Zinc!"

"Who killed Popa T.?"

"I killed Popa T.!"

"Who killed Baby O.?"

"Me, muthafucka, me!"

I went on to name a few others I had pushed off this planet, all the while trying to incite him to violence.

"Now," I said calmly, "who killed Twinky?"

"I don't know."

Out of control now, I grabbed him by the collar.

"Sissy, I'll slap yo' goddamn head off."

"If you do I'll still be from the big Six-O," he said.

I reared back as far as I could and slapped the hell out of him hard across the face. His hair net flew off from the blow. With little choice he stood up swinging, but he was just a gunfighter and had little skill with his hands. I beat him pretty bad. One of my uppercut blows landed directly in his eye, knocking his head back. He stumbled to a corner holding his eye and pleading for me to stop. I did only because he ceased to resist. All the while his homeboy said nothing, so I stepped over to him.

"What's yo' name?" I asked.

"Shakey," he replied. A fitting name, I remember thinking.

"How long you been from the Sixties?"

" 'Bout nine months."

"What you in here fo', shootin' one of my homies?"

"Naw, fo' shootin' some Brims."

In a flash one of the Bloods jumped up and said, "I'm a Brim," and rushed the Sixty with blinding quickness. For a moment I stood indecisive. After all, the Sixties were Crips. Shouldn't I help him get the Blood—which was *our* original intent? But the Sixties had showed little regard for my 'hood, my homies, or me. Why should I help him? "Fuck them Sixties," I decided, and sat back to watch the fight. Though both were my enemies, the Sixties were my worst enemies.

The rumbling was too loud against the door so the soldier-cops came in and seized both Shakey and the Blood. At this time the other Blood spoke up and made his exit to safety with his comrade. T-Bone stayed, and I pumped him for all the information I could.

That day in court my trial date was set. T-Bone was remanded to the custody of the sheriff's department, which meant he was coming to the juvenile tank. When he arrived the next day he had miraculously stopped banging. He was put on Able row. His eye was so discolored and bloodshot that he was given the new name of Tangle-Eye. After that, whenever any drama of significance took place with our 'hoods on the street, I beat Tangle-Eye for it. When Li'l Crazy De was shot—for the third time—I hurt Tangle-Eye bad. To offset my wanton abuse of him, Cyco Mike got Tangle-Eye claiming he was with Main Street, and because we had no beef with Main Street, he was able to enjoy a bit of immunity.

In the course of our slob game late one night we found the real Bloods. I was feeling at a loss for someone to beat up. One of the Bloods was Bingo from Bounty Hunter and the other was Weeble Wooble from Mad Swan. Both were from the east side of Los Angeles and neither had killed any of my homies, though we had suspected the Swans of desecrating our homie Cocaine's body while it lay in wake near their 'hood. We'd arrived late to find that Cocaine had been stabbed repeatedly in the face with a screwdriver and that multiple red flags had been thrown into the casket. But their part in this was mere speculation.

The most eager to put hands on the two Bloods were the

Grape Streets, whose worst enemy was the Bounty Hunters, and the East Coasts, whose worst enemy was the Mad Swans. Those poor Bloods. Up until the following day we had them believing that we were all Bloods. We'd lead into a topic about so-and-so having been shot, and they'd finish the story off. When our rumors proved false, they'd correct it for the record: "Uh-uhn, Blood, that was my homie so-and-so who kilt that crab." This went on through the night. We even signed off with "Blood love" before going to sleep.

The next day was Doomsday. We fell into the dayroom that evening feeling ecstatic, excitement in the air. Right up until we began tying blue flags around our knuckles, the Bloods thought they were among their own. No one said anything, everyone just prepared. The Grape Streets moved on Bingo first. The sight was inexplicable: within seconds he was unidentifiable. This was a standard beat-down. The other, however, is worth detailing.

Weeble Wobble was a stocky little guy with a full beard. Monk, from East Coast, said his name had a little weight to it on the east side. He, like the rest of us, had a murder. He had little beady eyes that darted around nervously, and the left side of his mouth quivered. I doubted it was because he was scared, though, because he didn't seem to be. He answered all our questions in an even voice.

Monk had a bit more tact than the Grape Streets, who just pounced on Bingo. Monk questioned Weeble Wooble at length about people, places, and events that had transpired over the years between their 'hoods. Weeble Wobble, as if knowing his fate and wanting to confess his sins, spilled his guts. But he did so admirably, proudly conveying the missions he had been on and who had fallen by his hand. Just as I admired Monk's professionalism in handling this prisoner of war, I had to acknowledge the sincerity of the prisoner. Not once did he falter during his debriefing, not once did he stutter.

When Monk was satisfied that he had bled him of all that he needed, he called for Dirt to bring a cup. Everyone looked baffled. It was enough to be civil in questioning the prisoner, but to now offer him a drink was a bit out of our range of diplomacy. Nevertheless, we all waited to see what Monk had up his sleeve. Monk had done some irrational shit in his day and was not beyond pulling a twist. When he got the cup from Dirt (Dirt's brother's name was Mud; they were both there for killing Jessie James from Blood Stone Villain) it was empty, which didn't seem to bother Monk too much. He simply pulled out his dick and filled the cup. And then, as if it were beer, he nonchalantly handed it to Weeble Wobble who, to our surprise, took it. Well goddamn, I thought, this shit was going too smoothly, almost as if rehearsed.

"Drink it," Monk ordered. Only now did his voice show strains of anger, betraying the cool look on his face.

"Wait a minute, Monk, I—"

"Drink it!" Monk exploded with fury, completely out of control now.

Without further protest Weeble Wobble drank the acrid liquid, spilling droplets on his beard as he tipped the cup. Once he had finished and put the cup down Monk tore into him with a vengeance. Everyone wanted to rat-pack him, but Monk insisted on it being head up. Weeble Wobble tried to dance about and put up a little resistance, but he had been so demoralized by the debriefing and the urine drinking that his response was simply no match for the swiftness and physical skill of Monk. Every punch Monk threw was with pinpoint accuracy, splitting

Weeble Wobble's lip with a left jab, then doubling back with an overhand right, opening a gushing wound above his right eye. Body blows rained in rapid-fire succession from his navel to his neck. When he fell to the ground, Monk proceeded to stomp and kick him all over—except, with any real intent, in the groin area—until his eyes rolled back in his head and he flopped around on the floor like a fish.

Bingo had long ceased any movement. Feeling somehow left out, I called Tangle-Eye over and slapped him up. Not to be outdone by Monk, I called for a cup. But I couldn't urinate, so I handed it to Taco, who quickly filled it up. No one said a word as I handed the urine-filled cup to Tangle-Eye.

"Drink it," I told him, "or come to the back and prepare for battle."

Tangle-Eye was looking around for Cyco Mike, who had gone to see a visitor. He then looked to Green Eyes for a reprieve.

"Hey, Green, you know I ain't no Sixty no mo'. You gonna let cuz do me like this?"

"Monster," Green Eyes began, "you know cuz claimin' Main Street now—"

"This muthafucka ain't from no Main Street! You know it and I know it."

And then, looking at Tangle-Eye, I held up both fists and repeated, "Now drink it, punk, or get these dogs put on yo' ass."

"You know you gonna have to answer to Mike when he get back," Green Eyes said.

"Drink it!" I said loudly, ignoring Green. And then as an afterthought I said, "Mike don't pump no fear here," slapping myself over the heart. "Just 'cause he got y'all scared 'round here don't mean I'm gon' be scared, too."

The dayroom was deathly quiet. The line had been crossed, my plan prematurely hatched.

"Muthafucka, what did I tell you?"

At that, Tangle-Eye tipped the cup and swallowed the urine. I slapped him anyway for being such a coward.

When the soldier-cops came to the dayroom door to let Cyco Mike back in, they saw Bingo and Weeble Wobble lying in pools of blood and called a 415—a distress call. Within minutes the dayroom was swarming with vile soldier-cops slinging threats and profanities around at random. We each were made to strip for examination by a sergeant, who looked for scratches, blood, welts, or abrasions that would suggest we had somehow been involved in the beat-down. Monk was the only one taken to the hole.

After the examination we were locked back into our cages. I heard Green Eyes sending Cyco Mike a briefing on what had happened with Tangle-Eye. But Mike said nothing to me.

Later that night I heard Cyco Mike order Li'l Fella from Five Tray to give up his breakfast in the morning. Li'l Fella, a small cat who weighed at least fifty pounds less than Cyco Mike, gave no response to this. It became apparent to me what was taking place. Cyco Mike knew he could not give Tangle-Eye full immunity under Main Street's jurisprudence for two reasons: Tangle-Eye had not joined willfully and with the required passage of the universal litmus test, and he had smut on him from not putting up a struggle for his props. This type of coverage only served to make Main Street look soft, as if anyone could join. Cyco Mike knew that I knew all of this. He also knew that he could not bring my latest act of aggression on Tangle-Eye to me without making himself look stupid. So he was using an indircct route to draw me out. All Trays—Four Trays, Five

Trays, Seven Trays, and Eight Trays—are natural allies, just as the Neighborhoods are. So by publicly taking Li'l Fella's breakfast he was actually sending a message to me.

I weighed the consequences of what I was about to do. How many troops did he have down there? There was Green Eyes, Cisco, Warlock, Killer Rob, Handbone, and Chicken Swoop—who was recently back from the clinic. He could also count Tangle-Eye on his side. I had Moman, Oldman, Taco, Poopay, High-Tower, Dirt, Mud, Bennose, Levi, Popa, and Perry. It's not quantity but quality that counts in such situations. We had a crew of quality soldiers who, quite frankly, up until my arrival, had lacked the proper leadership. To say I alone filled that vacuum would negate the role of all the others in forging our united front. We all, at different times, functioned in the seat of leadership. But I was the primary driver. Though I was nowhere near the physical condition I wanted and needed to be in, I had to respond to Mike. He knew what he was doing and I knew—that was enough. But before I could respond to him directly, I had to try to rile up some resistance in Li'l Fella. Although he had little chance against Mike, he could at least stand his ground.

"Hey, Li'l Fella, what you do, give cuz yo' breakfast or what?"

"Naw, homie, but fuck that breakfast."

"Yeah, but Trays don't do it like that," I told him. "If you ain't gonna eat it, throw it away."

Before Li'l Fella responded Mike spoke up.

"Monster, what tier you on?"

"Charlie row."

"Well, keep yo' ass up there. Don't worry 'bout what go on down here."

"I could give less than a fat rat's ass 'bout Able row. My concern is with my li'l homie," I said matter-of-factly.

"Yeah, well he live down here."

"You too big to be bullying on cuz anyhow."

"Who the fuck you think you is anyway?" Mike asked accusingly. "Coming here, thinking you that muthafucka somethin'. You too new here to be woofin' that shit, Monster."

"Nigga, fuck you!"

"FUCK YOU!" Mike shot back.

"So what's up then?"

"In the a.m., muthafucka, let the gates be the bell."

And that was it.

The silence weighed a hundred tons. It seemed that I could hardly move or breathe under it. I wanted to make small talk with Ben, but decided against it in fear of my voice cracking, showing strain, stress, and, honestly, fear. Fear not necessarily of Cyco Mike, but of possibly losing the fight. What then? Was I supposed to live with it? That just wasn't my style.

I remember before I went to camp in '79 my older brother, Kerwin, used to put hands on me. He'd feel quite content with bopping me around for any small infraction. But he didn't realize the radical transformations I was going through while in jail, where ass whippings just weren't tolerated by anyone. So when I was released and had committed my first infraction—something like failing to clean the bathroom—he went to pounce on me, and I quickly drew my strap and explained to him that those days were over. If he had any further notions of putting hands on me, he'd have to tangle with my gun. He nodded his comprehension and walked out of the room in somewhat of a trance. He hasn't touched me since.

Unfortunately, I didn't have a strap now. I did, however,

have my fighting skill. I lay there and went over some moves I could pull, trying to plan, which was ridiculous. How can one plan a fistfight? It's not like the combatants have the same choreographer. And it was clear this wasn't going to be a clean fight. This would be a stomp-down, drag-out brawl for the duration of wind, punches, and stamina. It had come to this, though prematurely, but in a way I was glad it was finally going to be on and over. Something had to break the tension. The situation had come to a head, and a new round of relations were about to be set in motion. I fell asleep with my mind full of these thoughts.

The following day, nothing happened. The next day, I observed Cyco Mike in the dayroom having war counsel with his troops. I saw Green Eyes wrap Mike's hand in blue flags and help him take down his jumpsuit, so I had Taco tie my hands up with flags and I took my jumpsuit down, too. Taco and I remained seated on the table in front of the old black-and-white television. Both sets of troops were fanned out about the dayroom eyeing each other skeptically. The tension was very, very thick. Cyco Mike and Green Eyes began to walk toward Taco and me, so we stood up. Mike spoke first.

"Woof that shit *now* that you was woofin' the other night."

"I ain't no tape recorder. You heard what I said."

We both were in strike-first positions, almost toe to toe.

"Fuck that, fool, we gotta get down," Mike declared, and went to step out of his shoes.

"I thought you knew," I said, and didn't let him get to the other shoe. Like lightning I was on him, hitting everywhere at once. My speed, fueled by great bursts of adrenaline, was surprising—even to me. When I stopped swinging he was down on all fours.

"Aw, you gonna try to hit me when I'm takin' my shoes off, huh?"

"Fuck you, punk, get yo' bitch ass up," I said vehemently.

When he stood up again he rushed at me, but not with swinging blows. Instead, he tried to wrestle me down. Each time he went to grab me I banked a blow across his face or head. I was backing up, sticking and moving, sidestepping and hooking. He was furious! Finally, when I had danced myself into exhaustion, he grabbed me in a suffocating bear hug. Using his strength and weight as leverage he succeeded in toppling me backward, falling on top of me. Once on the ground he tried to hit me a few times in the torso, but he left his face completely exposed and I took liberty with his mug. Taco moved to us quickly, as instructed, and pushed Mike off me. In a moment I was back up on my feet, dancing and shouting.

"C'mon, muthafucka, c'mon!"

Mike just stood there and then, to everyone's surprise, extended his hand in a peacemaking gesture. He said that we were both Crips and had no business fighting. Thinking it was a ploy, I backed away sayin' "Fuck that shit."

When I went back amongst my troops I saw pride, love, and admiration in their faces. The spell was broken. I felt like a world champion, a liberator, but didn't allow myself to get big-headed or pompous. Li'l Fella came over to me and without looking me in the eyes said thanks. Li'l Fella, like so many other noncrucial observers, thought that this was simply a result of the breakfast issue. Few knew that since my arrival this battle had been inevitable. Even I couldn't articulate it then. But I did know that the growing tension had precipitated a brawl because Cyco Mike was wrong in so many instances and hadn't the popular support to continue in his capacity as leader.

And so it went that I assumed responsibility for the juvenile tank. I didn't simply demote Mike, but let him carry some responsibility—not nearly what he had been used to wielding, but enough so as not to break his spirit. I had Handbone beaten and stomped for being a general coward. I reduced Tangle-Eye to a basket case and enjoyed the sight. And it was during my reign that I fixed it so that Sixties were outlawed from Able and Charlie rows. I allowed individual freedom and no one was misused arbitrarily.

The Darwinian theory of survival of the fittest continued to rule our existence. No one got a free ride. Our dayroom time was mostly spent going chest: Charlie row against Able row, everybody bombing everyone else with torso shots. We did this to enhance our physical skills, because so many had lost this ability, as the gun had replaced hand-to-hand combat. But here the strong survived and the weak were phased out. Within three months we were a quality contingency of sheer terror.

Lounging in my cage one morning, reading—or trying to read—I was disturbed by Fat Rat from One-Eighteen East Coast. He said that he had just seen and overheard two detectives down front talking about coming to search my cell. Fat Rat was known for his clowning and could hardly be taken seriously half the time, so I told him to fuck off and went back to struggling with my comic book. Not ten minutes later my gate opened and I was ordered to step out. When I stepped out on the tier, sure enough, two plainclothes detectives accompanied by a sergeant were walking briskly down the tier toward me.

"Kody Scott?" the blond detective asked.

"Yeah, wha's up?"

"We have a search warrant for your cell," he said, as the sergeant cuffed me to the tier rail.

"Fo' what?" I asked in utter disbelief.

"For murder, Mr. Scott, or should I say Monster Kody?"

"Man, y'all trippin'. I'm in here fo' murder already."

"Oh yes, we know that, but it seems that one of your homeboys has turned over on you for yet another murder."

"Yeah, right," I said, but now I knew that this was what Killer Rob had been talking about when I'd seen him in the Hall.

"So what y'all lookin' fo', guns? Oh yeah, I see, right here on this paper, a .32, a shotgun, a—"

"No, we're only looking for correspondence that you have possibly entered into with some of your homeboys."

They searched my cell for all of an hour. When they came out they had at least ten letters. While the sergeant uncuffed me, I told the detectives that I hoped they'd found what they were looking for, to which they replied that they had. As they were leaving, one turned back and said with a smile, "But we are going to wait until you are eighteen so we can gas your black ass."

"Fuck you!" I called after them, but they went out laughing.

In June I started trial for the murder and six attempted murders. The district attorney said that if I pleaded guilty he would be lenient and only give me twenty-five years. "Oh, is that all?" I asked sarcastically.

The Brims turned out en masse. One after the other they testified that I had blasted them in the park. When my attorney asked them what I was wearing, they all described my attire differently. All said that I had gripped the shotgun with both hands. When asked if I was wearing gloves, each said no, that both hands were bare. My attorney then produced medical files that clearly showed that I had been released from the hospital that very night and, most important, had a white cast on my left hand extending up to my elbow.

The jury deliberated less than an hour and came back with a verdict of not guilty on all charges.

It was June 22, 1981, and all that I had on my mind—before sex, drinking, and smoking pot or PCP—was to blast some Brims. Really blast them. Before the sun rose the next morning, they would feel me strong.

6

THE JUVENILE TANK

No one, least of all Taco, could believe that I was going home. I found it hard to believe myself, especially after the homicide detectives had searched my cage, confiscated letters, and made their threat of gassing me as they left. Since I had been acquitted in trial, I knew that the district attorney could not refile the charges for the murder and attempted murders. I was, however, worried about the D.A. notifying homicide that I had been acquitted and then having them come down and book me for yet another murder. When I was let out of my cage for release, I went first to Taco's cell and held counsel with him. He was my road dog and now would be in charge. We talked softly through the bars.

"Yeah, homie," I began, reaching through the bars to grab

Taco's hand, "I'm fin' to sky up and go get bent. Shoot up a gang of them snitchin'-ass Brims and get some pussy, ya know?"

"Yeah, yeah, that's right, cuz, go on out there and handle that shit. If you run into my big homie Honcho, tell cuz to get at me."

"Righteous," I said, looking now into Taco's eyes. "Damn, cuz, I kinda hate to leave you in this muthafucka. But I know you gonna be firm and do what you gotta do. But cuz, watch that fool Mike 'cause you know he ain't likin' us no way, no how."

"That's right," Taco said in a "Preach On" tone.

"So you gotta keep what we built up goin', ya know?"

"Yeah, but I don't think cuz gonna try to trip. But if he do, I'll give you a call and you can drop some of his homeboys out there."

"Righteous."

"Besides, we all like one now since you and cuz got busy. So for him to try to start somethin' now would only make cuz look real bad to the homies in the pen, ya know?"

"Yeah, you right, but just stay alert."

Easing away from Taco's gate was like trying to push away from a ten-course meal after not having eaten in five days. We both knew that he was not going home. He was charged with fifty-nine counts of armed robbery and a murder. Taco had heroically ridden into the Nickerson Garden Housing Projects on a moped armed with a .357 magnum and gunned down a Bounty Hunter. Only moments before, the Bounty Hunter had shot Taco's girlfriend. Although Taco was a hero in the Crip community for his successful mission, he was but a thug to the district attorney, who was, as usual, seeking a life term upon conviction. Taco took most of it in stride, but I knew, just as we all knew, that the threat of being in prison for life was a muthafucka.

What we did in the juvenile tank was reflected inside the prisons where we were headed. The rank system never ended. Just as it was on the street with continuous levels of recognition, so too was it in jail. Those in placement—foster homes—looked up to those in juvenile hall, those in juvenile hall looked up to those in camp, those in camp looked up to those in Youth Authority, and those in Youth Authority looked up to those in prison. Most of us in the juvenile tank looked up to those in prison, because that's where the district attorney was trying to send us. We were all under tremendous stress.

When I backed off of Taco's gate, still looking in his eyes but also taking in the larger scenery of his cage—his bars, bed, sink, desk, and toilet—he seemed so content, so at home. And I wondered, had I looked like him just weeks, days, hours before? I didn't want to stay here all my life, but I had no way to stop the wheels of fate, already set in motion long before I had a ticket to ride. If I just stopped gangbanging, perhaps I could avoid prison, an early death, and a few other occupational hazards. But to "just stop" is like to "just say no" to drugs, or to tell a homeless person to "just get a house." It "just wasn't happening."

Prison loomed in my future like wisdom teeth: if you lived long enough you got them. Prison was like a stepping stone to manhood, with everything depending on going and coming back. Going meant nothing if you never came back. The going was obligatory, but coming back was voluntary. Going didn't just mean prison, it circumscribed a host of obligatory deeds. Go shoot somebody, go take a car, go break into that house, go rob that store, go spray-paint that wall, or go up to that school. It never was "go and come back." "Go" was something that you *had* to do. To come back meant that you loved the 'hood and your homies, and that what you did was simply "all in a day's work." Being locked up was an inevitable consequence of banging. Your "work" brought you in contact with the police and, since jail was part of the job description, you simply prepared ahead of time for the mind-fuck of being a prisoner. The glory came not in going but in coming back. To come back showed a willingness to "stay down." It fostered an image of the set as legitimate, and each individual who could go and come back brought something new—walk, talk, look, way of writing—to add to the culture of the 'hood.

In prison, one is thrown in with all the other criminals, gang members, outlaws, misfits, outcasts, and underworld people from all over California. Since every jail I have ever been in seems designed to be recidivistic, as opposed to rehabilitative, the criminal culture is very strong. It saturates every level of every jail, from juvenile hall to death row. And so each individual going and coming back learns a new scheme to be used in the ever-growing arsenal of criminality. The 'hood also gains yet another expert in another field.

"I love you, cuz," I told Taco with a final salute of the "C" sign held high over my head.

"I love you, too, homie," Taco responded, hitting himself hard over the heart with the "C" sign.

I quickly moved to Levi's cell and rapped with him about standing firm in my absence. From his cell I went to Ben's, Dirt's, and Chico's before shouting my respects down to Able row. At that, I was on my way.

It took most of the night for me to be processed out of L.A. County Jail. Ever leery of the homicide detectives, who might pop out from behind some partition or desk with those "gas your black ass" smirks smeared on their faces, as soon as I was finally released I bolted like a track star to an awaiting bus. Once on the bus I darted straight to the back and crouched down in the seat. The police are notorious for letting you think you have gotten away, and then just when you think it's safe to go back in the water—*sharks!!* So I moved under cover of darkness like I had just broken into—or out of—1600 Pennsylvania Avenue. On the bus, traveling through downtown L.A., I began to ease a bit, but not much. I knew if I got into South Central, the police's chances of apprehending me would be slim, sort of like Marines hunting for Viet Cong in their native habitat. A mere academy-taught soldier-policeman would be put to shame trying to track me in the concrete jungle of South Central.

At Fifth Street a passenger of youthful age boarded the bus. On point, I scoped his dress code: blue khaki pants, white All-Stars, blue Adidas sweat jacket over a blue t-shirt, and a blue baseball cap with two golf-ball emblems fastened to the front. He definitely was a banger. The two golf balls could signify several sets. Back in the early eighties, we'd used numbers as codes of affiliation to circumvent police repression. All Trays, including three-time sets such as the Playboy Gangsters, Altadena Block Crips, and Marvin Gangsters, wore three golf-ball emblems on their hats. In contrast, Neighborhood sets and two-time sets like the 5-Deuces, 6-Deuces, and Raymond Avenue Crips wore two golf-ball emblems on their hats. Often, this alone would be a dead giveaway to set allegiance and quite enough to get one's brains blown out.

The banger paid his fare and started right down the aisle toward the back, toward me. He caught me scoping him and tensed a bit—not out of fright, but as a result, I'm sure, of an adrenaline rush in preparation for a confrontation. I had gotten my rush when I saw him board the bus. Before I saw any movement a small caliber weapon appeared in his right hand—a .25 automatic, I thought. He wasn't holding it in a threatening manner or aiming it at all. He was palming it as if to say "Yo, I'm armed, and if there is to be a confrontation this is my choice of weapon." He sat across from me and to the left, on the long, four-passenger seat. We eyed each other tentatively. All the while he palmed the weapon. After a few minutes that seemed like days, he hit me up.

"Where you from?" he asked in a serious, you-better-not-be-my-enemy voice. For the first time in my life I was scared of being shot, scared to die. Still reeling from the mental strain of being shot six months before, I couldn't summon the courage to die.

"I don't bang," I said and looked away in shame, fighting to keep down the bile pushing its way up. The banger broke his stare and looked elsewhere, totally dismissing me. I felt at a complete loss. Damn, I was trippin'. I couldn't very well say, "Uh, excuse me, I made a slight error. You see, I'm from Eight Tray." That would be even worse than not initially saying where I was from. I wanted to make it back to the 'hood, and not in a body bag. I would gladly die in a couple of months, but not now, not here.

We rode in silence the rest of the way. Then it dawned on me: the banger was probably unmoved by my disclaimer of affiliation and was going to ride the duration of the bus route to see where I got off. Then he'd know I was an Eight Tray and gun me down. Damn, I thought, while in the juvenile tank I'd had Termite, a Chicano from East Side Clover, write ETG on the back of my neck. For sure when I got off the bus he'd scope the set on my neck and unload his clip on me. Then I would die in shame.

Just as these thoughts were wracking my mind, he reached up and pulled the exit bell. As the bus slowed for his upcoming stop, he stood and pocketed the weapon and walked toward the back exit door. Pausing, he turned and said, "You should join a gang, 'cause you already got the look. Stay up."

And he stepped down into the street without a backward glance.

I wanted to shout, "Muthafucka, I got a gang!" but that would just fly in the face of what had already taken place. I rode on in silence, though I noted that he had gotten off the bus in an area of downtown where the only gangs were Salvadorans. This could mean one of two things: he belonged to one of the Salvadoran gangs, or he was just out riding the bus lines hunting for enemies. I quite possibly would have been one. What number, I wondered to myself?

The bus was now occupied only by myself and two other people, both elderly women. It turned right on Santa Barbara—now King Boulevard—and I wondered where the driver was going. When we got to King and Crenshaw, the driver hollered that this was the last stop. What? Last stop? Never familiar with the bus lines in L.A., I had apparently taken the wrong bus. Now I found myself on the corner of King and Crenshaw at 11:30 at night. This was the borderline between the Rollin' Sixties and Black P. Stone Bloods, and I had ETG on my neck and a folder in my hand saying the same thing. Shit, tonight just wasn't my night.

I milled around in the shadows, ever-watchful, shifting nervously from foot to foot. "Wasn't nobody on the street but police and fools, police not givin' a fuck and fools doomed by their own ignorance," Li'l De had said after my shooting. Now karma had reared its damn head and I was an ignorant fool, doomed. Every car was a potential tank manned by opposition troops. I had been dropped behind enemy lines and had to survive, had to get back to "my country." The mission of going to jail only proved successful if I made it back alive.

I was so far back in the shadows that I almost missed the bus going in the opposite direction. I was going to ride back down King Boulevard to Normandie Avenue, get a transfer, follow Normandie to Florence and then take my chances on foot at getting home. Mom didn't even know I was out. I could picture the utter surprise in her face when the police called.

"Uh, Mrs. Scott, this is Detective Joseph from L.A.'s homicide unit calling to regretfully inform you that your son Kody was murdered tonight."

Mom would calmly say that the officer was making a dreadful mistake. "My son Kody is in jail," she would say, probably right up until she had to I.D. my body in the morgue. She would never believe it could happen to me. But we had grown so far apart that if I were dying I would not have called her. Mom was the enemy at home. Mom was, to me, what antiwar protestors were to Westmoreland.

I rode to Normandie without incident, but while I was standing on Normandie and King, which is Harlem Rollin' Thirties neighborhood, a packed beige Cadillac rolled to a stop in front of me. Looking hard for recognition were the twisted, contorted faces of bangers from I-don't-know-where. I tried to look as unconnected as possible. The legal folder that held my letters and pictures from China—with the set scrawled blatantly across the front of it—was between me and the back of the bus-stop bench. I was being inspected for any signs of being a banger. Perhaps these cats were Harlems just patrolling their 'hood, something I have done a lot.

I've found some very out-of-the-way people in the 'hood on some of my patrols. One particular night I rode up on a carload of Miller Gangster Bloods sitting comfortably in an alley behind the Western Surplus. I was able to I.D. them by their loud talking. I was on a ten-speed bike, and once I confirmed they were enemy, I rolled up on the side of the car and emptied my clip into the faces and bodies of the occupants. Out of bounds, trespassing, free-fire zone—hell, I had a dozen reasons to fire on them. "Free country" never crossed my mind. Besides, this wasn't America—it was South Central.

The Miller Gangsters were from clear across town, 120th Street. It's possible that they didn't know where they were. Or it could be that they did know but had little respect for our 'hood, since they had never had open confrontations with us. I'd tend to believe the latter. This is why it's necessary to read the writing on the walls. Fuck street signs. Walls will tell you where you are.

Not seeing any clear signs in my face or dress code, the idling Cadillac began to ease forward. For identification purposes the passenger raised one hand out of the window with his thumb and pinky finger extended, the other fingers hidden in his palm. I recognized the sign immediately: Neighborhood Rollin' Twenty Bloods. No doubt they were on a military incursion through Harlem 'hood, their worst enemy. "Hurry up, bus," I found myself whispering. "Hurry up."

The bus came, and I rode attentively down Normandie, reading the writing on the walls, passing through several 'hoods. Normandie Avenue can be compared to the Ho Chi Minh trail. It is the main artery of well over forty sets, spanning from

Hollywood to Gardena. Normandie is a vital supply route. From dope to dynamite, Normandie has seen it. From King Boulevard to Florence, the bus made its way through the Harlem Thirties, Rollin' Forties, 5-Deuce Hoovers, 5-Six Syndicate and 6-Deuce Brims. Block after block, set after set, everybody belonged to something. The writing scrawled on the walls told fabulous stories. I knew most of the names written by face, but it was hard to picture the individuals writing them. Bending down, moving, scanning to see who's watching them . . . some cats just seemed too sophisticated for that. It's funny, too, because as much graffiti as covers our city walls, hardly anybody ever sees it being done. As much as I have struck up on walls, I've never been asked to stop or been asked what I was doing.

On Seventy-first Street, the street before Florence, I reached up and pulled the signal cord to be let off. I disembarked at a walking-run. Florence and Normandie was a hot corner. I turned the corner onto Seventy-first and trotted past Li'l Tray Ball's house and wondered if I should stop. No, I decided, make it home first. It was now well past midnight. Although there are more murders in the city on the weekends than the weekdays, it has nothing to do with gang members being workers. Gang members work all day, every day. This was a Wednesday, but that didn't mean I was more likely to survive. No, I was more likely to be killed any time and any place they caught me!

I scurried along, ducking and dodging into driveways and behind trees. Anyone in any other part of this country would have thought I had either stolen something or was a nut. But any resident here who clocked my antics knew I was just trying to get from point A to point B in one piece.

When I got home I went to the back door, but it was

locked. So I went back around to the front and knocked, but got no answer. I've never had a key, never wanted one. I never asked Mom for one, and she never offered one. I knocked again, harder. Still there was no answer, but Mom's car was there.

Suddenly I heard noises from across the street and saw flashes coming from Welow's garage. I went across the street cautiously. Welow was welding some pieces of metal together and working on his car. He was a civilian who worked at General Motors every day, but on the weekend he'd pull his 1974 Monte Carlo low-rider out and have a ball. He had a lot of tools and welding equipment. In fact, he would saw my weapons off for me and then smooth down the barrels on his grinder. When he saw me his eyes lit up. We rapped a bit before he broke out some pot. My system was clean from not doing any drugs while in jail for six months, so one stick of pot blew me over.

When I finally jetted back across the street I was really on paranoid. I banged on the door now.

BAM! BAM! BAM!

I was doing the get-the-fuck-up-it's-the-police knocks.

BAM! BAM! BAM!

And that's who Mom thought it was, because before they had come to my cell with the search warrant they'd gone to my house. Not believing Mom when she told them that I was already in jail, they still made her come out of the house and get on her knees on the front lawn like a common criminal.

I saw her now, peeking from behind the curtain. She couldn't recognize me, so she hit the porch light, splashing me with light. I freaked and bent down to avoid in-coming rounds.

"The light," I shouted, pointing, "turn the light out, Mom!"

Hearing my voice, she finally registered who I was. Just as abruptly as I was splashed with light, I was now doused with darkness. The light was screaming "Here he is," but the darkness said, "Shhh, it's all right, it's all right." Mom opened the door slowly, after undoing more locks than I ever remember having seen on that door.

"Hi, Mom," I said with a dopey marijuana smile. I know she smelled it all over me.

"You know they going to come get you, don't you?" she said with a look of why-you-keep-doin'-me-like-this.

"Who?"

"The police, that's who!"

"Fo' what? I ain't done nothin'."

"Boy, you done broke out of jail!"

"Naw, Mom, I beat my case. They let me out."

Mom assumed that because I was sixteen she had to come and get me, like always. But I was not in juvenile hall anymore. In the juvenile tank they just let you go.

"Boy, are you sure?" she asked accusingly. "'Cause I can't take them trigger-happy fools running up in here treating me like no thug. I work too hard for that shit, you hear me?"

"Yeah, yeah, I hear you, Mom," I said with my head down, wandering the length of the hallway feeling like "Damn, ain't nothin' changed, I see." "You been to see Shaun?" I asked, trying to get her off my back.

"Yes, I went last weekend. You know they gave him thirty-six years and life. My poor baby."

Uh-oh, I thought, here it comes. "Mom, I'm tired, I need some sleep."

"You need to stop smoking that goddamn weed," she hollered after me as I walked down the hall.

I closed my bedroom door and waited, hoping she wouldn't come into my room and continue preaching. I knew she meant well, but I wasn't up to it tonight. I wanted to be loved, to be missed, to be wanted, not scolded.

Now I was angry. I changed into my combat black, went out the window and into the garage. In a bag under the old chest of drawers, I had a .45 automatic that I had gotten from A. C. Rabbit, our Korean homeboy, before my capture. The .45 had only two shells in the clip. I went across to Welow's and he gave me eight more shells. I got on Li'l Monster's new ten-speed and rode quickly toward Brim 'hood, all the while cursing about my mother's disregard for my feelings, never questioning mine for hers.

From Sixty-ninth to Sixty-second I pumped furiously, needing to shoot somebody, eager to vent my anger. Rounding the corner on Sixty-second and Denker I encountered what looked to be two couples sitting on the back of a car playing oldies, hugging, being lovers. I slowed my pace and gave them the most evil mad-dog stare I could come up with. All four turned their heads and, I'm almost sure, prayed that I kept going. I made a tight circle in the street to see if any one of them were looking at me, but none were.

I peddled on toward Halldale. When I found no one there I doubled back. Noticing that the couples had vanished, I peddled on up Sixty-second to the other side of Brim 'hood by Harvard Boulevard. Getting halfway up the block, I noticed a furtive move to my left in my peripheral vision. Turning abruptly in the direction of the movements, I grabbed for my weapon. Before I could draw, the movement shot out of the shadows like fluid. "Damn," I said to myself, "a cat." Shit, the damn cat seemed to be doing just as I had been doing not more than an hour before, trying to get from point A to point B in one piece. I watched the cat momentarily before I continued my scan of the park.

Turning right on Harvard Boulevard, I saw two Chicanos leaning against a brown Gremlin, talking. Both, I guessed, were from F13. We had no beef with them. Further down the block I saw three cats who looked my age leaning against a van, talking and drinking beer. Bingo—enemies. I rode to within a house distance, approximately twenty to twenty-five feet, and made a circle to make sure they saw me. On my final loop I came up blasting.

DOOM! DOOM! DOOM!

"Ah, Blood, I'm hit!"

"Run!" screamed a distant voice. "Just keep runnin'!"

One Blood lay motionless in the street. The other two were pinned behind a tree. The van took the majority of my rounds.

DOOM! DOOM!

The .45 had the low, slow baritone of a big bass.

When I heard no other noise, I took off, retaining one round. Peddling as quickly as possible straight down Harvard, across Gage Avenue, and into the peripheral interior of my 'hood, I felt like a Native American on horseback retreating back to my camp after slaying the enemy. I made a left on Sixty-seventh Street and relaxed a bit. On Denker I turned right and made my way home. I put the bike in the garage and entered the house. I went to my room and fell asleep. I slept very well.

"You may tie your shoes in the morning, but the mortician may untie them at night," Alma, Crazy De's mother, was telling us as we waited for De to gear up. She knew we were up to no good.

Dressed heavily and in dark gear, Diamond, Tray Stone, and I sat on the couch, oblivious to anything Alma was saying. Our minds had long been locked on our upcoming mission. For once in a long time, we had gained the initiative in the conflict with the Sixties. We knew we had to keep up the pressure. Tonight would be but another offensive strike in a series of military maneuvers we had been conducting in the Sixties 'hood to wear down their resistance. We had made so many successful runs in and out of the Sixties that we arrogantly began calling ourselves the Demolition Squad. We had been seen so often by so many civilians that as of late we were getting waves and head nods. We simply waved back.

Our missions were successful largely because we had logistical help from the LAPD CRASH units. For four nights in a row now, we had been getting helpful hints from "our friends" in blue—as they liked to refer to themselves. "But," they'd quickly add, "we are from the Seventy-seventh Street gang, which just happens to not get along with the Rollin' Sixties."

Ignorant, very eager, and filled with a burning hatred for the "enemy," we ate that shit up. We never realized that the Seventy-seventh Street gang didn't get along with anybody in the New Afrikan community.

"Hey, Monster," a tomato-faced sergeant said, "I tell you, them goddamn Sixties are talking about murdering you on sight."

"Oh yeah, who?"

"Peddie, Scoop, Kiki, and a few others. If I were you I'd

keep my gun close at hand, 'cause those boys seem mighty serious."

"Yeah, well fuck the Sixties. They know where I'm at."

"Yeah, but do you know where *they* are? I mean right *now?*"

"Naw, you?"

Then, calling me to the car in a secretive manner he said, "They on Fifty-ninth Street and Third Avenue. All the ones I just mentioned who've been bad-mouthing you. I was telling my partner here that if you were there they'd be scared shitless. If you get your crew and go now, I'll make sure you are clear. But only fifteen minutes. You got that?" he added with a wink and a click of the tongue.

"Yeah, I got it. But how I know you ain't settin' me up?"

"If I wanted to put you in jail, Monster, I'd arrest you now for that gun in your waistband."

Surprised, I said, "Righteous," and stepped away from the car.

We mounted up and went over to Fifty-ninth and Third Avenue. Sure enough, there they were. And just as he had said, we encountered no police.

This was our fifth night out in collaboration with "our friends" in blue. We had a .22 magnum that shot nine times. I had loaded it myself with long hollow points. But first we went in search of a car to use on the mission. Jack at gunpoint for a vehicle with the .22. Once the vehicle was secured, we'd go and get more heavy weaponry for the mission.

It had been two weeks since I was released. China was complaining that I didn't spend enough time with her, that all I did was think about the Sixties. Since Li'l G.C.'s capture for murder, she seemed to have lost some of her ability to be confrontational with the enemy. She still walked, talked, and dressed gangster, but since my release she had not gone on one mission with me. In 1980, she was putting in much work. Now she wanted to be loved in a way that I could not approach seriously. I loved her, for sure, but I was far from being a romantic. I felt threatened by romanticism, thinking that perhaps I'd like it more than banging. So I shied away from it.

So much had happened since the start of the conflict. Before the war, we—as a set—were more like a family than a gang. Picnics, collective awareness, unity, and individual freedom abounded. Sure we struck out at foes, but it was all in keeping with traditional Red and Blue rivalries. Business, strictly business. We had one dead, one wounded.

Now, in 1981, we had three dead at the hands of the Sixties and numerous—too numerous to note—wounded. As soon as the war started, freak accidents seemed to befall us. Cocaine was killed by Mexicans in a burglary attempt. Bam was allegedly killed by one of our own. Dirty Butch was run over by a car. D.B. was stabbed to death by a wino. Some Bounty Hunters kicked in Joe Joe's door and shot his mother and brother.

Also, many had been captured. G.C. was given fifteen years to life. Big Spike, Dumps, Fred Jay, and Li'l Jay received sentences ranging from four years to twenty-five to life. Madbone had been captured for murder and given seven years straight. Time Bomb and Harv Dog had also been captured for murder.

Gangster Brown's house was being shot up three nights a week, and the summer hadn't even come yet. The set sagged miserably under so much, so fast. In as little as a nine-month period, we had gone from being a happy extended family with an infrastructure capable of meeting many of the needs of those driven to the street, for whatever reason, to an exclusive military machine. By June 1981 those who had stuck it out were well-seasoned veterans who could be compared to Long-Range Reconnaissance Patrol Soldiers in Vietnam. There was nothing else for us but war, total war.

After no success whatsoever in finding a vehicle to commandeer, Crazy De, Tray Stone, Diamond, and myself found ourselves clear up in the Rollin' Nineties—not one of our more cordial neighbors—before we decided to double back toward the 'hood. Diamond was in control of the strap. We walked down the adjacent alley off Western Avenue in twos, ever on alert. When we got to Eighty-ninth Street, we crossed Western hoping to catch a victim in Thrifty's parking lot. There were none.

We decided to try St. Andrews park. We walked the length of St. Andrews to Eighty-seventh Street, and there we found a civilian waxing a custom van. Just the thing we needed—a van. This meant more shooters could be secreted inside. More shooters meant more deaths. We stepped to the vic—the victim.

"Hey, man," I began spiritedly, as if I were really impressed by his van. "This is a clean van."

"Yeah, you like it?" said the civilian, who stood about six foot three and looked to weigh about three hundred pounds.

"Hell, yeah," said Tray Stone, "this muthafucka's tight."

The civilian then took in our attire and demeanor and, amped on adrenaline, looked everywhere but at his van.

"Yeah, I work hard for my things," he said nervously and then, as if expecting something, he added, "too hard."

At that, Diamond swung into motion. It all seemed rehearsed, we had done it so many times. One step back, draw the weapon, and instruct the vic to lie down on his stomach. Then, either Tray Stone or I would frisk the vic, taking anything he had. We treated the women much better than the men. We'd never rape the women, nor would we take the whole purse.

But this time when Diamond swung into motion his action was countered, as if the vic was a mind reader. When Diamond made his step backward the vic took one step forward, and when Diamond reached for his waistband to retrieve the strap the vic pounced on him with all of his height and weight. Diamond went down as if he wasn't even in the vic's way. De, Tray Stone, and I moved with alacrity to aid the homie who was now being pummeled by the vic, who was screaming something about him working too hard for his shit. Somehow, Diamond managed to wiggle free of the vic. He did so on his own, because the head blows we were delivering to the vic seemed to do little. The man had gone stone crazy on us.

When Diamond jumped up, looking like a frightened boy who had just seen a ghost, he started backing away mouthing something that we could not catch. The vic began to turn his big frame in our direction. Tray Stone hollered for Diamond to "shoot him, shoot the muthafucka." That's when Diamond found his voice and screamed, "He got the strap!"

By then it was too late.

"Now," the vic-turned-assailant said, "I'm gonna kill all you dirty, no-good little punks."

All I could think about was *Death Wish.* We each ran in separate directions, first for our lives and then to try and confuse the vic-assailant. I hadn't taken ten steps before the first shot cracked into the darkness.

POW!

Good, I thought, he ain't shootin' at me. And then the second shot cracked.

POW!

And I'll be damned if he didn't hit me in the back. Two other shots cracked off and I presumed them to be at the others. In the meantime, I dove for cover.

Within minutes of being shot my whole right arm was numb and I couldn't move it or my fingers. The shooting had stopped, but I was still reluctant to get out of my hiding place. My worst fear came from thinking about what the .22 bullet had done to me internally. All the stories of bullets traveling, ricocheting, and tearing up organs came rushing on me in every voice I had ever heard them in.

Suddenly I saw a shadow to my right and tensed. The shadow seemed to tense, too. Friend or foe? He must have thought the same thing I did, because simultaneously we both broke and ran. As I made distance I looked back. Shit, it was Diamond.

"Diamond," I hissed, "over here, it's me, Monster."

Diamond doubled back huffing and puffing, still wearing his frightened-little-boy face.

"Oh, what's up, cuz?"

"I'm hit," I said with all the it's-your-fault I could put into it.

"Damn, cuz," Diamond said, now looking out from our hiding place like we were trapped in Khe Shan. "I'm sorry, homie, but that big—"

"Don't sweat it," I interrupted him. "We got to get away from here. I can't move my arm."

"Damn," Diamond whispered with disgust.

"C'mon, cuz," I instructed Diamond, "we got to move."

We bailed out of our foxhole and into the lights of an on-coming car, Diamond waving his arms dramatically.

"Cuz, that's a van," I shouted. "It might be—"

"Muthafuckas!" was all we heard coming from the van. Then:

POW! POW! POW!

It was him all right, rolling on us. We darted to the left and ran through some apartment buildings, out the back, and onto Manchester Avenue. Once on Manchester we made our way over to the Boys Market parking lot. There we found Tray Stone and Crazy De. My entire right side now throbbed. With all the excitement making my heart pump faster I knew that I was losing a lot of blood.

Before I could say anything, Diamond told De and Stone that I was shot and that the man was rolling around looking for us. De looked like he was going to be sick. Stone kept mumbling threats about killing the man.

"We gotta get Monster to the hospital," Diamond said, feeling responsible for my wounding.

"How we gonna do that?" De said. "You done let fool take the damn strap from you. How we gonna—"

"Man, fuck you, De!" Diamond shot back. "You seen cuz over me, what I s'posed to do? Huh? What?"

"Cuz, fuck it, just fuck it," De said, waving Diamond off dismissively.

"Naw, ain't no just 'fuck it', 'cause you seem to—"

"HEY!!" I shouted. "I'm dying, man, we better do *something.*"

Stone spotted the father of one of our homegirls and flagged him down. We piled into his car and Stone told him to take us to the hospital. I objected, to everyone's surprise, and said to take me home. I had an irresistible longing to see my mother. Blue, our homegirl's father, was driving at a slower than normal pace, leaning in the seat—obviously drunk—and listening to old down-home blues.

After several blocks of this, with us looking from one to the other in irritation, Crazy De leaned over, inches from Blue's ear, and whispered, "Monster got shot tonight and we tryin' to get him home. Now, if he dies in this car because yo' old ass is drivin' too slow, you gonna die in this car, too." Then, more loudly, "NOW DRIVE!"

Blue drove so fast that I was scared we'd all die in an auto accident. He bent corners on two wheels, ran stop signs, and bullied his way through red lights. I don't know if he was driving this way for me or him. Moments later we came to a screeching halt in front of my house. When we piled out, Blue looked relieved.

We knocked on the front door and Kerwin let us in. He and Mom sat at the front-room table eating.

"Mom," I began with a stammer, "I'm shot."

"Boy, get outta here with that damn foolishness, I ain't got time for it."

"No, I'm serious, I can't move this arm," I said, pointing to my right arm with my left hand. I felt like a small boy trying to convince Mom that I had scraped my knee without there being a hole in my pants leg.

"No, Mrs. Scott, he really is shot," De said respectfully.

To this Mom balled up her napkin, threw it into her remaining food and said, "Shit, boy, you *always* into something. You gonna be dead before you eighteen." And she promptly stalked off to her room to retrieve her car keys—I hoped.

"Let me see," Kerwin said, getting up from the table.

"Man, fuck you!" I responded and sat down.

"What happened?" Kerwin asked, looking at the others, clearly not expecting an answer from me. But the homies already knew that Kerwin was a spy for Mom, so they said nothing. Every morning when I woke up I'd hear him in the front room telling Mom about things he had heard I'd done.

"Kody turned a party out on Eighty-fourth," or "Kody shot such-and-such," he'd say, so I knew not to tell him anything. If he heard it on the street, so what? It could be rumors.

When Mom came back up the hallway she had her keys, jacket, and purse with her.

"C'mon here, boy," she said, and walked right past me out the door. When I went after her, the troops followed. "And where y'all think you goin'?" she said, primping herself. "I am sure not going to be riding around this city with the four of you. It's bad enough that I got to ride with this one."

I rolled my eyes to the moonless sky and saluted the homies with the Tray.

"Three minutes," came their reply, and Mom and I were on our way. At the first corner she began in on me.

"Now what happened this time?"

"Nothin'," I said sullenly.

"Nothing?!" she shouted. "You got a damn bullet in your body, *somebody* put it there."

"You don't want to know," I said, staring out of the window, trying to disengage.

"Kody, I need to know what happened. These people are not stupid. They are going to need an explanation to this shooting. Now what happened?"

"Is that why you wanna know, just so you can have an explanation for them?" I shot back. "What about you? You haven't even asked me if I am hurtin'. No, you too busy fussin' to show me love, to say somethin' kind or nice. No, it's always fuss, fuss, fuss."

She gave no reply, just looked straight ahead. So I continued.

"You wanna know what really happened, Mom? Really?"

She didn't answer.

"We went to take a van for a move and the dude took the gun from Diamond and shot me in the back."

"My God," she said with disdain. "Kody, why do you want to take other people's property? That's not right. People work hard for what they have. You can't just—"

"Mom, can you drive faster, I think I'm bleeding to death."

"Oh, *now* you scared of dying. You should have thought about that when you had your bad ass out there, robbing folks. Now you want to worry about dying. I'll tell you."

I didn't respond and she didn't drive any faster. When we finally got to the hospital, well over an hour had passed since I was shot. We were made to sit in a waiting room. There were four people there: two New Afrikans, one Chicano, and one American. The American was called first. She had a cold. Mom went off.

"You stupid motherfuckers, don't you see my son has been shot!? You mean to tell me that a white woman with a cold is more important than my son with a bullet in his back? What kind of damn hospital are you people running here?!"

The receptionist, an American, was dumbfounded. Totally speechless, she sat safely behind the partition, thankful for her seclusion from Mom. Mom kept at it until two American doctors wheeled out a wheelchair and rolled me back through the double doors.

First I was X-rayed, then led to a room with a bed to await the results. The entry hole, they said, was very tiny and didn't seem to have done too much damage. I explained to the doctor about the numbness and he said it was a symptomatic response to shock and delay of treatment. He added that he doubted if it would be permanent. Mom sat on the side of my bed and gazed out the window.

"Yes, officer," I heard a female voice say, "he's right in here."

"Thank you," said a scratchy, still unseen voice.

Then in through the door came two American soldier-cops, one with a clipboard, the other with a Winchell's Donuts coffee cup. The one with the clipboard was older, redder, and more go-with-the-flow. His face was like worn leather, hair gray and managed as if he had just had it styled for a VO5 commercial. The younger one was straight off the beach, a surfer-Nazi from hell, all jittery and gung-ho, eager to make his bones in the department. I could tell right away that a conflict existed between these two. New versus old, traditional versus contemporary, professionalism versus personalism. I decided to have a little fun.

"What's your name, son?" asked Clipboard.

"My name, sir?" I asked, as if not overstanding the question.

"Yeah," Donut Cup snapped, "your name. You know, the legend you were given at birth?" His tone was pushy like "all you people are so stupid."

"Oh, yeah," I said, "my name. Kody Scott, sir." I was careful to be nice and respectful to Clipboard, while agitating Donut Cup with my feigned stupidity.

"Where did this incident take place?" asked Donut Cup.

"Incident?" I asked right back, looking from Donut Cup to Mom for an interpretation of "incident."

Donut Cup turned his head.

"Where were you when you were shot?" asked Clipboard with all the ease of a family doctor.

"I was standing alone on the bus stop at Adams and Western."

"Southeast, northwest?" asked Donut Cup.

"No," I began, as if he had it all wrong. "I was not at Southwest College, I was on Adams and Western."

"On which side of the street were you standing?" asked Clipboard.

"On the Adams side in front of the gas station going toward downtown."

"That would be the southeast corner, then," said Donut Cup, trying to hammer his point home.

"I just always thought it was the corner of Adams and Western," I said, trying to look perplexed. Donut Cup turned a shade darker.

"What happened while you were standing on the bus stop?" asked Donut Cup.

"Well," I began, imitating an old man by rubbing my chin in deep thought, "I wasn't really standing *on* the bus stop, I was standing *behind* the bus stop, in back of the bench on the sidewalk between the gas station and the street."

Donut Cup went flaming red, grabbing his head with both hands as if he were trying to stop from going mad. Mom put a hand over her mouth to suppress a laugh. Clipboard, ever-patient, just waited to rephrase the question.

"Look," said Donut Cup, his face a stricken mask of anger,

"all you have to do is answer the questions as we ask them. If you can—"

"Whoa, whoa," said Clipboard, turning full around to face Donut Cup, "if you'd let me ask the questions you would be better off."

"Yeah, but—"

"Ahh," said Clipboard with an upheld hand, waving Donut Cup to silence.

"Now, uhh, Kody, as you were standing behind the bench on Adams and Western," he began and paused for a second to turn and look at Donut Cup as if to say "this is all you got to do." Then he turned back to me and simply said, "What happened?"

"A brown Monte Carlo came by traveling eastbound." Now I looked over at Donut Cup as if to say "*you* people are so stupid." "A guy with a .22 rifle hung out of the window—"

"Which window?" asked Donut Cup.

We both ignored him.

"—and hollered something and began shooting."

"What was it that the shooter hollered out, do you remember?"

"No, sir. But I think it was some sort of gang language."

"Do you gangbang, Kody?"

As if he had just committed blasphemy in front of the Almighty, I said, "No!" with a look of are-you-crazy? Mom rolled her eyes to the ceiling and turned her head.

"Why do you think they wanted to shoot you?"

"I don't know."

"What kind of car was it?"

"A brown Monte Carlo."

"What year, do you know?"

"Seventy-four or seventy-five, I think."

"Any distinguishing marks, dents, primer, paint defects?"

"Yeah, now that I think of it, there was a huge, gray primer spot on—"

"The quarter panel?" said Donut Cup excitedly.

"Yeah, yeah, that's it." Fuck it, I thought, may as well send Donut Cup all the way out into left field.

"Oh my God," said Donut Cup to Clipboard, "Jimbo's out."

Mom was shaking her head as if to say "unbelievable."

When the soldier-cops had completed their report and were walking toward the door, I decided to use one of my old acting skits, which I had seen on an old TV show.

"Officer, officer," I said faintly, my voice barely audible.

"Yes, son?" answered Clipboard.

"You . . . you will get them, won't you, sir?"

And then just like in the movies Clipboard solemnly said, "Yes, son, we'll get them," and they left the room. Shit, that little episode threw me for a loop. Mom began right in on me.

"Boy, why you lie to them police like that? Don't you know they gonna find out that you were lying?"

"Mom, I ain't hardly worried about the police looking for me for lying. Besides, if I had told them the truth I would be going to jail for attempted robbery, assault, and possession of a gun. So I had to lie."

"I don't understand you kids today. Guns, robberies, and gangbanging. Where is it leading to? You don't even know, do you? You are just a blind passenger being driven wherever the gang takes you. Kody, I don't even know you anymore. You're not the fine little guy that I used to know. I just don't know what to do with you. You got Shaun into this shit, now he's locked up for the rest of his young life. When are you going to realize that you are killing me? Kody?"

I was faking like I was asleep so she would not see how effective her talk was. I was the same old person she used to know, wasn't I? Yeah, sure I was, I tried to convince myself. But if I were still that fine little guy, why didn't she smile at me anymore? Or laugh and joke like days of old? It wasn't me who changed, I wanted to say. It was the times, the circumstances dictating my rite of passage to manhood. All this was crucial to my development. I became, without ever knowing when, a product of the street and a stranger at home. Life sure was a trip.

"Mrs. Scott?" an American nurse said.

"Yes."

"You may as well go home and get some sleep, because the doctor wants to keep Kody here for observation tonight."

"Oh, thank you, but if it's all the same I'd like to stay with my son."

"Okay, that's fine. Would you like a blanket or anything?"

"No, actually I'm fine, thank you."

"All right, the doctor should be in any minute."

Mom looked at me and saw my eyes flutter.

"Boy, I sure hope you got on clean underwear."

Good ol' Mom, she never changed. Of course she had changed, I was just too preoccupied with my own little perverted existence to take in anything outside the gang world. The world could have been crumbling around me, but if it didn't affect the set, it didn't affect me.

When the doctor returned he explained that, miraculously, the bullet—apparently a hollow point—had exploded on impact. But instead of doing its job of ripping up my internal organs, it had simply stopped, and now there were thirteen small, detectable fragments throughout my upper back. He added that during his observation of the X-ray chart he noticed another bullet lodged in my abdominal cavity. I told him of my previous brush with death and he asked if I was a gang member. I said no. I was instructed to stay the night for further observation.

During the night I regained feeling and movement in my arm. The pain subsided under a stiff dosage of something shot into my hip. The next day, under the warm rays of the Southern California sun, Mom and I tooled out of the hospital parking lot. The radio blared with Stevie Wonder's new hit, "Hotter than July." It was July 2, 1981.

Once I got home and was safe behind the locked door of Mission Control—my bedroom—I called up Diamond to inform him of my clean bill of health. His grandmother said he wasn't there, so I phoned Tray Stone, who answered on the third ring.

"Hello?"

"What that gangsta like, nigga?" I said into the receiver, recognizing Stone's voice.

"West Side, the best side," Stone shot back.

"Naw, if it ain't North you short, fool."

"What's up, homie? You all right? What they say? Did the police come up there? What Mom say?"

"Wait, wait. Goddamn, man, ask one fuckin' question at a time, all right?"

"Awright, Mr. Important. You okay?"

"Okay all day and even on Sundays."

"Naw, I know that, I mean the bullet. What the Doc say?"

"I know what you talkin' 'bout. I'm cool. Fool say the bullet hit my back, broke up and stopped."

"You bullshittin'?"

"Naw, I ain't. Doc say I'm too strong for a deuce-deuce to stop."

"You puttin' too much on it, now."

"Naw, naw, Doc say, 'You must be some kind of Monster or something,' you know, so I said, 'Yeah, from the notorious North.' "

"Now I *know* you lyin'. Nigga, ain't nobody heard of no fuckin' North Side, 'specially no damn white-boy doctor."

"Yo' mama heard of the North."

Silence.

"Cuz, don't talk 'bout Moms. You ain't right."

"Yeah, you right, fuck her—"

"I'm gone, Monster."

"Naw! Awright, homie, I ain't trippin'."

"Oh, we handled that other thang, too," Stone said in a low voice, as if his father had come into the room.

"What other thang?" I knew what he meant, but I wanted to hear him say it.

"'Member that van that fool say he work so hard to get?"

"Yeah."

"Well, he gonna be workin' harder now, 'cause we fucked that muthafucka up!"

"What 'bout, fool?"

"He never came out and we didn't know what apartment he stayed in. And there was like a whole bunch of apartments, like fifty."

"Nigga, ain't no fifty fuckin' apartments on that damn corner!"

"Awright, 'bout sixteen then. Anyway, we kept fuckin' up the van and nobody came out. So Joker said 'Fuck it,' and shot up every apartment!"

"What?!"

"Yeah, cuz, the shit was crazy! People screamin' and shit. He shot one window and a fire started. Aw, cuz, it was just like the movies, I ain't lyin'."

"Right, right," I said, joining in on the excitement.

"But, cuz, you awright, tho'?"

"Yeah, yeah homie, I'm cool. I'll be at the blue apartments later."

"Awright, cuzzin, I'll see you then."

"Tray minutes."

"Wes—"

Before he could get "West Side" out, I clicked him. I felt good to know that the homies had responded. It was sad, however, that Joker had gone to such extremes, but I overstood his rage and appreciated his concern. I washed up as best I could with the bandage and the stiffness from the wound, put on my dark-blue overalls, a blue sweatshirt, black Romeos, and a black Bebop hat, grabbed my 9 millimeter, and hit the street.

When I got to the blue apartments Bam, Spooney, China, and Peaches were out in front drinking Old English and talking. When China saw me she eased away from the group, insinuating that she wanted to speak to me privately. Amid jeers and greetings from the other homegirls, China and I went to the side of the apartments. She seemed to have something on her mind.

"Kody," she began. Never had she called me Monster. "I can't take you gettin' shot no mo'. Baby, I be worried to death fo' you. Everybody dyin' and shit. I just don't know anymore."

"So, what you sayin'?"

"What I'm sayin' is we don't do nothin' together no mo'. You be wit' Diamond and them and I be all alone. I be worried 'bout you."

"Yeah, well it ain't like you don't know where I live, China—"

"You know *yo'* mama don't like me. You know that, Kody. So don't even try—"

"What?" I said accusingly. "Don't even try what? Huh?"

"You know what I—"

"No, I don't know shit. You know I'm out here, bangin', bustin' on muthafuckas daily to make it safe fo' you 'round here, and now you complainin'. You done changed like the rest of them sorry muthafuckas that's gone and left the set hangin'."

"No, baby, *you* have changed. This fuckin' war has really turned you into somethin'. You think you Super Gangsta or somebody, runnin' 'round tryin' to save the world. But look what it's doing to us! Look at us!"

She began to cry, dropping huge tears onto her smooth cheeks.

"Do you remember the last place you took me, Kody? Huh? Do you remember?"

"Yeah," I said, grudgingly. "I remember."

"Where?" she asked, hands on her hips. Then louder, "Where?!"

"To the drive-in," I said, but before I could stop the flow of words I knew I was wrong.

"No," she snapped, "you know where you took me? *To jail!* That's where!"

And, of course, she was right. Li'l G.C. and I had jacked a civilian for his car one night. A nice car, too, so I decided to take China out on a date in the stolen car. But then again, why waste a good G-ride? I'll just pick up Stone and Spooney, I thought, and we'll do a double date ride-by. Shit, why not? So China and I picked up Stone and Spooney, along with their gun—a huge double-barrel 12 gauge. We stopped at the 'hood store for drinks—Old English and Night Train, gangsta juice. As we made our way west toward the Sixties, a black-and-white patrol car got on our tail. Never one to comply with the law, I accelerated, and the chase was on. After ten blocks of high speed and a faulty turn, we crashed. Immediately I was out of the car and into the wind. I was the only one to get away. Stone, Spooney, and China went to juvenile hall.

"But—" I tried to say, but was cut off.

"But nothin', 'cause before that you stood me up when we was s'posed to go to the Pomona Fair. 'Member that? You got some new type of gun or somethin' and just left me behind. That was cold."

She was right again. The homegirl Dee Dee, whose boyfriend was in the navy, had given me a flare gun that looked like an ordinary ink pen, but shot a single ball of fire that she said would burn right through somebody. Well, that sounded like my type of weapon. She had given it to me on her way to the fair, and what better place to test such a weapon than at a fair? So I went with her instead of China.

"Yeah, but—"

"Naw, baby, 'cause there's no mo'—"

Then out of the night came a terror-stricken cry of "Sixties!!" followed by the rat-a-tat-tat of a rifle.

In an instant we both were belly down, looking at each other. She saw the anger in my eyes and said in a whisper, "Don't go, let somebody else play hero, baby, don't go."

"I gotta go, I gotta go."

"Fuck you!!" she screamed, but I was on my way. I heard her faint sobs as I mounted my bike and peddled off.

No one was hit, but the response would have been the same in any case. We mounted up and rode back with swiftness. After that, to beat the heat, I went to Compton to kick it with some homies from Santana Block.

A week later, word was out that the police were looking for me and Crazy De for robbery. Which robbery, I wondered? Shit, we had done so many robberies that I was at a loss to figure out which one we were wanted for. With the police out for us, I'd wake up early, get dressed, and be out of the house before 6:00 A.M., because that's their usual raiding time. I'd gravitate around homies' houses until their parents went to work, and then we'd kick it until the rest of the 'hood started stirring. Then I'd try to lose myself in the sameness of the community. I ran, ducked, and hid every time someone yelled "Rollers." I became so engrossed in escaping capture that my military performance slumped a bit.

The most frightening thing about being hunted as a banger is that you never really know what it is they are hunting you for. The banger's position is far from static, so one day you could be a robber and the next day you might be told to commit murder, only to be asked the following day to spray paint a wall. Controlled freedom—democratic centralism. The gang was all that.

De and I were both eventually captured and hauled off to jail. De was eighteen, so he went to the county jail. I was still sixteen, pushing seventeen, so I went to juvenile hall. At my first court appearance I was remanded to the custody of the sheriff's department and sent back to the juvenile tank.

Upon arrival I quickly saw that things had changed. Ben-nose and Levi were gone. Both had been sent to Youth Authority. Taco was still there, and so were about fourteen other Grape Street Watts Crips, all tight allies of Eight Tray. The difference was that Tangle-Eye was parading around there like a stalwart member of the community, as if his drinking of urine and set jumping was all in some other life. Cyco Mike had somehow regained his position as lord of the fiefdom and all the other bangers were catering to him like a bunch of oppressed serfs. And to top it all off there was an N-hood living on Charlie row!

The N-hood was Lucky from One-Eleven. He had two homies downstairs on Able row. After greeting Taco and the others I immediately went about the task of procuring a weapon to stab Lucky with. I wanted to make a strong point that I was back and shit was gonna be dealt with swiftly and harshly. After I had secured some iron—a steel flat of metal sharpened to a double-edged point—I told Taco of my intent and my utter hatred for all N-hoods.

"You ain't gotta stab cuz. If you say move, he'll move. But really, cuz is awright," Taco said.

"Fuck that," I told Taco. "This will send out a message to the rest of them punks."

The next morning I stepped to him and caught him asleep. I crept up, climbed on the stool and then the desk, raised my weapon like my fist was a hammer, and began my downward motion. His movement was swift and sharp. He rolled to one side of the bed and balled up. My downstroke pierced his blanket and mattress and finally stopped with a vibrating "pinggg!" on the steel bed frame.

"Monster Kody, wait!" Anyone who knows me calls me either Monster or Kody. Only enemies and strangers refer to me by my whole name.

"I'm gonna kill yo' punk ass," I said, making a mocking stab at him, enjoying the terror in his eyes. "You outta bounds, N-hood, this is Grape and Gangsta 'hood, fool." I made another swing in his general direction.

"Cuz," he pleaded, hands held high like I was telling him to stick 'em up, "I didn't know. Taco said it was cool if I live up here. Ask him, Monster Kody, ask him."

I stopped swinging but began breathing hard, looking around like a lunatic. I went into my madman routine.

"You got three minutes by Gangsta time to roll yo' shit up, bitch! You here me?" I said, eyes bugged like a crack addict's.

"Yeah, Monster Kody, I hear you."

"MOVE THEN!!" I yelled, waking everybody up.

"What's up?" somebody said from down the tier.

"EIGHT TRAY GANGSTAS!!" I yelled, and someone said, "Aw, shit, he's at it again."

Lucky moved down on Able row and I consolidated Charlie row, resuming control of the tank. I found out that Weeble Wobble had gone to the penitentiary after taking a twenty-five-to-life deal. In San Quentin, the United Blood Nation murdered him. Popa and Perry had received ninety-six and ninety-eight years, respectively, and were in Folsom state prison. Chicken Swoop had also been found guilty and sentenced to twenty-five years to life. Chico was given fifteen years to life, Moman was sentenced to twenty-five years to life, and Old Man was given fifteen years to life. A lot of new people were there, and a few of the old ones still remained.

De and I had been charged with a robbery that neither of us committed. The LAPD knew this, without a doubt. Apparently, a man had been robbed on Eighty-fourth and Western Avenue, his money and shoes taken, and he had picked De and me out of a mug book as the robbers. But we knew that it was a bogus charge. After putting out our feelers and finding out who had really robbed the man, we knew beyond a doubt that it was a setup. The actual robbers—two older homies—didn't resemble us whatsoever. It was impossible for that man to have been robbed by the other two homies and then have turned around and picked De and I. But it just so happened that De and I were the two hardest working bangers in the culture, committing crime sprees alone and together—a neighborhood's worst nightmare. So we surmised early on in the proceedings that all this was a game of get-us-off-the-street. Well, it worked. I received four years and De received five. Since I was a minor, I went to Youth Authority; De was sent to state prison.

While I was in the juvenile tank, my homeboy Eight Ball was murdered—blown up in a ride-by ambush. He died on 111th Street and New Hampshire while riding Devil from 107 Hoover on the handlebars of a ten-speed. He had not been out of Youth Authority a month before being killed. Because of who he was with, and the neighborhood they were in when the ambush occurred, it was easy to ascertain where the shooters were from. No doubt they were Neighborhood Blocks—the Hoovers' worst enemy. The next day I snuck into the dayroom and ambushed Crazy Eight from One-Eleven N-hood for Eight Ball's death. I beat him bloody.

Not long after that I was transferred to Youth Authority, going first to the Southern Reception Center Clinic (SRCC) in Norwalk. The day after my arrival I was summoned to the officer of the day's office. When I got there a big, dark New Afrikan man and a scrawny little American woman sat behind two huge desks, both cluttered with papers and books. The New Afrikan man eyed me suspiciously, while the American woman busied herself with writing, not turning to look at me when I entered the room.

"Kody Scott?" asked the New Afrikan officer, peering over the rim of his glasses.

"Yeah," I replied.

"Monster Kody Scott?" he asked again, to be sure.

A bit hesitant now, I finally answered, "Yeah."

"Well," the officer began, sighing, pushing his glasses up on his nose and sitting back in his chair all in one fluid motion, "we don't want you here. That is, in our institution."

"What you talkin' 'bout, man?" I asked, eyebrows automatically connecting in preparation for a mad-dog stare.

"Welp," he started, through another sigh. "Kody, you don't mind if I call you Monster, do you? It kinda keeps me focused here," he said, making a playful attempt at clearing his junky desk.

"Naw, it's cool."

"Good, good," he said, as if he were instructing someone who had done a good job at something. "I must admit you are nothing like I imagined." And then, as if to himself, "No, no, nothing like I imagined." He went on, "Well, Mr. Monster . . . ha, ha, ha . . . Mr. Monster . . . sounds funny, huh?"

I didn't smile.

"Yes, well, the point is every gang member that comes through here—and we get a lot—has something to say about you."

"Is that right?" I said, more bored than flattered.

"Oh, yeah, you betcha. And so from talking to them, and overhearing others, I've come to know that you have killed many people."

"That's a lie, I ain't kilt nobody!"

"Hold on now, Monster, don't get riled up now—"

"Naw, man, people be lyin' 'n' stuff, I—"

"Well, we just think it's best if you are sent directly to Youth Training School to complete your introduction up there, where there are more kids of your caliber around. Besides, the security is much tighter there. You'll like it."

"Like it?!" I shouted. "What makes you think that I like tighter security? You muthafuckas be trippin'—"

"Calm down, Mr.—"

"Man, fuck you!"

Just then the door burst open and in rushed two line-backer-sized Americans who grabbed me, kicking and yelling profanities, and cuffed me.

The next morning, before the sun rose, I was in chains and on a bus to Y.T.S. to begin serving my four years.

7

MUHAMMAD ABDULLAH

The Gray Goose, as the Youth Authority Transport bus was affectionately called, rolled through the double sally port gates at the Youth Training School under the watchful eyes of those prisoners who worked in 500 Trade jobs behind yet another chainlink fence. After meeting the security requirements of the last checkpoint, the Gray Goose chugged forward, further into the institution. Once this third fence was opened and we rolled through, the expansive sight of the landscape almost took my breath away. I saw the same effect on the faces of a few other prisoners aboard the bus. It looked like a huge college campus, or what I thought a college campus would look like from watching "Room 222" on television.

There was a standard football field of plush, green grass

surrounded by a red dirt 440-yard track. On one side of the track sat the bleachers, and behind them was a boxing gym. On the other side stood another huge gym containing Olympic weights and a full, hardwood basketball court. Adjacent to this was a swimming pool. After being locked in the concrete confines of South Central all my life—with the exception of youth camp—seeing such open spaces of well-kept grass surrounded by a track, gyms, swimming pool, and bleachers only conjured up beautiful images of college campuses and well-to-do students.

But, as with all things, that which looks good outwardly may be horribly ugly within. The well-kept face of Y.T.S. was but a facade, for behind the walls of the gyms and in the three units that stood around the outer track like mysterious statues on Easter Island, corruption of every kind was rampant—and for profit.

In 1981, the Youth Training School held 1,200 prisoners. No one, under California law, could stay in Youth Authority past the age of twenty-six. Y.T.S. was considered a senior Youth Authority. A maximum-security youth prison, it comprised three units, each divided into quarters. Each quarter was subdivided into halves, and each half was again divided into banks, or tiers. Every prisoner was assigned to his own cell. Each cell had a sliding door of solid steel with a small glass window for observation by the staff. The units were organized so as to meet the individual needs of each prisoner as set forth by the diagnostic researcher designated to individual casework.

Each unit had four companies, all structured alphabetically. Unit One housed companies A-B, C-D, E-F, and G-H. A-B was for orientation. One had to stay here at least two weeks without going anywhere else but to testing—math, reading comprehension, and so on. If your grade-point average was not up to par, you were made to go to school. If you did not have your diploma or G.E.D., you had to work half a day and go to school the other half until you got it. C-D was where you could be trained in fighting fires and then sent out to do easy time at one of the many Youth Authority Camps. E-F was for drug abusers and people who, when sentenced, were specifically ordered by the judge to complete the twelve-step program as a requirement for release. G-H was for alcoholics with the same presentence or board-recommended stipulations in their file.

Unit Two, consisting of I-J, K-L, M-N, and O-R, was the last unit of specifications. I-J was a medical unit for mentally ill prisoners and prisoners with rape charges or with character defects that had led to the charges and conviction. K-L and M-N were young companies. Young prisoners, even though maximum-security material, were kept together. O-R—better known as the Rock, was the hole, one of the strictest maximum-security holes outside of Pelican Bay's Security Housing Unit and Marion's MCU. Once on the Rock you had to practically jump through hoops to get off. Every week a bus came and took prisoners off the Rock and onto a state prison. The Rock loomed as the ultimate discipline for those considered fuck-ups. Whenever we passed the Rock, which was up above K-L, we gave sort of a thankful salute. The cool people just nodded respectfully.

Unit Three was considered *the* unit to be in: S-T, U-V, W-X, and Y-Z. W-X was where all the riders were. It had a reputation for everything from race riots to football, dope to weight lifting. It sat above S-T, which was a regular company, as was Y-Z. U-V was for those in 500 Trade. These were the upperclass sort of folks. Everyone in U-V got paid for their work. They kept the institution clean and functioning properly. Everyone wanted to be in 500 Trade. The Youth Training School also had a huge Trade Line, where everything from upholstery to plumbing was taught. Upon completion of the Trade Line, one was given a certificate.

As with almost every institution, correctional facility, or penitentiary, Chicanos and New Afrikans were in the majority. In Youth Authority, one began to learn about the larger prison culture that touched everyone's lives, including the staff who, after being in the institution so long, began to assume some of the characteristics of the prisoners.

Lines of race, of national unity that defied political logic and overstanding, were clearly drawn in Youth Authority, which served as a junior college for the larger university of prison. The most blatant was that of the Allied Forces of Southern Chicanos—"southern" meaning any land south of Fresno—with all Americans. The Americans could have "White Pride," "White Power," swastikas, lightning bolts, "100% Honkey," and such tattooed all over them, clearly stating they were stone-cold racists, and the Chicanos would be more than comfortable in their presence. New Afrikans allied themselves with the more cultured Northern Chicanos. The Northern and Southern Chicanos were, and still are, locked in a very serious war. The film *American Me* illustrates this. So, like the warring factions of New Afrikans, the Chicanos were split by geopolitical boundaries. What's striking is that the division of the two is signified in colors. The Northern Chicanos—Nuestra Familia, Northern Structure, and Fresno Bulldogs—wear red flags. The more numerous Southerners—Mexican Mafia, Southern United Raza, and South Side Government—wear blue.

The New Afrikans from Northern California—primarily

Oakland, Berkeley, Richmond, San Francisco, and Palo Alto—call themselves 415s, which, until recently, was the area code for most of the Bay area. As if the Crip and Blood conflict was not complicated enough, the Crips do not get along with the 415s. Actually, the 415s don't like the New Afrikans from 213—the Los Angeles area code—but for strategic purposes they have chosen the Bloods as allies over the Crips. So in Youth Authority, the ground rules of prison are set—your friends, your enemies. As a rule, all Americans get along with all North, South, 415, and 213. This, I believe, is because of their minority status in most institutions.

Tribalism was most prevalent amongst New Afrikans, who began as one then split into Crips and Bloods. The Crips, ever the majority, were then plagued—indeed, traumatized—by the internal strife of "set trippin'." There was also struggle within each set for leadership. In prison, beginning in Youth Authority, sets try to organize themselves on some level to deal with the new complexities of institutionalization. With this new quest comes the rise of antagonistic contradictions. Since most leaders were not politically equipped to properly recognize, confront, and resolve the contradictions in organizing the unorganized in relation to the larger society, their efforts usually failed, doomed from the outset, or were aborted in the early stages by those who opted for the old platform of anarchy. This start-and-stop process of organization was characteristic of most sets there.

When I was at Y.T.S., we began our organizing process when our numbers swelled beyond fifteen. Our critical concern was organizing around the larger reality of the war. I had been reading Mario Puzo's *The Godfather* and was devising a grand scheme for the set based on the Corleone family structure. Never did I take into account that first and foremost the Italians had a clear sense of who they were. That is, they overstood their heritage and their relation to the world as European people. We, on the other hand, were just Crips with no sense of anything before us or of where we were headed. We were trapped behind the veil of cultural ignorance without even knowing it. Yet here I was, trying to pattern our set after some established people, Europeans at that.

My opposition came primarily from Diamond. It got continually worse until 1983, culminating in my charges of set neglect against Diamond. This prompted a meeting of the entire set. Diamond was exonerated, but after that our relationship never recovered.

By this time, I had become very egotistical. My reputation had finally ballooned to the third stage and, by definition, I had moved into the security zone of O.G. status. My rep was omnipresent, totally saturating every circle of gang life. From CRASH to the courts, from Crips to Bloods, from Juvenile Hall to death row, Monster Kody had arrived. This, coupled with my newfound curiosity and interest in Mafia-style gangsterism, made me very hard to approach.

By 1983 I was physically the second biggest in the institution, second only to an old friend, Roscoe, the Samoan from the Park Village Compton Crips. We were weight-lifting partners. He had twenty-one-inch arms, and mine were twenty and one-quarter. He was bench pressing five hundred and ten pounds and I was doing four hundred and seventy. I heard after I left that he went considerably higher—five hundred and ninety, I was told. My size added to the Monster image, and I capitalized on it at every opportunity.

We had planned a righteous gangster ceremony of bloodletting for the year 1983—the year of the Eight Trays. But 1983 found the set in shambles. Most of our combat troops were locked away, dead or paralyzed by lack of motivation. We found ourselves compensating for this in Y.T.S. by vamping on the Sixties. What sped this process up, apart from it being 1983, was the fact that Opie had just been murdered by the Rollin' Sixties. Caught in a secured driveway trying to climb over a chain-link fence, he was hit once in the side and died waiting for an ambulance. We were incensed with rage, because other than Li'l Spike—who was the darling of the 'hood—Opie was our sort of mascot. He was always filthy and unkempt, which didn't seem to bother him at all. But De and I would always make fun of Opie's appearance and shabbiness. We even had the Opie National Anthem, which opened:

Where there's fire, there's smoke,
Where there's dirt, there's Op . . .

Opie would just look at us like he felt sorry for us, and De and I would double over in laughter. We'd take our hats off and place them solemnly over our hearts, looking very serious, and then fall into the Opie National Anthem. We loved Opie like a brother.

We needed to consolidate a meeting of all twenty-three of us in the institution so we could move simultaneously. The only feasible place we could congregate without the staff detecting our intent was in Muslim services, which was held every Monday night. We knew that the attendance was low and that our move to this service would not be viewed with alarm by the staff members who worked as operatives for the gang coordinator—the dreaded Mr. Hernandez.

When Li'l Monster came to Y.T.S. from Ventura for whipping a female prisoner, Mr. Hernandez called us both to his office. Li'l Bro was in Y-Z and I was on the Rock. I had been put there as a result of Li'l Fee from the Rollin' Sixties telling Hernandez that I had instructed Stagalee to beat him down, which of course was true. Li'l Fee had just come down from Dewitt Nelson and was trying to be hard. When I dissed his set, he surprisingly dissed back, though he was out of firing range. In fact he was clear across the front field. The diss was not verbal, and no one other than he and I knew it was going on. When I saw him looking in my direction I flashed his set's sign and then, still holding my fingers in place displaying his 'hood, I put them in my mouth and chewed on them, insinuating that "I be eating his 'hood up." He in turn did the same to my set. But my gesture was based on fact; his was empty. Nonetheless, he had done it. I would have charged him immediately myself, but he was in step with his unit, escorted by two staff members and clear across the field, and I was in step with my unit, accompanied by staff. The chances of getting him were slim, taking into account the distance and the staff coverage. Besides, had I gotten there, how long would the brawl last? Surely not long enough to punish him for the crime of disrespect. In addition, I was a "G." That meant I had people to handle this type of thing. No problem.

I sent word to Stag, who was in M-N with Li'l Fee. The very next day, Stag put an old-style gangster whipping on him. Li'l Fee informed Hernandez—who got involved in every fight that was gang related—of the dissing the previous day, and Hernandez locked me up on the Rock. Li'l Fee was sent back to Dewitt Nelson. The next time we would meet would be over the barrel of a gun.

When I got to Hernandez's office I was surprised to see Li'l Bro. I had heard that he was here, but had not seen him because I was locked on the Rock. Hernandez gave us some bullshit-ass speech about not wanting to allow two Monsters into his institution. I wasn't even paying attention to what he was saying. When in the course of his spiel about what he would not tolerate I jumped up out of my seat and shouted "Fuck it, I'm ready to go to the pen!" Mr. Hernandez was shocked and sat looking at me bug-eyed. Li'l Bro grabbed my arm and told me to "be cool." I sat back down and burned a hole right through Mr. Hernandez, who now knew that I was beyond his little threats. How could I be cordial with the same man who had locked me up and now sat before me espousing threats? I was escorted back to the Rock without further comment from Hernandez. I saluted Li'l Bro and exited the room.

From the Rock, I sent word for the meeting in Muslim services. The following Monday evening we fell into Muslim services twenty-three deep. Besides us there were seven or eight others, including the two Muslim ministers, Muhammad and Hamza. Although staff members escorted them for supervisory coverage, they left soon after the ministers began to speak. On this night, our first night, the Muslims had set up a film on slavery, which held no interest for us. As soon as the lights went off I began in on our needed sweep to rid the institution of the Sixties. During the course of my talk to the homies, the lights flicked on, and the film projector was turned off. We sat up from our hunched positions and were faced with a very angry Hamza.

"Check this out, brothas," began Hamza, who stood

before us in a black thobe over black combat boots and a leather jacket. "Y'all disrespecting our services, over here rappin' among y'all selves like little women—"

"Wait a minute, man," I said in quick defense of our status. "We Eight Trays, we ain't no women."

"Yeah, well the way y'all—"

"Naw, man, fuck that, we gangstas."

"Well, if y'all ain't gonna watch the movie, then y'all can leave."

"Oh yeah?" I said, standing up and slowly turning in the direction of the homeboys. "Let's bail." I stalked off without a backward glance, followed by the troops.

Once outside the Protestant church, which is where Islamic services were held, we made our way to the Trade Line's smoke-break area and stood around. All at once powerful lights hit us from the tower overlooking the facility, and moments later institutional cars and vans sped toward us, stopping within inches of our gathering. We were put on the fence and brick wall surrounding the smoke-break area and searched by irate staff members. When asked what we were doing "out of bounds," we said that the Muslims said we could leave. I was taken back to the Rock, while the others were locked in their cells pending an explanation by the Muslims, who had supposedly let us out of services without proper escort. The next day we found out that the Muslims had, in fact, backed up our story and, with the exception of me, all the homies were taken off lockdown.

The next week, while I was in the infirmary waiting room just wasting time out of my cell, Muhammad came through. At first I was a bit reluctant to approach him because of the disrespect issue. But I felt obligated to say something, because they had backed us up when the staff had asked them about the incident. I motioned him over.

"What's up, man?" I asked, not knowing how he would respond. "Don't you remember me?"

"Yeah," he said, "I remember you."

"Yeah, well, I just want to apologize for disrupting your services last week and say thanks for backing us up on our statement."

"Yeah, I hear you, but actually y'all didn't disrupt our services at all. And as far as the pigs trying to lock y'all up, naw, we ain't gonna contribute to that."

"Righteous," I said, noting that Muhammad's style of speech was straight out of the 1960s. He was about six feet even, with a very dark, shiny, well-kept blackness. He wore a full beard, gold glasses, and a turban. His dress code was militant. He was a black ayatollah.

"Isn't your name Monster Kody?" asked Muhammad.

"Yeah," I replied.

"From Eight Tray, right?"

"Right."

"Insha Allah, I be dealing with some of your older homeboys. Rayford, Bacot, X-con. You know them?"

"Yeah, them my O.G. homies," I said with pride.

"Was all them brothas with you last week from Eight Tray, too?"

"Yeah, we twenty-three deep here."

"Why y'all brothas fall to the services like that?"

"Huh?" I said, as if I didn't overstand his question. I didn't know if I should tell him the truth or not. If I said we were having a meeting he might feel that we really were disrespecting his services.

"You know, like why was y'all so thick? Somebody got killed on the bricks?"

He saw that I was perplexed and didn't want to say too much, so he talked on.

"You brothas looked unified and strong. Insha Allah, why don't you come and check out the services tonight?"

"Naw, I ain't into no religion or nothin'."

"Well here, read this. And if you ever feel like checking us out, come on by. You're welcome."

"Righteous," I replied, looking down at the pamphlet he'd given me, entitled *Message to the Oppressed.*

We shook hands and parted company. That night in my cell I read the pamphlet, which began with a quote by Malcolm X:

> Out of frustration and hopelessness our young people have reached the point of no return. We no longer endorse patience and turning the other cheek. We assert the right of self-defense by whatever means necessary, and reserve the right of maximum retaliation against our racist oppressors, no matter what the odds against us are.

It went on to list food, clothing, and shelter as the immediate aims of the struggle, and land and independence as the sought-after objectives. The pamphlet was not as religious as I thought it would be. I had been so conditioned to believe that religion was synonymous with passivity—from the Christian teachings to people of color—that I simply took for granted that Islam was like Christianity in this light. The material ended with another quote by Malcolm X:

> From here on in, if we must die anyway, we will die fighting back and we will not die alone. We intend to see that our racist oppressors also get a taste of death.

The language was heavy, and I was impressed by it. Of course I was trying to figure out how to fit my enemies into this language, for the word "oppressor" had little meaning to me then. Although I was, like every other person of color on this planet, oppressed, I didn't know it. I told myself that next week I was going to go and see just what was happening over there.

During the days before the services I read and reread the pamphlet. I had trouble clarifying words like "struggle," "revolutionary," "jihad," and "colonialism," but I kept on reading. It gave me a certain feeling, a slight tingle, and a longing sense of curiosity. Finally, the next week fell and I found myself walking down the ramp off the Rock and over toward the chapel that held Islamic services.

When I got there I was greeted by a brother named L.C., who was also a prisoner who lived on company S-T. There were about nine people altogether. After they went through their prayers, Muhammad read a short sura from the Holy Koran and then closed it. Standing there thoughtfully for a moment he played lightly in his beard, and then, as suddenly as thunder, he began a sharp tirade about the U.S. government.

"Brothas, it is incumbent upon you as male youth to learn of your obligation to the oppressed masses who are being systematically crushed by the wicked government of the United States of America. They already know of your potential to smash them, so they have deliberately locked you up in this concentration camp."

Now, heated up, he began to pace the length of the church.

"Insha Allah, you will not be sidetracked from your mission. You are young warriors who are destined to be free! But you must be prepared to jihad till death!"

I was totally awestruck by his strength and language, not to mention his sincerity. He talked on about the government's deliberate efforts to rid the world of people of color—black males in particular. All but the simplest things went right over my head. But what I was able to grasp slapped me hard across the face with such force that I got goose bumps. Damn, this shit must be real. It seems too heavy to be made up. And if he didn't know what he was talking about, how was he able to explain what I had been through in home, in school, in the streets, and with the law? No, this had to be real.

When the services were over I lifted myself up and floated to my cell, totally high on Muhammad's revolutionary speech. The week following the service, I must have read *Message to the Oppressed* thirty times. All I thought about was hearing Muhammad blow.

On Wednesday I got some devastating news. Crazy Keith from Harlem came for a visit and told me that Tray Ball was dead.

"What?" I said in utter disbelief.

"Yeah, Li'l Tray Ball just told me that cuz shot himself in the head playing Russian roulette."

"Where Li'l Tray Ball at?" I asked.

"I seen cuz on a visit."

"Damn!"

I felt at a total loss. I wasn't ready to hear that. Not Tray

Ball. I had dealt with other deaths in one piece, getting solace out of being able to strike back. But here, on the Rock, there was no striking back. No drugs, no loud music to put me in a trance, no revenge, nothing of the sort. Just me and myself. It was almost impossible to deal with—the reality of him being dead, gone, never to be seen again. All the good times came rolling up on my mental screen. Times when Tray Ball would act as mediator in disputes amongst the homies, using his influence to mend breaks in the clique. Or using his persuasion to recruit yet another homie. Ball gave us foresight, hindsight, and a deep-seated feeling of righteous worth. I couldn't imagine us without him. First we'd lost Eight Ball, and now Tray Ball. Symbolically, the set—Eight Tray—had been castrated by the removal of its balls, the Eight and the Three.

I cried like a baby for hours. Not just for Tray Ball, but for the set. The 'hood was dying, didn't people see it like that? Our symbols were falling and no one seemed to overstand the significance of this. My nerves were in total disarray. What do you do when your homie commits suicide? Who do you strike at? Who is to blame? We all played Russian roulette, that mindless game of stupidity sadly mistaken as courage. Fortunately, our chambers clicked empty against the ping of the hammer. But for Tray Ball, it was a full chamber.

From what I was able to gather, Tray Ball, along with two or three other homegirls and two members of the Compton Crips, were in the shack—Tray Ball's backhouse—getting high. Tray Ball started playing roulette with a .38 snub-nose. One round in the chamber, a quick spin, put the barrel to the temple, and *click* or *boom.* After several successful attempts—or unsuccessful, depending on the players' disposition, and I don't know what Tray Ball's mind-set was that particular day—he became bored with the game. He exited the shack and went into the house. While he was gone, thinking he was through with roulette, someone put five more rounds in the chamber. When Trayball re-entered the shack, he immediately picked up the gun, put it to his head, squeezed the trigger and BOOM! No one had time to tell him the barrel was full. Everyone fled the scene. Tragedy has no mercy.

Our first thought was of foul play. My initial instinct was to kill everybody who was there, including those from Compton. Later, I knew this was an irrational call based on emotionalism. I remained bitter the rest of the week.

When Tamu and my sister, Kendis, came to visit my brother and me on Sunday, I told them about Muhammad and the way he talked. I asked Bro to accompany me Monday night to services, and he agreed to.

On Monday Muhammad did as he had the week before, only this time he spoke more about the Black Panther party and its threat to the U.S. government. Seeing me and Li'l Monster there, he intentionally expounded on the lives of George and Jonathan Jackson, both members of the party. Jonathan was murdered in a heroic attempt to liberate three prisoners, including the Soledad Brothers—of which his Brother-Comrade, George, was one. Comrade George was assassinated the following year in a bungled attempt to escape from San Quentin.

"How old are you?" Muhammad asked, pointing at Li'l Monster.

"Seventeen," replied Li'l Bro.

"Jonathan Jackson was seventeen when he walked into the

Marin County Courthouse and took the judge and D.A. hostage."

He paused a minute for effect.

"What set you from?" Muhammad asked me.

"Eight Tray Gangster," I replied.

"George Jackson was the field marshal for the Black Panther party. He was eighteen when he was captured. He was given one year to life for a seventy-dollar gas station robbery. He served eleven years before he was killed by pigs. He was twenty-nine years old."

He turned to Li'l Monster. "What you in here for?"

"For murder."

"Who you kill?"

"Some Sixties—"

"Black people!" Muhammad shouted.

"Yeah, but—"

"George Jackson corrected, not killed, *corrected* three pigs and two Nazis before he himself was murdered!"

Muhammad seemed possessed.

"This is what I'm trying to tell you. As you kill each other, the real enemy is steadily killing you. Your generation has totally turned inward and is now self-destructive. You are less of a threat when you fight one another, you dig?"

We sat upright, clinging to his words.

"Jonathan knew chemistry, demolition, and martial arts. He was a man-child, a revolutionary. He felt responsible for the future of his people."

We sat there, stunned by the parallel between us and George and Jonathan Jackson. What made us sit up and take note of what Muhammad was saying about our self-destructive behavior was that he never talked down to us, always *to* us. He didn't like what we were doing, but he respected us as young warriors. He never once told us to disarm. His style of consciousness-raising was in total harmony with the ways in which we had grown up in our communities, in this country, on this planet. Muhammad's lessons were local, national, and international.

I put the word out that all Crips should come to Muslim services and hear Muhammad talk. Within three weeks attendance increased from nine to twenty-seven to forty and finally to eighty! The staff became alarmed, asking questions and even sitting in on some of the services, trying to grasp our sudden attraction to Islamic services. They never caught it.

Islam is a way of life, just like banging. We could relate to what Muhammad was saying, especially when he spoke about jihad—struggle. Of course we heard what we wanted to hear. We knew that Islam or revolution was not a threat to us as warriors. Muhammad didn't seek to make us passive or weak. On the contrary, he encouraged us to "stand firm," "stay armed," and "stay black." He encouraged us not to shoot one another, if possible, but to never hesitate to "correct a pig who transgressed against the people." After every service let out, it was a common sight to see fifty to eighty New Afrikan youths mobbing back to their units shouting "Jihad till death!" and "Death to the oppressor!"

The Protestant following totally evaporated. Reverend Jackson could not figure out where his constituents had gone. In these times, gang conflicts involving New Afrikans were at an all-time low. Mr. Hernandez began to pull on the strings of his informants, which, without fail, led him to me.

One day he called me into his office for a fact-finding chat.

He offered me a seat, but I declined. He then began his little probe.

"So, Mr. Scott—or is it Abdul or Ali Baba?"

I said nothing.

"Yes, well anyway I have called you in here because it is my understanding that you have been trying to subvert the institutional security."

The term "institutional security" is so far-reaching that whenever there is nothing to lock a prisoner down or harass him for, staff, correction officers, and most any figure of authority in any institution will pull out this ambiguous term. It is precisely this wording that has me locked deep within the bowels of Pelican Bay today. I am a threat, and proud of it. If I wasn't a threat, I'd be doing something wrong.

"Institutional what?" I asked, not yet familiar with the terminology.

"Security, Scott, security."

"Man, you trippin'—"

"No, Scott, *you* are tripping!" he yelled, slapping both hands hard on the table.

"I don't know what you talkin' 'bout," I answered with a blank stare.

"Oh, you don't, huh? Well how do you explain twenty-three Eight Trays, fourteen Hoovers, eleven East Coasts and a lesser assortment of other bangers cropped up in Moslem church for the past month, huh? Explain that!"

"Man, I ain't explainin' shit."

"Oh, no? Well how 'bout if I keep your bad ass on the Rock forever, huh? How 'bout that?"

"I already been there two months for some shit that didn't involve me—"

"You are a *damn* liar, you ordered that boy Layton to jump on Cox. And you been involved in a host of other shit. So don't tell me what you *ain't* done."

"You know what, Hernandez, do what you gotta do," I said low and slow, to let him know that I wasn't hardly giving a fuck about what he was stressing on.

"Yeah, I'll do that, I'll just do that. But you remember this when you go up for parole."

"Can I leave now?" I asked, bored with his threats.

Actually the Rock wasn't all that bad. I ate all my meals in the cage, showered every other day, and came out once a day for an hour, usually in the morning. I was able to have my radio and a few tapes. At that time I was exploring the blues. Jimmy Reed was my favorite. I still got my weekly visits, though I couldn't decide who I wanted to have come. At Y.T.S. they allowed prisoners to have only one female on their visiting list, other than mothers and sisters. Tamu really was not my first choice, China was. But she didn't have the mobility to be there every week, and riding the bus was suicidal. So I took her off my visiting list and replaced her with Ayanna, who was also from the 'hood. Her mother had moved her out to Pomona to get her out of the gang environment, and she now lived in close proximity to Y.T.S. Our visits went like clockwork, but eventually we grew tired of each other, so I took her off my list. For a short time I replaced Ayanna with Felencia, Tray Ball's sister. This didn't work out too well either, because she wanted me to stop gangbanging and I just wasn't having it. I was not giving up my career for no female, so I ended up putting Tamu back on the list. As long as I got my visits and could keep my music, the Rock wasn't shit.

In my cell on the Rock, I reread for the hundredth time *Message to the Oppressed.* Malcolm came on strong:

> We declare our right on this earth to be a man, to be a human being, to be given the rights of a human being in this society, on this earth, in this day, which we intend to bring into existence BY ANY MEANS NECESSARY.

As I read on I felt the words seeping deeper into me, their power coursing through my body, giving me strength to push on. I was changing, I felt it. For once I didn't challenge it or see it as being a threat to the established mores of the 'hood, though, of course, it was. Muhammad's teachings corresponded with my condition of being repressed on the Rock. Never could I have been touched by such teachings in the street.

The prison setting, although repressive, was a bit too free. But on the Rock, the illusion of freedom vanished, and in its place was the harsh actuality of oppression and the very real sense of powerlessness over destiny. Because there was no shooting war to concentrate on, your worst enemy was easily replaced by the figure presently doing you the most harm. In prisons this figure is more often than not an American. An American who locks you in a cage, counts you to make sure you haven't escaped, holds a weapon on you, and, in many instances, shoots you. Add to this the fact that most of us grew up in an eighty percent New Afrikan community policed—or occupied—by an eighty-five percent American pig force that is clearly antagonistic to any male in the community, displaying this antagonism at every opportunity by any means necessary with all the brute force and sadistic imagination they can muster.

It was quite easy then for Muhammad's teachings to hit me in the heart. However, my attraction to the facts involving our national oppression was grounded in emotionalism, and eight years of evolutionary development in Crip culture could hardly be rolled back by one pamphlet and a few trips to Islamic services. But I did feel the strength. I called off the move on the Sixties after Tray Ball killed himself. Everyone asked why, but I really had no answer. I told them that we'd handle it in a little while.

Stagalee was my neighbor on the Rock; he and I would talk through a small hole in the wall. I sent him over the *Message to the Oppressed* pamphlet and solicited a response from him about its contents.

"Cuz," I said bending down so as to talk through the hole, "what you think 'bout that paper I sent over there?"

"I don't know, some of these words too hard fo' me, cuz. But I can see that this is some powerful shit."

"Well, what you could catch, what did you think?"

"Cuz, really, I think Muhammad is some kind of terrorist or somethin'."

"Stag, you trippin'. Muhammad ain't no terrorist. Shit, Muhammad is down for us."

"Who?" he asked, "the set?"

"Hell naw, nigga, black people!"

"Ah, cuz, fuck all that, 'cause soon he gonna be tellin' us to stop bangin' and shit—"

"Stag, Stag." I tried to slow him down.

"Naw, cuz, I can't see me being no Muslim. I just can't see it. They be standing on corners selling pies and shit. Do you know how long one of us would live standin' on a corner, not even in our 'hood? Monster, let me catch a Sissy, Muslim or not, and I'ma blow that nigga up!"

"I don't know, homie, I just feel that there is something there."

"Yeah, muthafucka, a bean pie!" Stag answered and broke out laughing.

"Stall it out, cuz," I said, feeling myself getting angry.

"Monster, you ain't thinkin' 'bout being no Muslim, is you? Cuz, don't do it. Muhammad cool and everythang, but cuz, you Monster Kody. Ain't nobody gonna let you live in peace. Plus the set needs you, cuz. Here, cuz."

Stag had rolled up the pamphlet and was pushing it through the hole.

"Naw, cuz, I ain't thinkin' 'bout turnin' no Muslim. I'm just sayin' that what Muhammad be stressin' is real."

"Right, right."

"Well, I'ma step back and get some z's. I'll rap to you later. Three minutes."

"Three minutes."

I lay on my bed with the rolled-up pamphlet on my chest and thought about what Stag had said.

"You Monster Kody. Ain't nobody gonna let you live in peace. . . . The set needs you . . . "

My young consciousness screamed back in an attempt to exert itself.

"Who *is* Monster Kody? . . . *I* am Monster Kody . . . a person, a young man, a black man . . . Anything else? . . . No, not that I know of . . . *What* is Monster Kody? . . . A Crip, an

Eight Tray, a Rollin' Sixty killer . . . a black man . . . Black man, black man, BLACK MAN . . . "

The words reverberated again and again.

"Nobody gonna let you live in peace . . . "

"*Who* ain't gonna let you live in peace?"

"Black men, black men, black men . . . "

"*Why?!*" my consciousness shouted back. "WHY?!"

I had no answer. The confusion gave me a headache. I knew that I was reaching a crossroad, but I didn't know how to handle it. Should I accept it or reject it? In a perverted sort of way I enjoyed being Monster Kody. I lived for the power surge of playing God, having the power of life and death in my hands. Nothing I knew of could compare with riding in a car with three other homeboys with guns, knowing that they were as deadly and courageous as I was. To me, at that time in my life, this was power. It made me feel responsible for either killing someone or letting them live. The thought of controlling something substantial—like land—never occurred to me. The thought of responsibility for the welfare of my daughter or a nation, New Afrika, never crossed my mind. I was only responsible to my 'hood and my homeboys. Now I was being subjected to a wider reality than I had ever known.

Then I heard it. As I was struggling with this dilemma I grasped the point that Muhammad was trying to make.

"When you were born you were born black. That's all. Then, later on, you turned Crip, dig?"

In this light I found clarity. But, I asked myself, what was Muhammad really asking of us? Did I have to be a Muslim to be black? I surmised that it was like being a Crip or a Blood, as opposed to being a hook or a civilian. Where I came from, in order to be down you had to be "in." Did I have to be "in"—

that is, a Muslim—to be down with blackness? Surely much thought and internal debate had to go into this issue.

My thing was this: I didn't believe there was a God. I just had no faith in what I couldn't see, feel, taste, hear, or smell. All my life I have seen the power of life and death in the hands of men and boys. If I shot at someone and I hit him and he died, who took his life? Me or God? Was it predestined that on this day at this time I would specifically push this guy out of existence? I never believed that. I believed that I hunted him, caught him, and killed him. I had lived in too much disorder to believe that there was an actual design to this world. So I had a problem with believing in anything other than myself.

My interest here was drawn by the militancy of Malcolm X and Muhammad, not by the spirituality of Islam. The first book I got was *Soul on Ice* by Eldridge Cleaver. Most of it was too hard to grasp, but what I did get was militant and strong. I found that this was my preference.

I was subsequently taken off the Rock and put back in Unit Three, in company U-V. While attending school for my G.E.D., I met a brother named Walter Brown. Bro—who worked at Y.T.S. as a teacher but functioned better as a guiding light—had been a prisoner himself in the 1960s. He was stern but flexible and held great influence over most of us who were considered O.G.s. Brown was militant but responsible. Not to imply that militants are irresponsible, but Brown was specifically responsible for the upbringing of us—young, New Afrikan males. His degree of effectiveness can be measured by the fact that he was designated to "teach" parole classes. That gave him access to prisoners for one week, one hour a day, before they were paroled. This skimpy time frame could not possibly have helped prisoners deal with the multi-complex phenomena of society. Most of what was taught was useless, old institutional garbage that was not applicable to the streets. Brown, however, was beyond that and taught hard-core reality-politics that drew those of us who listened closer to the brink of consciousness. Some of us, those who Brown felt had potential, would stop by his class long before pre-parole and sit and listen to him talk about the raw reality of America.

"Kody," Brown would say, "these white folks ain't playin', man. They will lock you up, lock you down, lock you in just like they have locked you out of this society. If you haven't got any marketable skills to sustain an income on your own, man, your chances of survival are slim. You are high-risk living—actually just existing. You young, black, unskilled, strong . . . you smoke cigarettes?"

"Naw, just bo'."

"Well, that's good enough. You use drugs, you drink, and to top it off you gangbang! Man, how you gonna make it?"

"Man, I don't know . . ."

Brown, like Muhammad, had a great impact on my development, though it took a few years to appreciate their contribution. The strongest New Afrikan men I had known up until that time were bangers. Verbalizing was not an issue. Shoot first and let the victims' relatives ask questions later. Guns were our tools of communication. If we liked you, you weren't shot and we'd go to any length to shoot whomever disliked you. If you were not liked, you were hunted, if necessary, and shot—period. Instantaneous communication. That's all I had known for years. Words, I thought, could never take the place of guns to communicate like or dislike. But here I was, totally absorbed in the spoken words of Muhammad and Brown, and the written word of Malcolm X. Each emotional lash was tantamount to the resounding echo of gunfire. But unlike gunfire, no one was killed. This was my first encounter with brothers who could kill with words. Their words were not mere talk, either. Action followed in the wake of their theories, and their presence demanded respect long before their words were spoken.

One Monday night we fell to Islamic services to find another "Muslim" there. In appearance, this cat was totally out of sync with the Muslims we had known. First of all, he had a Jheri curl, which was dripping juice onto his collar and the shoulders of his Members Only jacket, which was black and collarless. He wore some gray double-knit slacks and black penny loafers. Standing approximately five feet, four inches and weighing a meager one hundred and twenty pounds, he was the opposite of Muhammad. As soon as we had taken in his dress and fried hair dripping nuclear waste, we knew we had been undermined.

"Where's Muhammad at?" I asked, walking up on him.

"Oh, well," he began stammering, obviously intimidated by my size, "Muhammad was suspended by the California Department of Corrections Youth Board and restricted from entering the institution until further notice."

"What?!"

"Sorry, fellas, but Muha—"

"SORRY?!"

"Yes, you see—"

"Man, we want Muhammad. You don't even look like no real Muslim. Where you from? Who sent you?"

"Please, please," he said, raising both hands like a jack victim. "If you all sit down I will explain everything to you. Please, just have a seat."

We moved slowly and reluctantly to our seats, murmuring "Fuck that" and "This dude is a fake" under our breath. Once we were seated it was apparent that the "Muslim" felt even more intimidated by standing in front of eighty irate youths demanding an explanation for the sudden removal of our teacher. He began with "Asalaam Alaikum" and not one of us responded with "Walaikum Asalaam." Why should we? He wanted us to be peaceful with him, but we had no intention of bidding him peace until a full explanation was brought forth about the removal of Muhammad Abdullah. The "Muslim" extracted a white kerchief from his pocket and wiped the sweat mixed with Jheri curl juice from his brow.

"I am George Muhammad and I have been sent by the American Muslim Mission. My job is not to teach you revolution, but Al-Islam. Mr. Muhammad Abdullah was a fomenter of violence and separating. He was—"

"Man, fuck you!" came a voice from the back, immediately followed by a balled-up piece of paper.

"We live in violence," said L.C., one of the original members of the services before we came. "Always have and, by the definition of ghetto, we already live in separation. Muhammad did not teach us violence and separation. He taught us self-defense and nationalism. And anyway, Al-Islam teaches us, by way of the Holy Koran, that it is our duty as Muslims to fight oppression everywhere it assaults us in this world."

"Yes, but—"

"Naw, ain't no 'yes, but,' see, 'cause you ain't right. I heard Muhammad talk about you one day. Yeah, yeah that's right. He taught us 'bout how you be lookin' like us, talkin' like us, and livin' with us, but all the time you be workin' with the oppressor. Yep, we already up on you. Yo' name ain't no George Muhammad. Yo' name is Uncle Tom!"

"Get that muthafucka!" yelled someone to the left of me, and we all rose and began to advance on Tom, who stood bug-eyed and motionless. Just before he was seized, the doors to the chapel burst open and staff in full riot gear came rushing to his rescue.

We were all sent back to our cells and put on C.T.Q.—Confined to Quarters—during which time I received a letter from Muhammad. His letter was my first lesson in counterintelligence activity.

> The pigs sent the Negro preacher to gather intelligence on me. He climbed in the air-conditioning vent and taped several of our services. He has always been our worst enemy, unfortunately, for the Uncle Tom is so hard to detect among us. I will not be coming back to Y.T.S. for some time, if ever. But I will always stay in contact with you. Insha Allah, don't be deceived by those who look like us but think like the oppressor.

I was stung by the reality of Muhammad's letter, by the prophecy of his "don't be deceived by those who look like us" when just this week I had witnessed the undermining of our services by the institution. I passed Muhammad's letter around to those who were responsible for informing their troops. For those who had a problem reading, I took it upon myself to explain what had happened.

Attendance at Islamic services under the guidance of the

Uncle Tom fell off completely. No one attended, so Tom packed up and left. Because of what we had found out about Reverend Jackson spying on us, no one attended his services, either. As for the staff bursting in and rescuing the Uncle Tom—he was wired! I later found out the staff had anticipated such a response.

My consciousness about the larger enemy was being raised bit by bit. Why wouldn't someone want us to learn about who we really are? Is our knowledge of self so threatening that such measures as sending a Christian preacher into an air conduit are necessary to hinder its attainment?

Muhammad and I kept in contact, and he sent me a lot of literature, mostly Islamic but always Afrocentric. The banging mentality was still uppermost in my mind, as demonstrated in my everyday relations with most people. But questions of right and wrong now came to my mind immediately after every action I took. Muhammad had made a tremendous difference in my life that was barely noticeable then, but cannot be overlooked today.

My time in Y.T.S. after the closing of Islamic services continued in a fashion characteristic of prison life. To occupy my time I had structured a daily routine that gave me little opportunity to be blue about confinement. It was 1983, and I wanted to make a statement for the set somehow, someway. But I didn't want to do it in a physical manner, which seemed uncharacteristic of me. Actually, it was uncharacteristic of Monster.

Diamond, Superman, and I decided to get tattoos for 1983. I wanted mine on my neck, in clear view for all to see. This, I knew, would be a status symbol, as relatively few New Afrikans had tattoos on their necks at that time. Today it's hard to find a banger whose neck isn't written on, advertising his or her particular allegiance. In 1983 it was unpopular to have your set written across your neck, but hell, was I into this for popularity or was I committed for life? My all-out commitment for life would, if I lived long enough, bring about popularity, as I was already experiencing. But with Eight Tray written across my neck, it would be an everlasting bond.

In Black August 1983, I had the tattoo put on my neck. Superman had his mother's name put on his neck, and Diamond had some shading done on his back. Against the lightness of my skin and the thickness of my neck, the tattoo stood out as a beaming testimonial of my lifelong commitment to the 'hood. One staff member said something adverse about it, but most people didn't care. I felt content about it, and to me, that's all that mattered.

Not long after I received the tattoo I got more depressing news from the 'hood. C-Ball, who had been in the 'hood for years, had shot and killed Tray Stone. From what I was able to gather it was over a cassette tape stolen out of C-Ball's car. But after doing a bit more research I uncovered a possible link in a relationship with a female whose brother was from the 'hood. It was my overstanding that C-Ball was jealous of Stone's flirtations with the female and that he'd only used the tape issue as camouflage. Supposedly Stone was confronted on the north side by C-Ball, who was armed with a .32 caliber revolver, as Stone had grown too large for C-Ball to fight. When C-Ball asked after his missing tape, Stone became belligerent. C-Ball then fired one round at point-blank range into Stone's torso. Stone fell to the ground and said, "Ah, cuz, he shot me," as if he could not believe it. He died thereafter.

C-Ball turned himself in and received eight years. Now the debate was about what to do with C-Ball. Tray Stone was the highest level of combat soldier and was loved deeply by those whom he fought for and beside. C-Ball, while not a combat soldier, had been in service to the set for years, much longer than Stone. Those of us in the combat wing who favored Stone were calling for the on-sight execution of C-Ball, while the voices of the traditionalists in their armchair posture rang just as loudly for the forgiveness of C-Ball for slaying "Tray Stone the bully." The set remained divided over this for quite some time. Even today there are those on both poles of the issue still debating what's right and what's wrong. I have let it rest. Stone was eighteen years old.

I was paroled out of Y.T.S. on March 7, 1984. Mom and Tamu were there to pick me up. Li'l Bro and I had been at Y.T.S. for one year.

8

TAMU

"Slow down!" I yelled at Tamu as she zoomed through traffic, dodging and darting between trucks and cars. I had been confined for three years and had lived practically at a standstill, moving from place to place inside the institution only by foot. Even then my stroll was slow and cool with an obvious sway of gang culture. But now here I was, stuffed into the back seat of this red Toyota Tercel with Tamu and Mom sitting up front, chatting away, flying along the Pomona Freeway headed for Los Angeles.

"Tamu, did you hear me? Slow this damn thang *down!*" I shouted, holding the seat for leverage.

"Babes," she said, almost turning completely around in her seat.

"Don't turn around, watch the road!"

"I'm only doing fifty-five. It's the regular speed limit."

"Why it seem like we doin' two hundred, then?"

"'Cause you ain't been in no car in years, babes."

"I ain't gonna never make it home, you keep drivin' like this."

"Oh, boy, relax," Mom said. "You picked a fine time to be scared of something."

"I ain't scared, I just—"

"Yeah, yeah," Tamu said, giving Mom a we-really-know look.

I tried to relax, but I couldn't shake the excitement of being out. The last thing I wanted was to crash on the way home and fail the mission of coming back. Besides, this damn Toyota was awfully small for me. I was huge, muscles bulging from everywhere. Tamu and I kept making eye contact in the mirror, both our gazes dripping with lust. What would it be like to be with her again, I wondered? Even that seemed a bit frightening.

Cars zoomed past, irate drivers flipping fuck-you signs in our direction. I looked over Tamu's shoulder at the speedometer: fifty miles per hour. She had slowed down, but still we seemed to be moving at an alarming pace. Of all things to die from, I didn't want to go out in a traffic accident.

We swooped through downtown and up and over into South Central. It was dusk, and the sun lay somewhere out beyond Venice Beach, slipping into the water and bringing the deadly night to Los Angeles. To my right I saw the lights of the Goodyear Blimp hovering over the Coliseum. Perhaps there was some function there. It always amazed me to see that huge football-shaped airship floating effortlessly through the air, displaying an unspoken peace of nongravitational bliss. Over to my left I saw two helicopters dipping, dodging, and cutting through the air in violent twists that telegraphed their aerial pursuit of someone. One helicopter was labeled POLICE, the other SHERIFF. Peace in the air to my right and war above to my left. Good old South Central: nothing really changed.

When we got on Normandie I started reading the walls. The Brims, it seemed, had resurfaced with a little force. Once we passed Gage and moved into our 'hood, the writing became more pronounced, more violently scrawled on things, no doubt the sign of a neighborhood at war. Graffiti, although mainly used for advertising, can also function as messages to enemies—evil spirits—that "this territory is protected and it's not like we didn't give you fair warning." BEWARE OF EIGHT TRAYS was written in several places along Normandie Avenue. I found that amusing. Turning onto Sixty-ninth Street, I felt a pang of nostalgia for the block, my stomping grounds—my space.

As we pulled into the driveway I felt a stab of pain and a sense of loss. None of the homies from my combat unit was there. No one. Although there were at least twelve people from the set, they were not of my clique. Tray Ball was dead, Crazy De was in prison, and Diamond, who I had seen go home from Y.T.S., was already back in for murder. Tray Stone was dead, and my li'l brother was still in Youth Authority. But I did see Joker and Li'l Crazy De, which made it a bit easier to deal with the group. A few people I didn't know at all.

When Mom opened her car door, a horde of homies rushed to help her out. Someone held the front seat up so I could lumber out of the constricting back seat. Once I had gotten out and stood to my full height, the comments from the homies fell from everywhere.

"Goddamn, cuz, you swoll like a muthafucka!"

"Damn, check dis nigga out."

"Cuz' arms big as my head."

"What was they feedin' you, Monsta, weights?"

I stayed out front a while, answering some of their questions and asking some of my own. Once this grew tiresome I shifted and asked to speak to Li'l Crazy De and Joker alone. We went into the backyard and left the others to mingle out front.

"Cuz," I began, "I need a gat."

"Yeah," responded Joker, "we got some shit for you."

"Right, right."

"So, what's up with them niggas across the way? Y'all been droppin' bodies or what?"

"Aw, nigga, I thought you knew!" said Li'l Crazy De. "Tell him, Joker."

"Monsta, we caught this fool the other night in the 'hood writin' on the wall. Cuz, in the *'hood!* Can you believe that shit? Anyway, we roll up on boy and ask him, 'Yo, what the fuck you doin'?' Boy breaks and runs and—"

"I cut his ass down wit' a thirty-oh-six wit' a infrared scope!" interrupted Li'l De. "Aw, Monsta, I fucked cuz up! He was like all squirmin' and shit, sufferin' and stuff, so—"

"I put this," Joker said, pulling out a Colt .45 from his waistband, "and KABOOM! To the brain, you know. Couldn't stand to see the bitch-made muthafucka sufferin' and shit."

"Who was he?" I asked.

"Shit, we ain't heard yet, but he was probably one of they Baby Locs, 'cause he looked young, you know?"

"Have they rode back?"

"Naw, not that we know of. Most of they shooters in jail like ours."

"Who killed Opie?"

"Word is that Sissy Keitarock did it. Anyway, cuz in jail fo' it."

"Oh, but De, tell cuz how we to' shit up fo' Opie," said Joker excitedly.

"Aw, cuz, we shot so many—"

"Cuz, I need a gat," I said, trying to insinuate to Li'l De that I wasn't really interested in his war stories.

"Don't sweat it, big homie, we got some shit fo' you, cuz."

"Anyway—" Li'l De tried to continue.

"When y'all get the gat for me come back. But like, right now, I want some pussy and some food. Now if either of y'all got some of that I'll stay back here with you, but if not, I'm goin' in the pad to get some," I said, smiling.

"Aw, man, fuck you, cuz, we gone."

"Oh, but Monsta, we be back in three minutes, awright?" Joker said over his shoulder.

"Yeah, but if I ain't here leave the gat in them bushes right there, okay?"

"All day."

"Righteous."

I went in the house through the back door and made my way through the kitchen. I watched as Joker and Li'l De told the other homies that I'd be out later. The small crowd went one way and Joker and Li'l De went the other. Joker had the big .45 in his waistband, so I didn't worry about them out in the street.

I had brought a collection of my best tapes home: Jimmy Reed, Otis Redding, the Temprees, Barbara Mason, and Sam Cook. I went into the den and put on Jimmy Reed. When it came out over the speaker it sounded foreign to me. Jimmy didn't fit home like he fit jail. I couldn't rightly put my finger on it, but I knew that I wasn't going to be listening to too much

Jimmy Reed out here. When I came back into the living room, Tamu was sitting there looking through my photo album. I sat next to her and played with her hair.

"Kody, let's leave. Let's go and be alone," she said, never taking her eyes off the photo album.

"Awright, but let me eat somethin'."

"I want to take you to dinner. I know a nice little place you'd like."

"Okay, let me tell Mom we're leaving."

"She already knows," Tamu said, looking up at me seductively.

"Well, well, what is this, a conspiracy?"

"No, babes, just natural instincts."

"And what about this?" I said and fell hard upon her, crushing the photo album between us.

"That is called smashing your girlfriend."

"And this?" I kissed her full on the lips, my tongue darting in and out of her mouth.

"That," she said between kisses, "is called animal instinct."

"Well call me King of the Jun—"

"Kody?" Mom interrupted, appearing in the doorway.

"Huh? Oh, Mom, yeah?" I stammered, struggling to get off Tamu.

"I'm going to lie down. If you leave, lock the house up, okay?"

"All da . . . I mean, yeah, sure Mom."

I had been so used to our natural response to "okay"—meaning Sixty-Ninety killer—which would be "All day," that it just came out.

Mom looked at me then turned on down the hallway.

"Let's go," I told Tamu, and we left.

She took me to a small restaurant on Crenshaw Boulevard called Aunt Fish. We could sit in the window and look across Crenshaw and watch the D.J. spin records at Stevie Wonder's radio station, KJLH. We ordered jumbo shrimp and red snapper. Tamu, who ate like a horse, matched my appetite, and we tore that food up. The entire time I was eating, the woman at the cash register kept making hardcore eye contact with me. Naturally I flirted back, though only when Tamu wasn't looking. We kept eating and the woman and I kept flirting, right up until it was time to pay the tab. The bill was forty-nine dollars. When Tamu went to pay she found that she was short ten dollars. The woman at the register gave me a look that clearly said "Help her," but I didn't have a dime. I was so embarrassed, as I'm sure Tamu was. But it was especially difficult for me because it became a "man thang" when I couldn't help pay the tab. It took all the strength I had not to shout "I JUST GOT OUT OF JAIL!!"

Surprisingly, the woman offered to pay as long as Tamu promised to return with her money. Tamu thanked her and turned to exit. As I turned to follow Tamu, the woman cleared her throat to get my attention. When I looked, she handed me a restaurant business card with her name, phone number, and address on the back side. I put the card in my pocket and followed Tamu out to the car.

In the car I tried to console Tamu, who was really bent out of shape about not having the money to pay the bill. I almost told her about the flirting and of the woman giving me her card, but decided against it. We went to Tamu's house and retrieved the needed money and drove back to Aunt Fish.

After paying the woman we went straight to the Mustang Motel on Western Avenue. From the moment I left the car I had a raging erection that threatened to tear a hole in the front of my pants. We hurried like eager children up to our room. Once behind the door we literally tore our clothes off. To my surprise, Tamu had on black stockings and garters. She knew I had developed a liking for such things while in Youth Authority. We wasted no time as we fell into one another immediately. We sinned for most of the night, taking occasional breaks to smoke pot, laugh, and joke. We really had a good time. By the time we were buzzed to leave we both were spent, and it was another day when we emerged from the room.

"You know, Kody," Tamu began, talking in measured tones as she drove down Western Avenue, "I want to get an apartment together, for us. You, me, Keonda. But you have to get a job, babes."

"Yeah, I know," I said, but I really had no intention of getting a job. Hell, I was going to do like Joker and Li'l De said they were doing: sell cocaine. Whiteboy Eric, who was like a cousin to me (we told everybody we were cousins) was already heavily into it. I knew he'd kick me down, but I didn't want to tell Tamu that.

"'Cause, babes," she continued, "with your job and my doing hair, we could get a nice little place somewhere."

"That's right, babes," I said, not really paying much attention anymore, as I was now watching a familiar face in the car next to us watch me. The man slowly began to roll down his window, so I started rolling down mine, all the while cursing myself for not getting the .45 from Joker.

"Hey," he hollered to me, "ain't yo' name Kody?" He didn't seem to have any venom in his voice, but it could be a ploy.

"Yeah, wha's up?" I said skeptically.

"Aw, nigga, you don't 'member me from Horace Mann, Terry Heron?"

Terry Heron, Terry Heron . . . I turned the name over several times before it caught, and when it did it was too late. *Enemy Sixty!*

He recognized the stages of change in my face and knew I had computed him amongst the damned. Not only had I fought him in school long before the Sixties–Eight Tray conflict, but during the conflict I had shot him. Luckily for him I was unarmed, because I had ample time after the recognition to aim and fire. But to my surprise he was making no threatening moves.

"Aw, Kody, man," he said as we drove along, "I ain't in that bangin' shit no mo'. It's all about that money now. Nigga, you betta get wit' it."

"Awright then," I said with a slight hand wave, more relieved than anything. Shit, I needed a gun. He turned right on Sixty-seventh Street and into his 'hood, and we drove two more blocks and turned left into our 'hood.

Tamu dropped me off and we made plans for later. It felt like my second day on a new planet.

The phone rang. It was Li'l Crazy De asking me if I had gotten the strap.

"Naw," I said, "where was it?"

"In the bushes where you told me to leave it."

I told him to hold on and went out back to retrieve the weapon—a .38 Browning semiautomatic pistol. I came back to the phone and told him I'd found it and asked how many hot ones—murders—it had on it.

"Oh, three or four," Li'l De replied, "but don't sweat it, 'cause you was locked down when they happened, you know?"

"Righteous," I said and spaced the line.

I checked the weapon for rounds and went into the den to jam some sounds. I took Jimmy Reed out of the tape deck and put in a tape my brother Kerwin had lying around. "The Big Payback" by James Brown came roaring out:

I can do wheelin', I can do the dealin',
but I don't do no damn squealin'.
I can dig rappin', I'm ready, I can dig rappin',
But I can't dig that back stabbin'.

To me, "The Big Payback" was always the Crip theme song. I remember going up to Tookie's house—he was the West Side Regional Commander of the Crips—to watch him lift weights and to hear the original Crip war stories. I couldn't have been any older than twelve when I'd eagerly get dressed and scurry up to Tookie's to hold audience with the general. A lot of us used to go to his house to get firsthand knowledge of Cripism.

Tookie was a Crip through and through—walk, talk, and attitude. He gave the name Crip a certain majesty and was a magnificent storyteller. For hours at a time he'd give us blow-by-blow rundowns on the old Tom Cross record hops at Sportsman's Park. Or he'd tell about slain members who would have loved meeting us, cats like Buddha, Li'l Rock, and Moe, to name a few. He had a Cadillac and never drove it, preferring to walk everywhere. And if the walk was too long, he'd call up one of his drivers. His entire living room was filled with weights. No furniture whatsoever, just pig iron. Tookie was huge, beyond belief at that time: twenty-two-inch arms, fifty-eight-inch chest, and huge tree-trunk legs. And he was dark, Marcus Garvey dark, shiny, slick, and strong. He had the physique, complexion, and attitude that intimidated most American people.

I met the Original Crips at Tookie's house: Monkey Man, Bogart, Godfather, Maddog, Big Jack, and Raymond Washington. I was a student of Crip, and Tookie liked me more than the others, as he saw that I was a serious soldier.

Every summer the city of Los Angeles held a Festival in Black at MacArthur Park and most everybody from everywhere would attend. Tookie and Jamael—who started the Avalon Garden Crips—would go to all the functions, concerts, parties, and parks and peel out of their shirts, amazing everyone with their size. Jamael's light skin contrasted hard with Tookie's dark complexion and made them look even bigger, like two gargantuans. During the festivals in Black, Rennis and I would be designated by Tookie to carry the straps, which was more than cool with me.

Another time Tookie and I walked from Sixty-ninth Street to 107th Street so he could retrieve his shotgun. Eight Ball had been lent the gauge to bust on some Brims but had never returned it. So Tookie and I started walking to Eight Ball's, but before we got there we went around to a homie's house whose mother was selling angel dust—PCP. Tookie got two seams (a seam was a ten-dollar package in tin foil) on credit. He rolled each seam into a joint and we got high as we walked. By the time we reached the Nineties we were both whacked out of our brains. Everything seemed to be moving in slow motion, blurry and dark. When Took got high he walked like a cowboy in a *High Noon* duel.

When we got to 107th Street we ran into some Original

Hoovers: Sam, Jughead, Andre Jones, Jinks, and Cobra. They talked with Tookie for a while and mostly ignored me. (Later on they would come to know me.) Took got his hair braided by a Cripalette—a female Crip—and we made our way over to Ball's house. I went to the door and got him.

"Cuz," Took said, "where's my gauge?"

"I put it under the mattress in the back where Bitch sleep." Bitch was Tookie's pit bull.

"You should've told me . . ."

"I knocked, but there wasn't no answer."

"If my gauge ain't there, I'm gonna kill yo' mama."

"It's there—"

"It betta be!"

And we left.

Although Eight Ball was my homie, Took was the general. On our way back down Normandie, the police stopped us. Automatically they handcuffed Took.

"What's his name?" the police asked me.

"Tookie," I said, like don't-you-know?

"No, his real name."

Now, I knew his first name was Stanley, because he told us that before he got the nickname Tookie. They used to call him Stanley Livingston. I also knew that his brother, Li'l Tookie, was Wayne. Wayne Holloway. So I took it for granted that because they were brothers, Took's last name was also Holloway.

"Stanley Holloway," I said.

The police came back over to me and said, "Hmm, that's funny. He says his name is Stanley Williams. Somebody's lying."

"Maybe I got it wrong, I just—"

"Why are you with this scumbag anyway, huh?" asked the officer, cocking his head.

"Well, he's . . . uhm . . . my friend," I said, but it didn't sound right.

"Bull-fuckin'-shit! Who you think you talking to? Huh?" he said, grabbing me by the collar.

"But he—"

" 'But' my fuckin' ass. He is going to have you shooting up every goddamn Brim in L.A. He don't give a shit about you. He just wants to make you a Crip, one of his soldiers. Wise up, boy, you're still young."

So he did know who Tookie was. They uncuffed Took and we began walking off. Took asked what I told them his name was and I replied Stanley Holloway. He slapped me hard across the back of the head.

"Williams, dumb ass, *Williams!"*

"Awright, awright, I got it," I said, rubbing the back of my head, which was stinging like crazy.

The payback song reminded me of Tookie. That's all he played over and over as he lifted weights. He and Big Jack, his roommate, had an old eight-track rigged up to a speaker in a milk crate. On one tape he had four songs: "Payback," "Girl Calling," "Happy Feelings," and "Reach for It." I learned a lot of Crip etiquette from Tookie.

Most Crips have not had the opportunity to meet him, or any other founders, so they tend to believe that they "created the wheel." No history whatsoever is attached to their banging. In early '79, Tookie and two other Crips, who subsequently gave him up, were captured for four murders. In 1981 he was given the death penalty, and he now resides on death row in San Quentin.

As the Payback song played on, I found it hard to shake my trancelike thoughts about the old days. I soon became depressed. I wanted to sleep, to dream, to escape. For the first time I felt South Central choking me. I didn't want to die without having made any substantial contribution to something. But what? Where was I taking this?

I slept as much as I could. That night the homegirls came by to see me. Spooney, who had a baby by Tray Stone; Bam, who was pregnant by Diamond; Prena, Crazy De's sister; and Sharon and China were all there. The first thing Spooney said was, "Monster, don't die on us!"

I promised her I wouldn't.

"Why would you say that?" I said.

"Because," she explained, "everybody seems to be doing it, like it's cool or something. Monster, just be careful, okay?"

"All day!"

"We know that, just be careful, all right?" Bam pleaded.

We talked late into the night. Bam kept asking me if I had fucked any dudes in the ass while I was in prison. I assured her that I hadn't, which I doubt she believed. The fire between China and I had died. It seemed that our only union gravitated around banging and it was quite apparent from our conversations that both of us had grown up and a little out of the banging circle. She even had a job.

"Where's your daughter?" Prena asked.

"Over her godparents' house. She'll be here tomorrow if you want to see her."

"I do," said Sharon. China just looked away. I saw a glimmer of pain in her eyes. It still affected her.

When they finally left it was three in the morning. It felt good to see them. I called Tamu and we talked until the sun came up.

That afternoon Tamu brought Keonda to see me. She was three years old and I was scared to death of her! She looked just like me. We played and rolled around on the carpet together and bonded. Still, the responsibility of being a father hadn't sunk in. How could it have? Mom was still taking care of me. Tamu was still living at home, too. We both were young, but I knew I had to do something to generate revenue to provide for Keonda.

One day while I was still on the Rock in Y.T.S., I wrote to Mom in one of my militant moods, stressing as best I could the dominance of the white power structure over us as a people, something I had learned from reading *Soul on Ice* by Eldridge Cleaver. She had shown the letter to a Muslim friend of hers who, she said, wanted to meet me. She told me that when I got out he would give me a job. After seeing and being with Keonda I figured what the hell, let me see what this cat is talking about. Tamu had taught me to drive a stick shift so I would have access to her car whenever I wanted, which gave me the freedom to go see him.

The following Monday I drove over to his office. I felt awkward, because applying for a job just wasn't the gangsterish thing to do. You either jacked for money or you sold dope. Working was considered weak.

The business was a computer school called Trans-Western Institute. The position I applied for was recruiter, which meant I would be sent to designated areas to recruit students for the school. Students were eligible for government grants, student loans, and other financial help. For every student I recruited I would be given a fifty-dollar commission.

The first place they sent me was the unemployment office downtown, which was cool because I wasn't in danger of being recognized. I didn't want anyone I knew to see me with a job and I surely didn't want to be caught by some enemies while recruiting.

My first day I didn't try to recruit anyone, I simply walked around, amazed at the unemployment lines snaking around inside the tiny building. Hordes of people, mostly Chicano and New Afrikan, stood around, shifting from foot to foot, waiting, hoping, trying to find something to do. Utter despair was marked like tattoos on most of their faces. I guess this was the look that people said Reaganomics caused, but I doubted the truth of that, because as long as I could remember I had seen Mom wear that same fixed expression of hopelessness. The striking thing here was that there were so many of these expressions together in one room. Certainly the pain in those faces was not the result of just four years of Reagan, nor could the sudden shift to conservative economics be the result of one bad man in office. I sat back on a dirty bench and watched until it was time for lunch, at which point I went home.

The next day they sent me to Garfield High School in East L.A. I never went. The following day I didn't show up at all, and I never returned again.

Instead I went to Whiteboy Eric. He gave me some drugs to sell. The first thing I bought with the proceeds was a '68 Chevy and some sounds. Then Tamu and I got an apartment on Eighty-fourth Place and Western Avenue. After being out of Y.T.S. for only three months things were smooth.

Since I had no comrades from my unit out in the field, I

bonded with those whom I had the most in common: Gangster Brown and Tracc. Both Brown and Tracc were still heavily into PCP, so as a social link I too fell heavily into it. For almost two months straight we'd smoke whole Sherman cigarettes dipped in PCP every day, sometimes two and three times a day. I had gotten a blue flag from downtown that was as big as a bed sheet. Oftentimes while I was high on PCP I'd arrange the huge blue flag on my head in Arab fashion, secured by a black stretch belt. I'd put on my Locs, roll down all the windows in my car, and fly around the city looking stone-crazy! Everyone thought I was a nut.

That summer we all got skinheads. We'd pile into my car four deep, bald-headed with dark shades on, and ride around L.A. We'd never smile. We actually had a good time, though we were heavily armed. After all, you can only play so much in L.A.

Finally Stagalee got out of prison and I was grateful, as the Sherm was starting to take a toll on me. Stag and I subsequently became road dogs. He was at least four years younger than me, and I found myself in almost the same role with him as Tray Ball had been with me. Although Stag had been with the set before he and I met in Y.T.S., his clique was a noncombative unit of wannabees. By hanging with me, he got turned onto some righteous soldiers. He was a tragedy waiting to happen. Like Tray Stone, he was a sleeper who just needed someone to coach that ruthlessness out of him. Once I'd tapped into it, he roared to life like an age-old volcano. I knew we'd be good friends.

One afternoon, much to my surprise, Muhammad came by my mom's house and he and I rapped awhile about the circumstances surrounding his suspension from Y.T.S. He also showed me a letter he'd received from Warith D. Muhammad that forbade him further entry into prisons in the capacity of an imam. The letter said, "You are teaching hatred and breeding terrorists."

Muhammad asked if I would attend Salat with him the following day. I agreed. He left me with two books—*Black Panther Leaders Speak* and *The Autobiography of Malcolm X*. I went in the pad to look over the material.

"Who was that?" Mom asked as I entered the house.

"Oh, that's Muhammad. He used to teach us at Y.T.S. Remember I told you about him?"

"Uhm, I'm not sure. You got so many friends. What's that he gave you?" she asked, reaching for the books.

"Books on us, black people. Mom, you should hear him talk. He can get off!"

"Yeah, well he needs to take that turban off before someone mistakes him for the Shah of Iran."

"Naw, Mom, the Shah of Iran was a U.S. puppet. You mean the Ayatollah."

"Well, whoever, shit," Mom said and handed me back the books.

I had surprised myself by remembering what Muhammad had told us so long ago about the Shah being a U.S. puppet, but as soon as it was fitting to speak on it, it just came out. Muhammad was always able to bring out the sharpness in me.

The following day we went to the Islamic Center on Fourth Street and Vermont Avenue and I totally tripped out. I saw Muslims from all over the world. Sisters my age—nineteen—wore traditional Afrikan dress from the continent. There were Iranians, Saudis, and Libyans, too. I saw flowing thobes of various colors, turbans, jewelry, and manners unlike any I'd ever seen or known. I was standing there in 501s, Puma tennis shoes, a Polo shirt, and a Raiders cap and felt like a damn fool! I got a few looks that today I would define as Third World people seeing me as a benefactor in their oppression, but at that time I thought they were just curious about my dress code.

Muhammad went in and did Salat and I milled around by the shoes. The women and girls went to another part of the center to pray.

"You know," Muhammad began as we walked out into the noonday sun, toward the car, "Al-Islam is not compulsive. Allah will raise up those he sees fit. Insha Allah, you have a mission."

"I always thought that only actors in Hollywood wore those geni shoes that curled up in the front."

"Brotha, the European has twisted and turned everything to fit his warped way of thinking. He has made himself the center of the world, indeed of the universe. Have you ever heard the words Oriental and Occidental?"

"I heard of Oriental. Don't that mean Jap?"

"No, now listen," he said, with a precautionary finger up. "Orient means East and Occident means West. Now here's the twist. Europe, as put forth by the European, is the center of the world. Therefore, anything to its east is Oriental, while anything to its west is Occidental. This is what is meant by Eurocentric."

"Yeah, but if Europe is not the center of the world, then what is?"

"Check this out. When a baby is born what is the most essential thing needed for its survival?"

"Uhm, food?"

"Food! Right. And where does that food come from?"

"The mother, or the doctor."

"All right, therefore what's central to the baby?"

"The mother?"

"Right. The cradle of civilization is Afrika. Afrika *is* the *mother*land. Therefore, Afrika is central to all of humanity."

"But—"

"Wait, wait, let me explain this. Now those whom we know today as Europeans are actually mutants who left the safe confines of the Motherland and evolved in Europe. Their food for survival was doctored by an unnatural mother. The side effects of their development outside of the natural womb has been albinism, aggression, and universal weakness predicated on their minority status in the world."

"Well, if that's the case, why don't we just tell everybody what's really going on?"

"I wish it were that simple. Hey, ever heard the words mankind and human?"

"Yeah, I've heard 'em."

"Do you know what hue is?" he asked, looking at me now over the top of the car.

"Hue? No, don't know what it means."

"Color, it means color!"

"And?"

"And? Bro, can't you see it? Look . . . human . . . hue-man."

"Oh," I said with a big grin of recognition, "color-man, man of color, right?"

"Right! Now, that means humans are people of color, all people of color. Brown, red, yellow, et cetera, dig?"

"Yeah."

"And melanin is the ingredient that produces skin color. Europeans, mutants—"

"What's a mutant?"

"Something produced from . . . or an out-growth of . . . Anyway, these mutants don't have any melanin, therefore they are colorless."

"White," I said.

"Right, white is colorless. And to be without color is to be abnormal because the majority of the world's people are hue-man."

"Colored!"

"Right! So it's normal to be of color. Which means they are, as mutants, a kind of man, therefore mankind, you dig?"

"Damn, that's *heavy*!" I felt stuck on stupid.

"Brotha, we as Afrikan people are weak because mankind has cut off our nutrition from the Motherland. He has twisted the world so that Europe, the Mad Doctor, looks like the center. And *we* look abnormal. Oh, it's deep."

"That's a trip."

"You'll learn, Brotha. Insha Allah, you'll learn."

We drove back through South Central with Muhammad speaking on other issues; he always inspired me to search for the truth. When we got to Mom's house he asked if I had started on either one of the books he had given me the day before. I told him that I hadn't, but that I intended to. He said I should start with Fred Hampton in the Black Panther book. I said "Cool" and closed the car door. Muhammad asked through the open window if I wanted to go with him to a seminar the following week and I said yes, that I'd be glad to. "Righteous," he said, and drove away.

I just stood there looking at the back of Muhammad's car thinking about what he had said. Actually, I was trying to get it right so I could tell Mom. I never heard the car roll up.

"Yo', what up, muthafucka?"

Damn, I knew that voice but was reluctant to turn and see who it was. Just shoot me in the back, I said to myself, but I turned around and I'll be damned if it wasn't Huckabuck.

"Cuz, what's up?" I said. "Get yo' black ass out the hoop. Park that piece of shit. Uhh-uhh, not here in front of Mom's pad 'cause I know that muthafucka's stolen."

"Nigga, this my shit, it ain't stolen!"

"Well how I'm s'posed to know that?"

I hadn't seen Huck in years, and it was like seeing a long-lost brother. He was missing all of his top teeth, a result of a high-speed chase with the police in which his car flipped completely over. He said that Fly and Lep had been in the car, as well. Lep broke his arm, and Fly escaped with minor abrasions. I asked where Fly and Lep were now, hoping to get a reunion going, which seemed like a great idea in the light of what had happened in the past nine years, since my recruitment. Huck said that Fly had dropped out of sight, though his baby brother had joined up with the 'hood. Lep had fallen victim to the new enemy—crack—and was doing everything and anything to get a blast.

Huck and I kicked it about Tray Ball's death and G.C.'s life term. Things were developing every which way. Who was to say that because we were still here we were any better off than Tray Ball or G.C.? We talked about the successful double murder of two Sixties that Slowpoke, Fish Bone, and Football—Damian "Football" Williams' older brother—put down recently, which stunned me. The obvious karma of it was startling.

Two Sixties—Kenbone and Kid—had come into our 'hood prowling for a victim and run across Li'l Frogg at the gangster store on Florence and Normandie. They'd stood outside and demanded that Li'l Frogg "bring his tramp ass out." Of course Li'l Frogg refused, knowing that any enemy on Florence and Normandie had to be well armed. Unfortunately for Li'l Frogg, some of our homegirls were in the store, which made it a "man thang," so he had to go face the music. And he knew the tune would not be nice. To his surprise he got hold of Kid and beat him before Kenbone could shoot him five times. Once Li'l Frogg lay wounded, the two fled.

The next day at approximately the same time a Search and Destroy team spied both Kenbone and Kid exiting the Taco Bell on Sixtieth and Crenshaw, rolled up on the unwitting pair, and shot each sixteen times with .22 rifles. Now that was something.

"So what else is up wit' you?" Huck asked.

"Oh, a little bit of this, a little bit of that."

"You seemed to have slowed down some," Huck said with a look of "I told you so" on his dark face.

"Yeah, a bit. Shit, really ain't nobody out here to kick it with. I was kickin' it with Brown and Tracc, but cuz, them be havin' me smokin' that Sherm and that shit make me crazy."

"They still doin' that shit?"

"Every day. I be kickin' it with Stagalee now, though."

"Who?"

"Stagalee."

"Oh, cuz that stay over on Sixty-sixth?"

"Yep, he straight down, too. Last week we went up to Fat Burger on Crenshaw to try and catch some Sissies and cuz almost blasted some Main Streets. Droopy and them was out there, too. If I hadn't known cuz, they would have got blasted!"

"Where Li'l Monster? Still locked down?"

"Yeah, he in Y.T.S."

"What they give cuz for that murder?"

"Thirty-six to life, but you know he's a juvenile, so he can only do seven. He been down fo' already. What's up wit' Li'l Huck?"

"Cuz live in Swan 'hood. He be fuckin' up. Just the other day he blasted some Swayhooks"—a disrespectful term for Swans—"who lived next do' to us."

Huck and I rapped on in this manner until he had to go. Before his departure we swore not to let another six years see us apart. No sooner had Huck left than Joker rode up on a beach cruiser. I could tell by his facial expression that something wasn't right.

"What's up?"

"Monster, cuz," he began, literally fighting back tears, "them Hoovers be trippin', man. We gotta get wit' them niggas, cuz."

"What happened, homie?"

"Cuz, last night me and Li'l De fell to one of they parties on One-oh-fourth, Big X-ray's pad, right? And cuz, I was all drunk and shit, but you know, I ain't trippin' on no Hoovers. But Macc from Eleven Deuce start woofin' some way-out shit and—"

"You and Li'l De was the only two gangsters there?"

"Naw . . . well at first, 'cause Li'l Harv's bitch-ass came later. But anyway, cuz go to woofin' that shit, right? And you know how Hoovers get when they deep . . . "

Joker paused and turned his head. I could see he was really hurt.

"So anyhow, me and cuz get to scrapin'—"

"Who?"

"Macc from Eleven Deuce. And Monster, you know cuz a G, he 'bout yo' age. Well, like I said, I was drunk, you know, and cuz, like he got the best of me."

When he said that I could have sworn I saw him shrink a few inches.

"So then what happened?"

"When we was leavin' they started bustin' at us—"

"What?!" I said in disbelief.

"Aw, cuz, since you been in jail them muthafuckas been trippin'. But Monster, I want that fool Macc. Cuz, just take me over there. We gotta do somethin'. They made the 'hood look bad."

I called up Stag and he came right over. I had Joker explain again what he'd told me. Stag was fuming. His solution was gunboat diplomacy, but I didn't think that would mend Joker's pride. He needed to battle Macc personally. I decided that we'd roll over into Hoover eight deep—four in each car, symbolizing the Eight Trays.

The Hoovers had recently consolidated themselves under a new dynamic program called "Hoover Connection." Their foundation was crack, the new high-profit commodity. All Hoovers who were part of the "Connect" saw Eighty-first as the hub of their new union. Thus at any time of any given day there could be well over two or three hundred Hoovers in attendance. Eighty-first Street between Hoover and Figueroa was without a doubt Hooverland. Ground zero. Everybody would be armed with their weapons openly displayed. When night fell, this street made *New Jack City* look like a boys' club.

We had been tight allies with the Hoovers since we'd both broken away from Tookie's leadership. Their enemies—which there was no shortage of—became our enemies. We'd entered five wars with them as allies. We went to war with the Neighborhood Blocks, the Underground Crips, the Rollin' Nineties, the Watergates, and the Raymond Avenue Crips, who had never killed any of our homies. But on the strength of our alliance we'd taken up the call to colors and gone to war on their enemies. When the Hoovers and the East Coasts fell out and began their shooting war, the Hoovers automatically thought we'd go to war with them against that gang. When we opted to sit that one out, it soured our relations with Hoover. To get involved in the Hoover–East Coast conflict could be potentially disastrous for us, as our neighborhood had blood relations in both the East Coasts and the Hoovers. As a result of our nonaggressive posture and steadfast refusal to support either side, emotions were strained all around. It was in this climate that we rolled into Hoover Connect for a head-up fight.

In my car was Stagalee, Joker, and Preacher. In Li'l De's car was Li'l Stag—since removed and replaced with a firmer soldier—Bink, and Cyco Mike. We rolled to a stop in the midst of some fifty Hoovers standing in the street listening to music. We piled out of our cars. Herm from Eight Tray Hoover recognized me and came over with his hand extended. I took his hand and shook it.

"Where's Macc at?" I asked, looking for signs of hostility in Herm's face.

"Oh, cuz 'round here somewhere. Cuz, y'all seen Macc?" he asked of some of his Baby Locs.

"Cuz got point, there he go."

Macc came strolling across the street with an M-1 strapped across his back. When he saw me he broke into a wide grin. Me and Macc went way back together. When I got kicked out of Horace Mann and sent to Henry Clay, Macc was my road dog. He took me to his 'hood and made me an honorary Eleven Deuce. He and I were friends, and in this light I could not overstand his maltreatment of my li'l homie.

"What's up, Big Monsta?"

"Ain't nuttin', just coolin'."

"Eh, cuz, we fin' to groove to the beach. You wanna bail?"

"Naw, cuz, we got problems. Check this out. Last night you slapped up my young homie, Joker, at X-ray's party. Now that cuz ain't bent, he wanna go head up wit' you."

"What?" Macc said in disbelief, easing the carbine around so that it was now across his chest.

"You know what's up, nigga!" Joker blew up, coming through the crowd.

"Cuz, I'll blow you' brains out—"

"Naw," I said, "ain't gonna be none of that. Cuz wanna scrap head up."

"Yeah, well, you know what? Like I would get down wit' you, but my hands is all fucked up from beatin' yo' ass last night," Macc shot back to Joker, but in his statement I heard fear.

"Macc," shouted a Hooverette, "fuck that nigga up. He don't come in the Connect talkin' that shit."

"Hoova!" shouted another voice. The situation was deteriorating to a lynch-mob atmosphere. The gathering crowd was getting larger and more hostile by the minute. I saw Li'l Crazy De and Stoney from Eight Tray Hoover shooting daggers at each other.

"So what up, Macc?" I asked, eager to turn Joker loose on him.

"Cuz, if you really want to scrap, let's get it on."

At that, Macc eased the carbine over his shoulder and handed it to Junebug. A circle was cleared and the scrap was on.

Joker tore into Macc with a vengeance. Macc was outclassed, out-punched, and almost out cold a few times. When

Joker knocked Macc to the asphalt he attempted to stomp him, but the crowd surged and it was all we could do to keep from being swarmed. At that, I stopped the fight, which from the jump was clearly one-sided. The only reason that Macc got the best of Joker at the party was because Joker was sloppy drunk.

When Macc gained his composure he grabbed the carbine from Junebug, who had taken off his shirt like he wanted to fight. Macc, whose lips were busted and bleeding, was heaving deeply and looking hard at Joker, who was relaxing against my car.

"All right now, y'all shake hands. That shit is squashed," I said, trying to break the deadly silence.

"Naw, cuz, this shit ain't over. I'ma get you, Joker—"

"Naw you ain't, Macc, 'cause should my li'l homie come up dead behind this, I'ma get *you.* Now, if you—"

"Cuz, what you sayin', Monster?"

This was Junebug piping in.

"Y'all on Hoova turf, cuz. Macc could blast y'all right here right now, or Macc could call it cool. But it's on Macc."

"Macc," I started again, totally ignoring what Bug was talking about, "so what's up? If you still got beef with Joker, y'all can scrap again, but this time it's gonna be in *Gangstaland* at St. Andrew's Park."

"Nigga, you ain't said nuttin'. Saturday, three o'clock, St. Andrews!" Macc blurted out over swollen lips.

And with that we piled into our cars, but only after we heard several weapons being cocked and loaded. We drove off without incident.

For the entire week that followed we made sure we told everybody about the upcoming brawl with Macc and Joker.

Given the tension of the previous Saturday, it could easily develop into a full-scale gang fight.

The following Saturday the turnout in support of Joker was tremendous. Old homies came out of the woodwork in short pants and sweatsuits. G's nobody had seen in years were there. Hillbilly, Robert Finch, Bacot—who had just served eleven years—Hoodlum, Harv, and Captain Wino were there. Also present was Smokey Joe, Sodici, Sidewinder, X-con, Sneaky T, Bo-Pete, Red Bone, and Goat Mouth. The park was filled with three generations of Eight Trays ready to rumble. Joker was being pampered by the homegirls. Weapons were planted around strategically.

"Here they come!" shouted our sentry, who spotted Moo Moo's blue truck bending the corner of Eighty-ninth Street. I saw it too, but it was the only vehicle to turn the corner. They were alone. It is not Hoover policy to do anything alone. Something wasn't right.

The truck pulled to a stop and eight Hoovers came forth, one Hoover representing each street of the Hoover Connection—43nd, 52nd, 59th, 74th, 92nd, 94th, 107th, and 112th. As they lumbered out I recognized hardly any, except Bennose from 107th Street and Macc. But still something wasn't right. Their faces were disfigured. All of them had been beaten, and bad.

"Cuz," stammered Macc in barely audible syllables, "we came to squash that shit we got goin' on wit' y'all. We fin' to get wit' these Sixty niggas. Cuz, they mopped us at the Gladys Knight concert last night."

"Damn, how many of 'em was it?" I asked.

"Man, they was like two hundred deep."

"So what's up then?" asked one of our Baby Locs.

"Come to the truck," said Ben, and he turned and walked away.

"Bring a gat," I whispered to Stag, who promptly retrieved the .45 from Bam. We followed the Hoovers out to the truck. When we got there Macc pulled back a burlap covering to reveal a cache of rifles. Not shotguns, but rifles! There had to be at least two dozen there.

"Cuz, is it Hoova-Gangsta or what?" asked Macc to the crowd.

"It's Gangsta-Hoova, if anything!" someone yelled back.

"Well, let's show these Sixty niggas what it's like!"

At that, homies started climbing into the truck, grabbing weapons, and running to their cars. Some stayed in the back of the truck and rode with the Hoovers. When we pulled away from St. Andrews Park, the caravan was sixteen cars deep, with the Hoovers heading it up. The week that followed would be one filled with rumors of sheer terror and mayhem.

It was Sunday, August 27, 1984. As we headed out we ran into Ping from Santana Block, who had two females with him. After we explained to him that we were on our way to the races, the females asked if they could ride with us. I said no, but Li'l Harv simultaneously said yes. We ended up letting them roll with us. We introduced ourselves as Monster and Li'l Harv, which is all it took for them to link us with Eight Tray. They were Sixties and never told us.

When we got to the races, which were largely huge Crip meetings, we asked the two females if they wanted something to eat from Golden Ox across the street. They declined and we walked over to the restaurant to get some food. In front of Winchell's Donuts we met up with Li'l Marstien and Godfather from 69 East Coast. We talked for a while to Baby Gangster, Twin, and Mondo from Santana Block and when we returned, the females were gone. Harv was upset, as he felt they owed us some pussy for the ride. I said "Fuck 'em" and settled down with my pastrami sandwich. I hadn't taken two bites before I was frozen stiff with fright.

"Aw, shit!!" is all I heard Li'l Harv say.

And damn, right in front of us was Li'l Fee—Tyquon Cox—and at least twelve other Sixties dressed in all-black suits walking toward my car. I was sitting in the driver's seat with the door wide open, eating on the pastrami, and Harv was next to me in the passenger seat. By some stroke of good luck they walked right past and never looked our way. The slightest look to the left would have meant a bullet to the head. My weapon was not even reachable from where I was seated. I recognized not only Li'l Fee, who looked like a reptile with almond-shaped eyes that were green or hazel—depending on his mood—but Crazy Keith from Harlem Thirties, who had brought me the horrible news of Tray Ball's death while we were in Y.T.S. Back then, only a year before, he was talking that "Tray love" shit, using semantics, knowing that Harlem's allegiance as Thirties was not to the "3" but to the "0," which automatically allied them with the Sixties and Nineties. On his own, Crazy Keith was likable. But now I saw his true colors.

"Cuz, let's go. We can get away!" said Li'l Harv, excited, relieved, and happy that we had escaped.

"Fuck that," I said, reaching for my .38 under the seat. "You know they up here lookin' fo' me."

"Yeah, but they ain't seen you. We can—"

"Shut up! Listen, take my car to the end of the alley and wait fo' me. I'ma give these niggas what they come fo'."

"We could get away." Li'l Harv was mumbling more to himself than anything else as I got out and he slid over into my seat.

I went into the alley the same way they had and walked to the end, looking slowly out. There I saw two cars parked, both drivers facing the same way. I thought about blasting the drivers, but opted for bigger fish instead. I eased back into the alley and waited for the group to come back my way. It didn't take long. I heard them laughing and talking amongst themselves and let them all walk past. I let them get about twenty-five feet before standing and taking aim.

"GANGSTA!" I yelled, and squeezed the trigger.

Some ran, some fell, and others hollered. One turned and fired back. It was Li'l Fee. But he had a revolver and was out-gunned. I squeezed off nine rounds then broke across the alley, dropping the clip and pushing in a fresh one. I fired four more shots before the others found the heart to return fire. The big blue dumpster I was behind was catching hell. I spent my remaining five rounds and discarded the empty clip, then slammed in another one and continued my assault. When I had three rounds left I began my retreat.

Their shots came far apart now. I heard screeching tires and screams all around us. A siren wailed in the far-off distance. The Seventy-seventh Division of the LAPD is less than five minutes from Florence and Main. When I was out of danger and able to stand and run, I bolted to where I'd told Harv to wait. He was gone!

I ran back around the side, taking fire from those who were retrieving their wounded, and out onto Florence Avenue. Luckily, I saw Whiteboy Eric and flagged him down for a ride. Back in the 'hood I found Li'l Harv sitting in my car in front of Tray Ball's house. I opened the door and immediately started pistol whipping him. Disgusted at his cowardice, I left him in the street and went home.

All that night I thought about Crazy Keith. The next morning I called around and got April's number. She had resurfaced and was supposedly claiming Harlem. If that was the case, I knew she had a line on Keith. I got in touch with her and asked where Keith lived. She claimed not to know, but added that he'd be over her house at eight that evening. Before I hung up she said, "Monster, don't kill him at my house," which sent chills through my whole body. If she had set up Twinky, had she been that cool about it?

I called Stag and ran down the previous night's episode. He was hot. I told him of my plans for that evening and he was all in. Just then Tamu rolled over.

"What was that all about?"

"Nothin' really. Just gettin' at Stag."

"About what? And what did you do last night?"

"Oh, just shot a few people."

I knew that would stop her from asking questions, and it did.

I took a shower and watched some cartoons with Keonda. She asked if I'd take her to the park and I said I'd see. She was so pure, so clean, so honest. We contrasted sharply. I hoped then that she'd never know her father was a monster, a hunter, and often the hunted. I watched her more than I did the cartoons. Fatherhood. How? When? And most importantly *where?* The park she knew was a vast grassland with a sandbox and swings. In actuality, it was a meeting and mounting place for one of many warring factions in South Central. It was a target area for rivals and a cemetery for the ignorant. She was oblivious to all that made up her surroundings.

" . . . did you hear me?"

"Huh? What?"

"I said, are you hungry?"

"No, I'm good, thank you."

"Babes, what's wrong?"

"Nothin'," I said, and went on watching Keonda watching TV. But I knew what was wrong. I just didn't want to tell her. I didn't want to worry her. I was back in the thick of it and knew that after tonight there'd be no turning back. My neighborhood right, my neighborhood wrong. Right or wrong, *my neighborhood.*

At 7:30 P.M. Stag and I rolled out in the red Toyota Tercel for undercover purposes. I had the .38 in my waistband and Stag had the .44 Bulldog. We headed north on Western Avenue. Our intentions were to correct Keith with minimal damage to others and space back to the 'hood.

We pulled to a stop on Thirty-ninth across from April's house, facing west. Crazy Keith pulled to a stop in front of her house facing east. He was in Baby Brother's white '61 Chevy. We waited to see if he would notice us. He exited the car with a bag that appeared to be a forty-ounce bottle of beer and began walking up to April's house. The very real possibility existed that April could be setting us up—after all, we weren't the best of friends—so we moved cautiously.

When his back was turned we left the car and began to creep up on him. He never heard us coming. The only thing that saved him was April answering the door and calling our names. He turned in surprise, so we had to play off like we were just seeing how easy it was to get him. After that he began to relax, never thinking that he had been clocked last night with his cohorts in pursuit of me.

"So, what the Tray like, homie?" he said, popping the top on the Olde English.

"E-T-G, R-S-K!" I said without humor, reminding him I was a Rollin' Sixties killer. His fake smile started to fade.

"What's up, Stag?" he said, trying to switch-hit, hoping to find some humor in Stag, or at least a reprieve. I'm sure that at that point he suspected I knew, as I had said it.

"Cuz, what you got against me?" I asked Keith. April excused herself and went into the house. "Or, what you got against my 'hood?"

"Nuttin', Monster, you and me been cool. You know I ain't beefin' wit' you." He was taking big gulps of the forty, perhaps his last drink.

"Keith, Keith, Keith," I began, doing the Michael Corleone scene with Rocco, who had set Sonny up. "I saw you. Now don't lie to me."

"Cuz, they said it was just business. That's on the 'hood, they said it was strictly business—"

"Who said that?"

"Li'l Fee and the Raymonds. They—"

"Raymonds?!" asked Stag.

"Yeah, it was us, the Sixties, and the Raymonds. But cuz, it wasn't nuttin' personal."

"So it's just business when I blow your fuckin' brains all over this muthafuckin' porch, huh?"

"Uh . . . uh . . . "

"Huh?!"

"Naw, Monster, wait. I know where they be hangin' out at. All of 'em. Cuz, they there right now. They tryin' to start this syndicate thang on the west side and say you a problem, so you gotta go. It's for the betterment of the Crip Nation!"

"You believed that punk shit? Nigga, you out yo' fuckin' mind. They can't kill me, fool, I'm already *dead*, muthafucka!"

I drew my weapon and grabbed Keith by the collar, putting the barrel to his temple. I watched the sweat pour down over his face.

"Monster, wait, please man, hold it. We can go right now and bust on them niggas. I ain't down wit' them."

"Man, I wouldn't do shit wit' yo' sorry ass."

Just then a Cutlass came to a halt in front of April's house. It was impossible to see who was inside. I put my weapon away and pushed Keith out in front of me. The driver, who it appeared was the only occupant of the Cutlass, got out and came up to where we were.

"Keith, who these niggas and what's wrong wit' you?"

"Cuz, that's Monster Ko—"

And before Keith could even get it out, the dude, who I later found out was Brandon, started to draw a small chrome revolver. But his movements were slow and obvious, and Stag had him on bead with the .44.

"Cuz," Brandon said when he saw we had the drop, "Harlem ain't got no beef wit' Gangsta."

"Then why you pullin' yo' gat?" asked Stag, who still had the .44 trained on him.

"'Cause, shit, I ain't knowin' what's up wit' Monsta."

"Yo, homie, Keith was wit' some Sissies and Raymonds last night when they call theyself ambushin' a muthafucka."

"What?! Keith, what I tell you 'bout hangin' wit' them niggas when they set trippin'? Huh?"

POW!

Brandon slapped Keith hard across the face.

"Cuz, I didn't know they was—"

POW!

"You a damn lie, Keith, you love them niggas!"

SWOOSH!

Brandon swung at Keith, but missed. Crazy Keith hobbled a few feet away like an old, sorry dog.

Stag and I started to leave but were stopped by Keith.

"Monster, watch yourself, 'cause cuz and them is serious."

"What you know 'bout serious when every time someone stronger than you around, you do whatever they say? Get out my damn way."

"Naw, cuz, wait . . . " Keith tried to explain further.

"Let 'em go, Keith," Brandon said.

We got into Tamu's car and left. We contemplated rolling on the Sixties, but I didn't want to bring any more heat on Tamu's car. It was bad enough that Keith had seen it. And lived.

After a while, Stag asked what I thought about what Keith had said about the West Side Syndicate thing. I actually had no opinion about it. I knew that if they tried to hit me, I was going to hit back. West Side Syndicate. I did feel an awkward kind of fear that I had never felt before. This stemmed from the fact that if it were true that they were forming some new union inside of Crip and that my removal was, in some way, for the betterment of the Crip Nation, then there must be someone other than the Sixties, the Raymonds, and the Harlems behind it. That was not their language. This was the language of older people, people I didn't know. That was a problem. How could I put up an adequate defense when I didn't know who was coming? Or worse yet, how they were coming? The previous night's maneuver was typical Sixties—bungled. I could always out-think them.

But if they were, as Keith had said, starting something new, the next group of shooters might not be Sixties, henceforth creating a blind spot in my ability to predict what would happen.

"We gotta find out who is pumpin' this West Side Syndicate shit, you know?" I told Stag.

"That's right," Stag replied. "We should kidnap that fool Li'l Fee. His grandmother live off of Seventy-sixth Street."

"We'll see what's up."

I dropped Stag off and went home. Tamu wasn't there. I peeled out of my combat black, took a shower, and watched the news. I dozed off on the couch.

I was awakened by Tamu, who had Keonda in her arms. She told me to go get into our bed so she could put Keonda in the couch bed. I stumbled to our room, but couldn't sleep. Tamu eventually came in.

"Do you believe in God?" I asked.

"Yep," she said, and then added, "why would you ask me about that?"

"No real reason." I propped myself up on my elbow. "And what is your God's name?"

"Name?"

"I mean what do you call him?"

"God. Or Father, I guess. But I don't really get into names. I just believe in a higher power. Why are you asking me these questions?"

"Do you know what Allah means?"

"Isn't that the name of the Muslim's God?"

"No, it just means God in Arabic."

"Oh, 'cause one of my mother's friends was a Muslim."

"I'm tired, very tired," I said, lying back on the bed and looking up at the ceiling.

"Well, babes, get some sleep."

"No, not that kind of tired. I'm tired of living. Tired of killing. Tired of acting like people want me to act. I'm tired of . . ."

"What's wrong, Kody? Don't talk like that, you're scaring me. It's gonna be all right. Things will get better. Hey, remember that Temprees song you like so much, 'We've Only Just Begun?' Remember that?"

"Yeah, that's a bad jam."

"It's gonna be all right, babes, you watch."

She held my head to her breast and rubbed the side of my face with her soft hands, all the while humming "We've Only Just Begun."

When I awoke the next morning, Tamu was up cooking and playing music. The fresh, wholesome aroma from the kitchen coupled with Anita Baker's new song, "Angel," made me feel good. The sixth sense of my melanin was catching some good vibes. Keonda came into the room and she and I talked awhile. When I was in Y.T.S., Tamu or Tamu's mother had taught her how to say Ronald Reagan. When I was released I taught her his third name—pig. Now, over and over, she would say "Wonal Wagan pig!" and I'd say "Yeah!" I finished playing with Keonda, ate, showered, and geared up. The phone rang.

"Telephone, Kody, it's Muhammad."

I went to the phone.

"Asalaam Alaikum," he greeted me.

"Walaikum Asalaam."

"So, are you ready to roll?" he asked.

"Roll? Where?"

"To the seminar."

Damn. I had completely forgotten about that.

"Yeah, I'm still down."

"Great," he said, "I'll be right over to pick you up."

Thirty minutes later I heard his horn. When I got to the car there was another brother inside who looked vaguely familiar. He introduced himself as Hamza. Hamza, yeah, that's right. I'd met bro in Y.T.S. on that first encounter during the slave movie. We saluted each other as Muhammad pulled out into traffic.

"So, what's been up, Monster?" Muhammad asked.

He always used my gang name, I believe to make me feel comfortable. Even when he introduced me to brothas and sistas in the movement he said, "This is Monster Kody from the Eight Trays." He never downed where I was coming from and never made me feel ashamed. I must admit, though, that when he'd introduce me to revolutionaries I'd feel uneasy being announced as Monster Kody from Eight Tray. Like most bangers, I felt that the revolutionaries wanted to stop gangs, which is seldom true. They want to stop gang violence, which is ninety percent black-on-black. And the way they try to stop it is to show that black-on-black violence is a result of white-on-black violence. I knew none of this then, but felt uneasy all the same.

"Ain't nuttin' up, man, just dealin' wit' this madness out here."

"Have you read anything on Chairman Fred?"

"Who?" I asked, not catching who he meant without the last name attached.

"Fred Hampton. The brotha in the Panther book."

"Oh, naw, man. I ain't read nuttin'. Been havin' a few problems out here, you know?"

"Yeah, I heard. Someone told me you shot the street races up Sunday night."

"Either me or them."

"You gotta check out Chairman Fred. The brotha was dynamic and strong, sort of like you. How old are you now?"

"Nineteen."

"Yeah, Chairman Fred was twenty-one when the pigs assassinated him. You know, Chairman Fred used to say, 'They can kill the revolutionary, but they can't kill revolution. They can kill the liberator, but they can't kill liberation.' Ain't that deep? Pigs killed Fred 'cause Fred was serious. Fred was hard as nails, brotha. You should read up on the brotha. You'll dig him strong."

"Yeah, I intend to. But lately, man, I've just been wantin' to turn myself in to the graveyard and sleep."

"What?! Brotha, it ain't never that bad. That's what the beast want you to do. Check out what H. Rap Brown say: 'We are starting to realize what America has long known. And that is every black birth in America is a political birth, because they don't know which one is going to be the one to raise the people up.' Bro, don't let the beast pressure you into taking yourself out. You got a mission, remember that."

"Righteous."

But still I felt tired, overburdened. Today I know what that weight was, but then I didn't. It was my conscience struggling under the weight of constant wrongdoing. Not wrongdoing in any religious sense, but doing things that were morally wrong based on the human code of ethics. Also, it was my subconscious telling me that my time was up. I knew it, I felt it, but I just couldn't face it. No professional can. "You're too old," "You can't move like you used to," "You're slippin'." No one wants to hear that, especially when that life is all you have known.

At nineteen I felt like thirty. I didn't know what to do.

Dying on the trigger didn't look so appealing anymore. I needed to do something that would be as satisfying as banging once was. Banging had taught me that I like the feeling of fighting *for* something. My greatest enjoyment from banging came from the sense of power it gave me. To be armed and considered dangerous felt good, but to stand in my turf that I fought to make safe was the climax of banging for me. So I knew that whatever I did after banging had to involve fighting for power and land.

When Muhammad dropped me off I began reading about Chairman Fred Hampton from the Chicago chapter of the Black Panther party. Just like Muhammad said, Fred was *raw!* Fred and eight other Panthers, including his pregnant fiancée, were set up by an informant and ambushed in their residence. Fred Hampton and Mark Clark were murdered. The informant and Fred's killer were both Negroes. After reading about Fred, I really got into the book.

On September 27, a month after the street race shoot-out, our door was kicked in by the soldier-cops. They found a .25 automatic and hauled me off to the county jail. I was charged with mayhem and two counts of attempted murder. Three people had gotten shot. One, Li'l Eddie Boy, had positively identified me while in the hospital. He was the mayhem victim. The irony of this was that he and his unit had come into East Coast 'hood—sovereign territory—gunning for me. I'd defended myself and shot him in the ass in a dark alley as he ran away, yet he had positively identified me. I guess their thinking was, "If we can't kill him, we'll lock him up. But he *must* go."

When I got to County I was immediately rushed to 4800,

the Crip module. Out of 18,000 inmates in Los Angeles County at that time, all wore blue jumpsuits except the 150 Crips who were in 4800—they wore gray. Everyone who wanted to take a shot at us could, as we stood out like flies in the buttermilk. When I arrived, Li'l Fee was there, as was Big Eddie Boy, the victim's brother. A sort of détente existed between the sets, since the Consolidated Crip Organization (CCO) had members sprinkled throughout the module keeping the peace. They did this by keeping our rage focused on the pigs, who were always antagonistically aggressive toward us—and our dicks.

I told Fee that Li'l Eddie Boy was a witness against me and he assured me that he would not come to court. At that time, Li'l Fee only had a gun charge, but a week or two later he was on the front page of the *Los Angeles Sentinel* wanted in connection with five murders—the Kermit Alexander family murders. The story was that it was supposed to have been a hit but that he'd gotten the wrong street, only even we weren't doing hits. It made the Syndicate story carry a little more weight.

Li'l Fee was taken to High Power, maximum security, and Big Eddie Boy got released. Thus my contact with Li'l Eddie fell off and, surprisingly, he came to court to testify.

Slowpoke, Football, and Fishbone were in County for double murder. Diamond and Nasty were there for murder. Diamond had caught a Swan writing on the wall at St. Andrews Park and beat him to death with a baseball bat. Ckrizs was there, too. In fact, Crips from all over were there.

We were housed in Denver row and Charlie row in four-man cells and in Able row and Baker row in six-man cells. The pigs were so complacent that often there'd be six members from the same set in the same cell. A command booth was situated in the middle, and a glass catwalk ran the length of the tiers for observation by the pigs. Communal showers were located at the entrance to each tier.

For all of us, 4800 was a new testing ground, and there was always something going on.

9

48 HOURS

Module 4800, the relatively new (to us) attempt by the Los Angeles County Sheriff's Department's Operation Safe Street (O.S.S.) to curb the gang activity in the L.A. County Jail, wasn't working. Their attempt to isolate us in a module, alone and out of the general population, was an impossible task.

The reasons they gave for such "preferential" treatment were initially cloaked in emotional rhetoric and sprang from the April 1984 rebellion, in which seventeen Crips erupted into rampaging headbangers in the 4000 floor chow hall. Heron, an O.G. from Spooktown Compton Crips, had been beaten by the pigs for some infraction and the other bangers just weren't going for it. Fed up with the wanton abuse from the pigs, the Crips seized the chow hall. After the pigs were beaten and one temporarily detained for questioning, the rebels went after the trustees, the faithful servants of the pigs, who were notorious for shorting everyone on food. The trustees had also jacked up the price of donuts, which they stole from the main kitchen and sold to general population, from the established price of two dollars a bag. All were beaten and ran from the chow hall. Then the doors were barricaded and the demands began.

During the five-hour siege, the misinformation agents in the sheriff's department told the media that the "riot" was only due to overcrowding and the breakdown of the air-conditioning system. While the pigs videotaped those in the chow hall from an elevated Plexiglas tower, acting sympathetic to the righteous complaints of the resisters, other pigs were busy evacuating the module adjacent to the chow hall—4800.

For five hours the resisters demanded to be "treated as men" and to be given "better food" and some protection from the "Nazi police"; for five hours they heard "Okay, gentlemen, you're right," and "Of course we are all men." Then the resisters were made to leave the chow hall naked, walk through a gauntlet of pigs in full riot-repression gear for their well-deserved whack with the P-24 baton, and directed into 4800. The seventeen stayed naked, with no bedclothes, no visits, no showers, for three days. After that they were given bedclothes, visits, and gray jumpsuits.

The other eleven thousand prisoners wore blue jumpsuits, but the Crips had to wear gray. Every time they went to court, on a visit (under heavy escort) to the doctor, anywhere, they were subjected to the abuse of sadistic pigs who were looking for revenge. The Bloods, camouflaged in blue like the general population, also took liberty and attacked gray suits when they were caught alone or in isolated pairs.

Directly across the hall from 4800 the pigs set up the O.S.S. interdepartmental office. Ironically—or perhaps not at all—this was around the same time that the F.B.I. released a study on Crips that stated "one out of every four Crips is in jail for murder, or has done time for murder. And three out of four Crips have been arrested for weapons-related charges." The counterintelligence of the Crips was kicked into full swing, and 4800 became the "Crip Module."

It's quite clear to me now what was taking place at that time. But then, in 1984, I was deaf, dumb, and blind. We helped the pigs gather intelligence on us and had no idea we were doing so. Instead of 4800 being a module to contain us and keep the general population safe, it became an intelligence satellite for law enforcement—probably the true purpose for which it was originally designed. For us, it became the 'hood, a place to call ours—another testing ground. The most astonishing thing I remember about 4800 was that there weren't any books in the entire module, and we weren't allowed access to the library. The decibel level was so high that when I didn't have a headache, I felt funny.

Every set desperately tried to get their own set deep, because a deep set wielded power and could protect itself. Whenever, on our way to see a visitor or the doctor, we'd see one of our homies in blue out in the G.P. (general public), we'd tell the escort pig that the homie was a Crip, and the pig would get his name and booking number. That same night the homie would be moved to 4800, doomed like the rest of us. G.P. was smoother, much better than 4800. You could walk around unattended to visits, other modules, practically anywhere. Many

Crips shunned the module for this reason. Some didn't want to be labeled as Crip, and others couldn't stand the stress. There were also those with dirt on them who had to dodge their homies for fear of a beating or stabbing. But when we'd see a homie in G.P., we felt like "Yo, man, bring yo' ass home, to Cripville."

The process of getting into 4800 was overwhelming, so cats tended to circumvent it for this reason, as well. You were made to stand and hold a placard with your name, your set name, and your 'hood on it for a series of pictures. The pictures were no doubt distributed among the pig population for intelligence. A lot of cats just didn't want to deal with that. Inside the module were Crips ranging in age from eighteen to forty. The deepest sets were the Hoovers and the East Coasts, a deadly mixture of power. In the beginning, all the sets tried to get along, each individual making an effort to suppress his disdain for enemies that he was now face-to-face with—sometimes in the same cell.

In January 1985 this thin line of love and hate evaporated in the face of unfolding developments in the street. The first major eruption of violence occurred on a slow day, a day that looked and felt like any other day. I was in Denver-8 and my cellmates were Oldman from Nine-Deuce Hoover, Kenny Mitchel from the Sixties (he was arrested in the 1970s for robbing the Commodores), and Joe Dee from Atlantic Drive Compton Crips. We had just finished making a batch of pruno—jail-made wine—and were preparing to get drunk when we heard a voice.

"Cuz, who is that down there from East Coast?"

"Marstien," the voice replied. I had seen Marstien at the

street races on Florence and Main before the shoot-out with Li'l Fee and his crew.

"Eh, Marstien, what up, nigga? This Li'l Sad, cuz. I'm gonna come down there later and rap with you, homie."

"Awright, cuz."

Li'l Sad was on Denver row and Marstien was on Baker row below us. I was going to send my regards, but decided to wait until later, as I was enjoying my drink. Everyone had heard about Lajoy (Li'l Hoov) being killed days before, supposedly by East Coasts as he drove through his 'hood. So when Marstien came in, along with Vamp, for murder, it was believed that he must be in for killing Lajoy. Marstien now had two murders, as he was already in for killing a Swan.

There were at least eighteen Hoovers in 4800 at that time, and equally as many East Coasts. There were four tiers in the module, each housing sixteen cells. Those on Able and Baker were six-man cells, while those on Charlie and Denver row were four-man cells. We were not allowed in the chow hall any more as a result of the rebellion, so we ate in the dayroom. Each tier had its own dayroom, and the inhabitants ate there respectfully. Of course, every cell was full.

When Able row was let out to chow, the East Coasts fell into a tight circle around Marstien and Vamp, creating a group eight deep. The largest contingency of Hoovers in the module was also housed on Able row, so no sooner did everyone get into the dayroom than the violence erupted.

"HOOVA!" someone shrieked, sounding like a deadman's charge.

Crudely constructed knives were drawn and the Hoovers proceeded to stab and beat the East Coasts. The Coasts resisted, but were no match for the fanatical Hoovers' aggression. From my cell I could see the battle. Some Hoovers had two knives in hand and were making daring dives into the crowd of retreating East Coasts, who looked more terrified than hurt. Other Hoovers had whole bars of county soap in socks and were swinging them into the heads and bodies of the reachable East Coasts. One East Coast—Snake, from Seven-Six—was armed with an ice pick, but in his attempt to strike at the charging Hoovers he slipped and stabbed his homie Vamp.

The battle was quick and decisive. When the pigs rode down, the Hoovers stood on one side of the dayroom, victorious, proud, and, as usual, arrogant, some still holding weapons. The East Coasts were crumpled in the opposite corner, wrecked, beaten, and shamed. Six were stabbed and all sustained bruises. The other Crips in the dayroom stepped back to let the inevitable take place.

O.S.S.'s response was a devastating blow to the Crip Module and gave some of us a glimpse at the type of control they really exercised. Marstien and Vamp were sent to the more constricting, High Power 1750 module. The Hoovers went to the Hole. But the real twist was that all West Side Crips were moved to Able and Charlie row and all East Side Crips were put on Baker and Denver row. Although the conflict did involve the West Side Hoovers and the East Side East Coasts, it was not an issue of East vs. West, but rather that these two sets—mere chapters of their respective sides—were at war. Their conflict entailed nothing else. But when O.S.S. split up the Crips, it gave the Hoovers and the East Coasts the opportunity to agitate each side into a war between East and West. And that's exactly what happened.

At night the chanting began, with everyone from both sides participating.

"EAST SIDE!" Baker and Denver row would chant, repeating it three times and finishing with a set roll call.

"East Coasts, Avalon, Main Streets, Grape Street, Eight-Seven, PJ Watts, Fo' Tray, Five Tray . . . "

And in response the West Side would chant, "WEST SIDE! Hoova, Eight Tray, Sixties, Shot Gun, Raymond, Playboy, West Boulevard . . . "

The threat of the East Side became real. So real, in fact, that East and West Side sets that had never clashed began to do so under these conditions. All the while O.S.S. was conducting "interviews"—actually interrogations—to find out who was trying to bring about the long-lost unity of old.

In these times, many disappeared from the Crip Module. One afternoon we were all told to gather up our personal property and go into the huge communal showers. No one had any idea of what was taking place. We all crowded into the showers with our meager property. We waited for hours to find out our fate. Looking around at one another, at friends we had met while in this shark tank, at enemies we had forgiven in the light of a new "enemy"—the East Side—we felt like a family being torn asunder. Eventually, a pig came in with our JRC cards and began to call off names.

"Scott?" the pig shouted into the shower.

"Yeah," I replied, wondering why I was being called first. "What'cha call me fo', man, I ain't—"

"Shut up. You are going to Charlie-10. Get your shit and move, now!" shouted the little pink-faced pig, who weighed no more than 150 pounds. I would have slapped the shit out of any other American for talking to me like that, but this scrawny little pig had the armed forces on his side.

I gathered up my property and moved down the tier to C-10. This didn't make much sense to me, because I was in C-8 before they rolled us up into the shower. It felt strange to walk past cell after empty cell, striped bare to the concrete and steel. I felt like the only Crip on earth. I got to the cell, it was electronically opened and I stepped in.

"Davis?" I heard the little pig say.

"Yeah, here." That was Fat Rat from Five-Deuce Hoover.

"Charlie-10."

Shit, that was my cell. Now I was tripping on what these pigs had in mind. Fat Rat came down the tier, laboring heavily under his crushing weight. Fat Rat was huge, with muscular arms and chest and a fat belly that, coupled with his dark complexion, made him resemble a potbellied stove. He and I were friends from juvenile hall.

"Cuz, what they doing? I mean why they movin' us all around?" I asked Fat Rat as he plopped down on the bunk across from mine.

"Shit, cuz, I think they fin' to mix us up. I pity the Cheese Toast"—disrespectful for East Coast—"that come in my cell."

"You think that's what they up to, huh?"

"Yeah, 'cause I heard one cop tell another."

Another name was called.

"Anderson?"

"Right here."

"Charlie-10."

Fat Rat and I looked at each other, and Fat Rat smiled. Anderson was B.T. from East Coast.

"I got one," Fat Rat said as he began to make his bed.

I didn't know B.T., but since he had come to the module I had seen him around. He stood in front of the cell and waited to be let in. B.T. was six foot one, muscular, and dark—almost like a fit Fat Rat, but taller. He had been in the dayroom when the Hoovers vamped on the Coasts, but he'd hit the wall when it jumped, claiming he was under paperwork (Crip constitution) and couldn't participate in Crip-on-Crip violence. He was one of the two who didn't get stabbed.

"What up, cuz?" B.T. said to me as he hoisted his bedding up on the bunk above mine.

"Ain't nothin', just trippin' off these canines."

"Yeah, these devils is on one," he said, then turned to Fat Rat. "What up, cuz?"

"HOOVA," shot Fat Rat in a hard-core confrontational voice, "and I'ma tell ya right now, nigga, I ain't likin' you or yo' homeboys."

"Yeah, well I ain't on no set trips and I ain't into no tribalism. I'm hooked up and therefore forbidden to involve myself in that. In other words, I got no beef with you, just like I ain't got no beef with Master Kody."

"*Monster* Kody, not *Master,*" I said, annoyed.

"Yeah, yeah, that's right, I'm trippin'."

"Yo sho' is if you think I'm goin' fo' that old bullshit you talkin' 'bout, nigga. Fuck that. This is Hoova," Fat Rat said stubbornly.

"I ain't even trippin' that." And B.T. went on making up his bed. I knew that a confrontation between the two was inevitable.

I had heard about the Crip constitution, but that was the extent of my knowledge. The constitution was the latest topic on the wire. It was said that members of the organization were coming down to 4800 from San Quentin and Folsom to get things together in the Crip Nation. By this time I was moving toward that mind-set of unity. I had been living hard and could not expect to continue to do so and live or miss a life term in prison. The rumors surrounding the coming of the constitutionalists had the ring of truth to them. When people spoke of "them" or "those under paperwork," they invariably did so with great respect. "They" seemed to us like descending angels coming to redeem the lost souls of Cripdom.

Some felt nervous. I could see it in their eyes when "they" were spoken of. Perhaps they had done wrong or feared the responsibility of having to handle some business. Some seemed relieved and eager for the constitutionalists' arrival—those who were under everyday attack by vultures preying on setless individuals and shallow sets.

What the pigs had done was mix everyone up. As much as they could, they put one member from each set in each cell. They were now trying to force us back together after they had intentionally torn us apart, creating conditions for massive distrust and confusion.

Big Hog from 107 Hoover was a tier tender and went up and down the tiers trying to get those assigned to cells with oppositional members to refrain from any tribalistic violence. Most complied, but Fat Rat could not be deterred. He wanted to find out more about B.T.'s affiliation. He wanted to see who he was really connected to. The remaining East Coasts in the module had severed ties with B.T. because of his failure to act in their defense when they were attacked by the Hoovers. I had learned that day that the Coasts had put a "blue light"—a hit—on B.T. for his inactivity. Fat Rat knew that the Coast Car would not defend B.T., so he had little to worry about on that front.

When Big Hog came down the tier, sweeping up, Fat Rat called to him and began whispering something in his ear, no doubt about B.T.'s authenticity. Big Hog had been to the pen already and had been under the old constitution, so he'd know if B.T. was really hooked up or not. Fat Rat repeatedly insisted he was faking. After Fat Rat had spoken to Hog, with B.T. looking on in suspicion, Hog called B.T. over to the front gate. They began whispering. Fat Rat beamed as if to say "Now, the test of fire." The conversation with B.T. hadn't lasted but two minutes when Big Hog spoke up.

"This nigga ain't hooked up in shit, Fat Rat, serve this nigga!"

B.T. backed up to the gate, facing us in the cell. His face said it all: coward. Fat Rat read it and moved in.

"Eh, hold on Fat Rat, cuz, I ain't got no beef wit' you, man."

He knew he was doomed and was begging. Fat Rat had a reputation for being a "booty bandit" and thrived on weak men with tight asses. Poor B.T.

"Fuck that, why you lie, huh?"

POW!

Fat Rat smacked B.T. hard across the side of the head.

"Aw, cuz, I just ain't into Crip-on-Crip, cuz, I—"

SMACK!

Another whack came down, this one across his face. The tiers grew quiet.

"Eh, Hog," B.T. began, turning to Hog for relief, "tell Rat to stall me out, cuz."

"I'm gonna stall you out awright."

And with that Fat Rat grabbed B.T.'s boxer shorts by the elastic waistband and yanked them with one powerful tug. They tore right off of him. Surely, I thought, B.T. was going to mount an attack now. He *had* to.

"Bitches don't wear boxer shorts, punk, men do," Fat Rat shouted, throwing the ripped shorts on the floor near the steel toilet.

"Aw, Rat, you trippin', cuz," B.T. said, but made no move that telegraphed strength.

"It's *Mister* Fat Rat to you, bitch. Now what you wanna do, huh? You wanna get 'em up or what?" Fat Rat eased into a strike-first position.

"I ain't got no beef wit' you, Fa—Mister Fat Rat."

And that was it. His last vestiges of strength. He had yielded his manhood by calling Fat Rat "Mister," a cardinal sin. In that instant, Fat Rat connected fist to face, knocking B.T. hard against the bars, where Hog took the liberty of grabbing his cheeks. B.T.'s knees buckled; until Hog had fondled his cheeks he was going down.

"Ahh," B.T. gave a start when Hog's hands touched his ass. "Cuz, what you doin'?"

"Shut up, punk. You know you like that," said Hog.

Catcalls began coming from the adjacent cells. B.T. looked around like a frightened, trapped lamb. But in contrast to a meek, feeble-bodied person, he stood there six foot one and buff. Yet he had no inclination to defend himself from what was definitely a head-up situation.

Hog was out on the tier and could not get in the cell. And I was not going to get involved. I had no beef with East Coast or B.T. Could I have prevented it? Yes, and I intended to, but it would be interesting to see how far this would go. I can't now qualify my thinking at the time. In my mind it was kill or be killed, live and let die, law of the land.

Fat Rat had backed to the rear of the cell and begun to disrobe. I thought then that B.T. would strike, but he didn't. He still seemed to think that Fat Rat could be deterred by reasoning, by appealing to his intellectual morality. B.T. had been to the pen and had gotten "tamed." He'd learned manipulation and vocabulary skills. But shit, Fat Rat, like me, was uncut street, straight out of the bush. The only language Fat Rat knew or respected or could be persuaded by was violence. Everything else was for the weak. Action and more action—anything else paled in comparison.

Fat Rat stood wide-legged in tattered shorts, belly hanging over them. He looked like an enraged Buddha. He was ready to fight or fuck, and knowing Fat Rat, he planned on a bit of both.

"Oh, Hog, you just gonna let yo' homie trip on me like this, huh?"

"*You* lettin' him trip on you, nigga! I ain't in that cell. My name is Hog, not Fat Rat."

"Hey, Fat Rat, cuz, I don't wanna fight wit' you, man."

B.T.'s pleading was reduced to a whimper, clashing hard with his appearance. He was evenly dark from head to toe, and standing there naked he looked like a Zulu warrior.

"Nigga, you gonna do somethin'," Fat Rat said, massaging his groin and stepping up on B.T.

"Cuz, you *trippin'*. Fat Rat—"

POW!

Fat Rat punched him hard in the solar plexus.

"*Mister* Fat Rat, punk!" Fat Rat exploded as B.T. doubled over in agony.

"Oooh . . . awright, awright," he said, barely getting the words out.

"Now, what you gonna do? You ready to get 'em up or what?"

Fat Rat forced his way behind B.T. and made him move to the back of the cell.

"I don't wanna do this, Fat Rat," B.T. said, straightening up to his full height, towering over Fat Rat by at least three inches. Even Fat Rat had to take a small step back.

B.T. put his guard up and positioned his feet in a fighting stance. Then swiftly, like greased lightning, Fat Rat rushed into B.T. and began pounding him everywhere at once with furious blows. Fat Rat's hands were hammering blurs, reducing the formerly upright B.T. to a pitiful clump of flesh under the steel sink. B.T. hadn't thrown a blow, hadn't said a word, hadn't resisted with one fiber of his being, but Fat Rat didn't seem to recognize this. He continued to hammer away at B.T.'s defenseless body as if he had put up a ferocious struggle. I believe he continued out of sheer fear of B.T., from when he had finally stood to do battle.

Fat Rat clearly wanted to make sure that B.T. never resisted again. When Fat Rat ceased hitting him, B.T. lay unconscious on the cold concrete floor. The entire side of Able and Charlie row was deathly quiet. Everyone was listening.

Winded and crazed beyond any reasoning short of death, Fat Rat began tearing his sheet into shreds. I knew what this meant. Once he had torn enough he dragged B.T. out into the middle of the cell. He then rolled him over onto his stomach and proceeded to tie his hands behind his back, then his legs; then he tied his bound limbs together. Only after he had been securely bound did B.T. start to squirm against the tension of the sheets, which held him in a hog-tied position. Fat Rat, in all his brutish arrogance, put one foot on B.T.'s back like a big-game hunter who had bagged a tiger and shouted from the depths of his lungs.

"HOOVA!"

And it seemed to echo forever, bouncing off wall after wall.

"Hey, Monster," Snake from Seven-Six said to me from the lower tier, "what's goin' on?"

"Head up," I replied, which also implied that there was nothing I could do.

Big Hog had to lock it up, but before he left he told Fat Rat to save some for him.

Fat Rat, enjoying his audience, wanted to make an impression as being a total brute. He looked over, as if just noticing me in the cell.

"Monster, what's up, cuz? What should I do with this punk?"

"I don't know Rat. Cuz is a coward-ass muthafucka, huh?"

"Hell yeah," Fat Rat replied and looked down at B.T. with disgust.

"Let me up, cuz," B.T. said, trying to sound irritated. A bit late for that shit. Fat Rat responded by pissing on B.T.'s back and head as he lay on the floor. I couldn't believe it.

"Ahh, cuz," B.T. cried, "you wrong Fa—"

BAM!

Fat Rat kicked B.T. hard in the side.

"Oooff . . . *Mister* Fat Rat."

"And don't even say 'cuz' no mo', you ain't no Crip."

"Fat Rat," I said, "who gonna clean this shit up, man?"

"Him," Fat Rat said, indicating B.T.

I knew Fat Rat wasn't going to untie him and expect him

to clean up. Surely B.T. would make an attempt on Fat Rat's life now. Wouldn't anyone so treated?

"You gonna untie cuz? Man, Fat Rat, you on one now," I said.

"Monsta', this nigga broke. He ain't wantin' to see me. Shit, I should change my name to King Fat Rat."

I rolled my eyes to the ceiling at Fat Rat's insanity. He then bent down and began to untie B.T. I slid back on my bed so as not to be in the way of what I was sure was going to be some stomp-down action. Once B.T. was loose, he stood up and went peacefully over to the sink.

Uhn-uhn, no you don't," Fat Rat said in a fatherly voice. "Befo' you clean yo' self you fin' to clean these walls, the toilet and . . . Hey," Fat Rat hollered over the silent tiers, "anybody need they drawers washed?"

"Hell, yeah," several voices replied from down the tier.

"Send yo' line down here," he shouted. "What you lookin' at, punk?" he said to B.T., who flinched each time Fat Rat spoke. He was totally conquered.

B.T. washed the graffiti-packed walls, washed several pair of underclothes, braided Fat Rat's hair, massaged Fat Rat's back, and finally, Fat Rat made him eat a bar of County soap and drink some perm-repair shampoo. Rat was ruthless. After B.T. had done all of this without so much as a flicker of resistance, Fat Rat body-slammed him, tied him up again, and slid him under the bed on his stomach. Fat Rat had done all of this without an inkling of shame or remorse. B.T. was his de facto servant-slave. He followed through on every demand like a robot. The life had left his eyes and his swollen face showed no feeling. All of his movements seemed to be under the supreme command of Fat Rat's verbal remote control.

It was at times as amusing as it was scary and pitiful. How could B.T. let this happen? How had he grown up in South Central and escaped being tested for weakness? His will to resist was sapped like soda from a glass slurped through a straw. Fat Rat pranced around the cell like a proud little Buddha who had just converted another disciple. He kept trying to explain to me the process of the "breaking stages" he was putting B.T. through. He had actually developed a little science to it.

"You see, Monsta," he said like a college professor, "the first thing I did was strip him of his clothing, dig? This make him feel less than strong. Then I degraded him by pissin' on him, you see? And then I wouldn't let him wash it off, ya know? So he was feelin' pretty fucked up inside, and wit' a punch now and again, sheeit, fool ready fo' anything."

"Where you learn that from, Rat?"

"Slavery."

"Slavery? Nigga, you ain't never been no slave, fool."

"Naw, but I read that in a book befo', 'bout how the slaves wasn't 'loud to have clothes or wash they self so they lost they self . . . esteem, yeah, that's it. So I took his self-esteem, see?"

"Yeah, I seen that."

And when I looked at B.T. his expression was one of utter helplessness. I felt a little sorry for him, but I was a hard-line conservative and felt that this was the life he'd chosen. Unlike the slaves, he had *joined* the Crips. He knew the job was dangerous when he took it. Module 4800—this testing ground—was for some a breaking station. We had started calling it Forty-eight Hours, because if you could survive the first forty-eight hours—the noise, fights, stabbings, cross-burning by the pigs, tribalism, set tripping, interrogations, and being crossed, doubled-crossed, and triple-crossed—then you were in. B.T.

couldn't handle it and froze up on the first occasion of hand-to-hand and knife-to-body combat. He'd left his homies out there alone—a fatal mistake. Now his homies left him to Fat Rat's desires.

"Monsta, you can go on to sleep now, cuz. I can handle it from here."

Fat Rat said this as if I'd actually been helping him work B.T. over.

"Yeah, I guess I'll kick on back now. I've seen enough for today."

I knew what Rat was up to. He was ready to sodomize B.T. and felt reluctant while I was awake. It made me feel like a conspirator. I hadn't said a word in protest to Fat Rat about his treatment of B.T., and by not saying anything I felt like I was condoning it. Silence gives consent. When I opened my eyes to protest, Fat Rat had B.T. out from under the bed and was ready to rape him.

"Naw, Rat, I can't let you trip that hard. Don't do cuz like that." I'd swung my legs over the side of the bunk and was looking directly at Fat Rat.

"Aw, Monsta, this ain't got nuttin' to do wit' you, homie. Hey look," he said, grabbing B.T. on the ass, "he got enough ass fo' the both of us, Monsta."

"Stall cuz out, Fat Rat. You done already ruined him in the gang world. He can't go home. Now you wanna take his manhood, too? Stall him out, Rat."

"Damn! Monsta . . ."

Fat Rat looked genuinely disappointed. I guess he figured he had done all of this and rightly deserved a piece of ass. But I couldn't let that happen, not while I was in the cell. Fat Rat slid B.T. back under the bed and went to sleep.

The next morning he untied B.T., broke his jaw with a short right hook, and put him out of the cell. Twenty minutes later our names came blaring over the module's P.A. system.

"Kody Scott, Ray Davis . . . roll it up for transfer."

"Damn, Fat Rat, now look what you done," I said. "Fool went and told."

"Goddamn!" exclaimed Fat Rat.

Now he looked awfully silly as his pride over what he had done shrunk to a peevish little glare. We rolled up our property and went to face the music.

We got our customary whacks from the pigs, a few stomach blows and a slap across the head, which we could do nothing about as we were handcuffed. They sent us to the Hole for ten days. We were given "joot balls" during our entire stay. These are brick-shaped blocks of all the preceding days' leftover food mixed together. They were terrible!

I had my gray jumpsuit on the bars one day and a Blood, who was also in the Hole, came by, snatched it, set it aflame, and threw it over the tier. He shouted to his comrades that he had burned up a "trashman uniform." Long before we had recognized and taken gray as one of our colors, the Bloods had zeroed in on it as symbolizing Crip. So my gray jumpsuit was just as good as a captured blue flag to the Bloods.

We were allowed out of our cells one at a time to shower. When I came out for mine I threw a milk carton of urine on the Blood who'd burned my jumpsuit.

"Burn this, slob!" I shouted and gassed him full in the face with my warm piss.

"Aw, Blood!" he cried, running to the back of his cell.

"Aw-my-ass, punk. Shut up," I said and kept on stepping.

That day he was let out of the Hole and I got no additional

flack from the others. In fact Pee Wee from Swan was my neighbor, and he and I got along fine. He had given me the names of some East Coasts that were telling on him. He said one of them was in Forty-eight Hours. I told him I'd get on it. A rat was a rat. Pee Wee was charged in the deaths of two East Coasts. He eventually got the death penalty.

When we got back to the module things had changed. It had only been ten days, but as soon as I came in the door I sensed it and saw it on every face in the rotunda. "They" were here, is what the faces said. I began to sweat a bit as I wondered about B.T. What if he really was hooked up?

I went to Denver row, and Fat Rat went back to Charlie row. I was assigned to Denver-7. My cellmates were Sam from Santana Block, Killer from 107 Hoover, and Li'l Bubble from Six-Deuce East Coast. I had known Killer from the street and Li'l Bub from the hall. The conversation inevitably came around to B.T.

"What happened?" Killer asked seriously.

"Fat Rat just dogged dude out," I said.

"Did he fight back?"

"Naw."

"Did y'all fuck him?"

"Hell, naw! I ain't into that shit."

"Oh, 'cause that what we heard. I just wanted to be sure 'cause people been askin' 'bout him."

"Who?"

"Just some people . . ."

Damn, B.T. *was* hooked up! I wondered what this meant.

Were Fat Rat and I—the silent observer—going to be blue-lighted?

"Was B.T. under the constitution?" I asked Killer, who had been to the pen.

"No, but he was one of our prospects."

"Our? Are you in, or under it?"

"Yep," he said proudly. "Been in the organization for three years now."

I had one right in my cell! I didn't really know how to talk to Killer after I learned he was in the organization. It all took on an air of mystery. No one really knew much about it, and most were reluctant to speak about it. This only caused more confusion and hyped speculation surrounding the means and goals of the organization.

I didn't want to ask Killer outright about the group for fear he would take it wrong, so I just observed him for a few days. His attitude had changed tremendously. He had none of the old craziness that I remembered him for when we were growing up. He had gone to camp back in '79 for kidnapping a Nine-0 when the war broke out. His demeanor now was humble and sure, with an air of confidence. He was respectful to the point of being almost silly. "Excuse me" and "please," he'd say, and instead of thank you he'd say "asante," which is Kiswahili for thank you. I was tripping out on his actions. Every morning he was the first one up, cleaning the cell, wiping the floor with a wet rag on his hands and knees! And each morning he'd say "Habari ya asubuhi"—good morning in Kiswahili—to Elimu (Honey Bear from Venice Sho-line) and Ronnie T. from West Boulevard. Throughout the day they'd speak to one another in Kiswahili over the tier. When they did so, the whole tier would fall quiet and just listen. They were upright, respectful, physically fit, and mentally sharp. They used "Afrikan" in place of "Black," and never said nigger. They were socially conscious like Muhammad, but they weren't Muslims. I finally asked Killer about his change one day when we were alone.

"What changed you, Killer?"

"Actually the process took some time," he said. "At first it seemed strange to me. You know, having someone tell you what to do or how to act, what you can say and what you can't say. But by reading about our Afrikan heritage I learned that the things that my comrades were saying were right and that most of what I learned in school or in the 'hood was wrong. Through our heritage I learned what it really means to be a Crip. A *real* Crip."

"Wha'cha mean, *real* Crip."

"We in the Consolidated Crip Organization, or C.C.O., believe that CRIPS means Clandestine Revolutionary Internationalist Party Soldiers. And with this knowledge of ourselves we believe we as a tribe have an obligation to our people. We don't disrespect our people and we don't fight against the United Blood Nation."

"Who?"

"The U.B.N.—United Blood Nation, which is the vanguard organization representing the Blood Nation."

"They got a constitution, too?"

"Yep," Killer replied.

My head was spinning with all of this. Clandestine Revolutionary Internationalist Party Soldiers—CRIPS. That was heavy. Nation and tribe, Kiswahili and unity—words that when spoken in isolation from anything tangible were meaningless.

But when they were applied in sync and sequence to concrete developments and everyday circumstances, they held meaning and could be seen as clearly as the bars that held us captive.

"Monster, Crip is a bad word only because we have turned inward on our community, preying on civilians and turning them against us. We are our own worst enemy. So C.C.O. has set out to re-establish CRIP as a positive influence in our community."

"Yeah, but how you plan on doing that?"

"With people like me and you who have clout and pull in our 'hoods. But we gotta be sharp, ya dig?"

"Yeah, yeah I hear you."

From then on Killer would pull me to the side and drop little lessons on me. Elimu talked to me, too. He was especially strong academically and was a great inspiration to all of us in the module.

There were ten C.C.O. members in the module, spread out on different tiers, all working their magic on the uncultured Crips. They began to transform Forty-eight Hours into a training station teaching military science, political science, Kiswahili, and Crip history. People knew more about American history than Crip history, so that was definitely an area of concentration. Most of us were receptive to their knowledge, but as always, there were those hardheads who had to "be their own man." They were tolerated initially, but when they began to disrupt the program they were dealt with and removed. Most complied out of the realization of C.C.O.'s presence in the population. San Quentin was the C.C.O. headquarters—though recently the Central Committee has been moved to Folsom—but they had well-disciplined cadres in every prison who, upon order, were ready to plant some steel in anyone's chest. More important, they were educators, teachers, and protectors of the Crip Nation.

It's a trip how fast their language became our language and how their ways became the ways of us all. Together we were a nation—the Blue Nation. The tribalism all but ceased. One cell was designated as the Community Canteen; everybody had to donate something out of their share of store-bought items to the Canteen. It was used for those who had nothing and no one to send them anything. At night—every night—instead of East Side–West Side chants we did the Universal Crip Cadence. Initially Elimu would lead, but he eventually taught me the words so I could conduct them. Everyone would be up on their feet, facing the tier, repeating the words, shouting after me. The sound was earth moving. We called it Machine in Motion.

"Monsta Kody!" Big Rebo from Compton would holler every night.

"Yeah?" I'd say.

"MONSTA KODY!" he'd holler again, just to make sure everyone knew what was going on.

"YEAH?" I'd reply again.

"MACHINE IN MOTION!" which came out with a rhythm like "MAH-SHEEN-IN-MOE-SHUUUN!"

And I'd answer "MACHINE IN MOTION!"

Then, from my left, Elimu would yell, "Handle that shit!"

And I'd begin.

C-R-I-P, C-R-I-P
Crip! Crip!
Minds of steel, hearts of stone,
Crip machine is movin' on.

Blue steel, blue flag,
Crippin' hard, no turnin' back.
Raise the "C" and hold it high,
Forever forward, do or die.
Spread yo' wings, raise yo' head,
We are risin' from the dead.
Who say?
"C" say!
Who the greatest?
"C" the greatest!
Can't stop, won't stop,
Will not ce stopped!

Soldiers! Soldiers!
War! War!
Lose one, kill two,
Never rest until you do.
Hear the spirit from the grave,
Got to Crip every day.
The "C" is strong, the world is weak,
Strength and loyalty is our key.
Across the sea and over the hill,
Gauge in hand we come to kill.
Coast to coast, state to state,
C-machine is on its way.
Who say?
"C" say!
Who the greatest?
"C" the greatest!
Can't stop, won't stop,
Will not ce stopped!

In sixty-nine the "C" was born,
Sixteen years and growin' strong.
From out the east came the "C,"
From the west came the rest.
East Side, West Side,
North Side, South Side,
Nationwide, unified,
CRIP! CRIP!

Raymond Washington did his best,
Cripped for years, now he rests.
Big Took, ce like him,
Dare to struggle, dare to win.
Mac and Satiy, they were down,
O.G. Compton, strong and proud.
Hoova Joe, he was right,
Cuttin' throats day and night.
Up the hill, down the hill,
Through the land, kill the Klan,
Kill the dog, on the wall,
Bring him down, bust his crown!
Who say?
"C" say!
Who the greatest?
"C" the greatest!
Can't stop, won't stop,
Will not ce stopped.

Keep the busters on the run,
If you catch him slice his tongue.
Back him up against the wall,

To his knees he will fall.
Hold your sword, make him beg,
No compassion, take his head!
Plant the "C" everywhere,
For we are those who will dare.
Uptown, downtown,
Blue flags all around.
Chitty-chitty bang-bang,
Nothin' but a Crip thang.
C-R-I-P! C-R-I-P!
Whata'ya want? (Freedom!)
When you want it? (Now!)
How you get it? (Power!)
When you need it? (Now!)
UHURU, SASA! UHURU, SASA!

Everyone would beam with jubilation at the close of each cadence call. The Nation lived!

The pigs were furious, and word was that still more C.C.O.s were coming down from the pen. Meanwhile, word also came down that there was a rat among us. I had searched out those whom Pee Wee had told me about, but they were not in the Forty-eight Hours. Another cat's fate was sealed when paperwork arrived—transcripts—revealing his testimony. I volunteered for the mission. The C.C.O.s wanted him stabbed, which was fine with me. Elimu, however, chose Rebo for the mission.

Later that day, in front of the nurse and everyone else, Rebo stabbed Richie Rich eight times with an ice pick. We went on immediate lockdown and O.S.S. began "interviews." Nothing was yielded, so we stayed on lockdown. For two weeks we were given no roof time, visits, showers—nothing. On our fourteenth day we were allowed visits. Then Sam from 107 Hoover, who was under investigation by C.C.O. for collaboration with O.S.S., knocked out a trustee in the visiting room and we went back on lockdown.

But this time we protested. We were instructed by C.C.O. to tear our wristbands off and refuse to give our last three— our I.D. numbers—at count time. We threw our wristbands on the tier, and when the pig came to our cells we went mute.

"Scott, last three?" asked the pig, looking down at the count board for confirmation.

Silence.

"*Scott,* what's your last three?"

Silence.

"Let me see your wristband."

Silence and no movement. I just gave him a cold stare, as did my cellmates, who flanked me wearing identical stares that said We ain't having it.

The pig started off to the next cell but never made it. An anonymous hand reached out and busted him in the head with a bar of soap. The pig dropped the count board and bolted for the grill gate.

"Monsta Kody?"

T-Ray from Nine-four Hoover had taken Rebo's place on the initiation of the cadence.

"Yeah?"

"MONSTA KODY?"

"YEAH?"

"MACHINE IN MOTION!"

And I began the cadence, knowing that the pigs would be back. But instead of coming on the tiers they were up on the catwalk, trying to identify the caller of the cadence. They stopped in front of our cell and stared. I got louder. A minute later my gate opened.

I stepped onto the tier, never stopping the cadence. Three pigs stood at the end, beckoning me to come to them. They would not come on the tier to get me, so instead of moving toward them I went in the opposite direction, continuing the cadence until it was over. Only then did I walk to them. My cellmates hung back as I moved past cell after cell, giving and receiving dap handshakes from the troops.

When I got to Elimu's cell he said, "Can't forgive, won't forget."

"Righteous," I replied and went on down the stairs to the red-faced pigs, who held huge flashlights.

"Unbutton that top button," one of them demanded.

I did that, no big deal.

"Turn around . . . "

I turned toward my cellmates and raised both hands high in the air, displaying a clenched fist with my right hand and a "C" with the left.

"Motherfucker," said one of the pigs, grabbing me by the back of my collar. "Didn't you—"

BAM!

I swung on the one closest to me, hitting him square in the face. I tried to swing my body around to get to the one behind my back, but he had a death grip on me. When I charged another instead, the one behind me literally jumped up on my back, choking me as he did. Briefly I heard the troops shouting in the background.

"Cuz, they fightin'! Monster's gettin' 'em up wit' 'em!"

The wrestling match was on, and we were all over the floor.

I was kicking, elbowing, scratching, jerking, and swearing, while simultaneously trying to protect my private parts. In less than a minute the cavalry arrived and I was swarmed by pigs. The only thing that saved me from being beaten to death was that there were too many pigs vying for a punch, kick, groin shot, or insult. I don't even remember hearing "nigger," but I'm sure it was said fifty times.

After they'd beaten the hell out of me, I was cuffed and whisked off to a holding cell. I screamed the whole way.

"CAN'T STOP, WON'T STOP, MUTHAFUCKAS! CAN'T STOP, WON'T STOP!"

I wound up in 1750 High Power, maximum security—the story of my life.

The troops tore the module up, burned their blankets and mattresses and, where possible, engaged the pigs. I was charged with conspiracy, assault, and arson, but the charges were later dismissed.

While in High Power I met Suma, the general of C.C.O. He said he had heard of me and that if I needed anything to let him know. He and Tony Stacy, another C.C.O. member, had come down from Folsom, but O.S.S. had locked them in 1750 right away. Peabody, general of the U.B.N., was there, too.

On a visit one night, Tony said that they had come down to try to hook me up. They wanted me and Insane from Playboy Gangster. I was flattered but skeptical. Once in the organization, you were in for life. He asked if I wanted to take a stand and I told him I'd think about it.

"Monsta," he said frankly, "you've done too much damage to the Crip Nation. We can't let you continue to kill our citizens. Either you hook up or you must be destroyed for the good of the C-Nation."

I was dumbfounded. I couldn't speak, couldn't hear. It was practically what Crazy Keith had said after the shoot-out. Was C.C.O. also the new West Side Syndicate?

"Was that . . . " I started to ask, but couldn't.

"Let me know what you decide so I can inform Suma."

I walked back to the module in a trance.

The following day I called Big Frogg and asked him what he thought. He was under the old constitution of Blue Magic, which had been combined with Blue Machine to form the Consolidated Crip Organization—a synthesis of the two.

"No," said Frogg angrily. "Don't do it, homie. It ain't for everybody."

"What'cha mean?"

"I'll be down there to see you tomorrow, all right? But don't do nuthin' till then."

I hung up and went to my cell, confused.

The next day I went to court and missed Frogg's visit. The following day I told Tony I was ready—that I was in. When I went to court again the following day I met Bwana from Hoover—a C.C.O. member who had also come down from the pen. He filled me in on small things. When I got back from court, the constitution was on my desk. To this day I don't know how it got there, as Tony and Suma were clear across the module in another section.

I was trembling even before I began to read it. I had to be sure about this, but it really was do or die. Though I wasn't actually being forced into it, I did feel a little pressured. In the end, it was my choice, and I took it. I read the constitution and afterward burned it, as instructed. I was *in,* hooked up, a member, a comrade, a soldier. I turned all of this over again and again in my mind. I didn't feel much different and didn't feel like I knew any more than before I'd read the constitution.

Late that same night a new brotha came on our tier and was put in the last cage. When Maurice from Five-Six Syndicate asked his name, he replied Salahudin Al-Muntaquin. He was a member of the Black Guerrilla Family—B.G.F.—a quasi-revolutionary organization with an awesome military machine. They had clashed with Crips several times in prison and supposedly had killed Pee Wee from East Coast in Tracy in 1983. My intelligence was up to date on him and when he said his name I knew who he was. I made immediate plans to stab him. Oldman, who was my neighbor, made a knife out of plastic and sent it to me. I was the tier tender and planned on spearing him the following morning when I came out to pour the milk.

The next morning I went down to his cell, the knife tied to a broomstick, hoping to catch him asleep. When I got there he was up doing Salat. He was a Muslim. He stood up and came to the bars.

"How you doing this morning, brotha?"

I was momentarily dazed by his humbleness, for we had always heard that B.G.F.s were antagonistic toward Crips, offensive and hostile.

"I'm fine," I said, looking for an opening. I had the broomstick on the head of the broom, but not screwed in. At the other end, covered by my hand, was the knife.

"You a B.G.F., ain't you?" I said, hoping he'd get hostile.

"I am a revolutionary," he said, "and the weapon is unnecessary. I'm not your enemy."

"What?" I said, noting that my hand was no longer around the weapon, but on the handle.

"Do you know Suma?" he asked.

"Yeah, that's my comrade," I declared proudly.

"Ask him about me. He knows me well."

At that I went back down the tier and repeated everything to Oldman. He agreed we should wait on Suma.

That afternoon I got a note from Suma saying that C.C.O. had no beef with B.G.F. and that if I could, to watch out for Salahudin. I'd almost made a costly mistake.

Salahudin and I eventually became good friends, and it was he who named me Sanyika.

Not long after that I left County with a sentence of seven years in state prison. My life has never been the same.

10

RECONNECTED

I arrived at Chino state prison on June 5, 1985, eager to begin serving my seven-year sentence. As soon as I got off the bus a confrontation started brewing with a Chicano who kept looking at me. We were herded into R & R like cattle. "Nuts to butts" is how the Correctional Officer (C.O.) explained the way he wanted us lined up. I was relieved that he didn't have a flashlight. We were crowded into a cold, dim room with puddles of water on the floor, as if the ceiling had been leaking.

"All right, listen up," the C.O. said in a deep baritone that seemed to shake shit loose from the walls. "The first thing I want you to do is take off your wristbands and throw them in this box. Next, I want you to strip naked and have a seat. If you want to send your clothes home, hold on to them. If not, throw them in this cart. Once you've stripped naked, we can follow through with the procedure."

All the while this Chicano kept staring at me. Every time I looked at him he was looking at me. Even when I looked elsewhere, keeping him in my peripheral vision, he was watching me. I had already been briefed on our relationship with the Southern Mexicans: C.C.O. and the Mexican mafia—the Southern Mexican vanguard—were at war.

"If you think one of them has detected you," Suma had told me on a visit, "take off first."

Now here was this dude burning holes in the side of my damn head. I played it cool and went through the procedures that the C.O. was explaining.

"Put your hands over your head. Let me see your armpits. Open your mouth and wiggle your tongue. Lift up your nut sack. Turn around, bend at the waist, spread your cheeks and give me five big coughs. Let me see under your left foot. Now your right . . ."

This was nothing new. We had to do this every time we came from court in L.A. County Jail. At first it bothered me a lot. I felt like a diseased piece of meat being examined by some pigs at an auction. A bunch of guys getting their kicks off of watching forty naked men moving into different positions of humiliation at the command of a voice. In all my days, months, and years of being a prisoner, I've never seen one of these searches yield anything.

What are they expecting? Some pig says, "Okay, bend at the waist and give me five loud coughs," and *plink!* a knife falls out of a man's ass? Although I know that prisoners do secrete weapons, drugs, and other things in their butts, the pigs haven't ever found anything on the searches I've been involved in. This process is just another ritual designed to degrade.

When I got dressed I started walking over to the Chicano who kept looking at me, but the C.O. asked me where the fuck I was going. I said to the head, to which he replied that it was behind me. And I'll be damned if it wasn't. A small urinal hung on the wall, closer to where I was than the Chicano. I acted as if I was using it, then sat back down. I had to be slicker.

But now the Chicano knew I was trying to get to him. To my surprise, he stopped looking at me, and as I looked more and more at him he seemed vaguely familiar. I knew I had seen him somewhere, but because there were no Chicanos living in or around my 'hood, I knew it had to be from a jail. But which one, and when? I continued to eye him, much like he had eyed me. I pulled up face after face, place after place on my memory bank's screen, but I kept drawing blanks. In my enemy file I saw only the faces of Chicano gang members who had been running with the Sixties and, more than ever, dying with the Sixties. We've always tried to be equal-opportunity killers.

"Everybody stand up and follow the man in front of you. You are going to be fingerprinted several times and have your photo taken. One set of prints goes to the Justice Department, one to the F.B.I., one to the State Capitol, one to the . . ."

I didn't even try to hear the rest. Hell, I had heard it all before in Youth Authority, where prints are taken and sent to the same groups of people. In youth camps run by the county, you are treated as a statistic by group. But in Youth Authority, which is run by the state of California, you become a potential case study as an individual. The F.B.I. and the rest of the authorities have the names of everyone who has ever been to

Youth Authority in a huge data bank in Washington. When you go to state or federal prison, they simply update their data bank. If you get involved in anything they think is noteworthy—and everything is noteworthy to a hunter—they put it in your file in their data bank. They know what you may do long before it happens, as well as what you have the potential to do. Because gang actions are seen as self-destructive and not a threat to the security of this country, it's not necessary for them to stop you. But if you begin to question the right of those in authority or resist the chains that constantly bind you, then you'll be elevated as a security risk and more than likely put in the Agitators Index file. I've been in the Agitators Index since 1986.

I took the photos and went through the mundane routine of prints. (As if mine had changed since I'd left Y.A.) At my first opportunity I stepped to the Chicano, surprising him.

"What's up, man, you know me or somethin'? Huh? You got a problem wit' me?"

He was shorter than I and weighed thirty pounds less, which really didn't mean a thing, because in prison, fighting was for those you liked. Stabbing was for the enemy.

"Ain't your name Kody, Monster Kody?"

"Yeah, that's me. Why? What up?"

"You don't remember me?"

"Naw," I said, eyeing him suspiciously. "From where?"

"Juvenile hall and camp. I'm Cooper from El Monte Flores." And he broke into a wide, boyish grin.

Yes, I did know him! He and I were friends from the seventies. Every time I went to the Hall he was there. When I went to camp, he was there. I missed him in Y.A., but now here he was again in prison.

"Goddamn, yeah, I'm knowin' you. What up, Copper? How much time you got?"

"Fifteen to life. And you?"

"Just seven."

"I'll be here when you get back!"

"Fuck that, I ain't comin' back."

We talked a bit more before we had to break it up. This was not camp or juvenile hall, where our relationships were not governed by politics. This was state prison, where talking to the wrong person could very well get you killed. I wondered if he had gotten hooked up.

The group of us went through a few other stages of questions and answers before having to go get blood tests, immunizations, and physicals. After that we were given our bed numbers. Chino is the reception center for southern California. You go through all your indoctrination there: school testing, health testing, and a visit with a counselor for placement in a permanent prison. One usually stays at Chino for a month or two before being transferred. It is old, dirty, rat and roach infested, and always cold. I was sent to Cypress Hall and put on the third tier. My cellmate was a civilian.

"How you doing, black man?" my cellie said with a big smile.

"Cool, asante."

"Oh, you speak that Swahili, huh?" he asked.

"A little. My comrades have been teaching me. You?"

"Naw, but I want to learn."

"Right."

"Do you smoke cigarettes?"

"Naw, never have."

"Oh, 'cause I have some tobacco. But if it bothers you I'll smoke only on the yard."

"Naw, it's cool, it don't bother me," I replied.

He seemed like a cool cat, right up until he noticed the knife in my hand.

"Man, where you get that? You gonna get us put in the Hole, man!"

He was bug-eyed with hysteria, frantically crossing and uncrossing his arms, and his feet would not keep still.

"I keistered it and brought it from L.A. County Jail. It's better to be caught with one than without one. We are at war, haven't you heard?"

"War?!"

"Shhh," I said and reduced him to silence with a mad-dog stare.

"Look, man," he began in a lower tone, "I don't know what you talkin' 'bout. I ain't involved in no war. I ain't got no enemies. I got two years, man, and I want to go home."

I looked at him and remembered what Salahudin had told me about brothas in the pen.

"Sanyika," he'd said, which was what he always called me in place of Monster once I'd accepted it, "Afrikans in the pen will use every excuse they can think of to avoid aiding you in a crisis. They will cite the Bible, bad health, the weather, any and everything to get out of having to endure perhaps a little hardship as the expense for saving your life. We are neglectful like that. But let a Chicano give a distress call and you'll have a hundred of them to deal with." Prophecy.

"Check this out," I said to him. "This is my weapon, my beef. I'm not getting rid of it. If you feel safe without one, fine. I don't. If I had known you was gonna trip out I never would have let you know I had it. I'm a soldier and I ain't gonna let nobody stick shit in me without me stickin' somethin' in them, ya dig?"

"Aw, man, it ain't like that in here. Everybody cool with one another. Man, we—"

"How long you been here?"

"A week, but I—"

"You been to the pen before?"

"No, but I—"

"Well shut the fuck up then, 'cause you don't know shit, man. You don't know nothin' 'bout the politics here, man, *nothin'!*"

"Politics?"

"B.G.F., E.M.E., A.B., N.F., C.C.O., U.B.N., V.G., T.S., Four-fifteen . . . You ever hear of them, huh?"

"Naw, sound like some code or somethin'."

"Fool, they run these muthafuckin' places, man. At any time they can have you murdered, man. But you don't hear me, do you? You think just because there ain't no guns going off 'round here now that everybody cool? Huh? All it takes is one order and any one of the cool people you kick it with will put a piece of steel right through your neck! Ain't no 'cool' in here."

He was visibly frightened now. I had brought the raw reality of our situation fully down on his shoulders and said, in effect, Carry this! He was already sagging under the weight.

"Let me see that weapon," he finally said.

The next day I was told to roll my property up and move to another hall. I still don't know why. I was put in Sycamore

Hall in a one-man cell. I was then called to the lieutenant's office.

Lieutenant Ballard, the gang coordinator, held the briefing. He was a huge, dark-complexioned New Afrikan with a contagious smile.

"Monster Kody Scott," he began, with a knowing grin. "I been hearing about you. I knew you was coming and I'm supposed to lock you up in the Hole. But seeing how you ain't done nothing—yet—I got no cause to slam you."

"Who wants me locked up?" I asked seriously.

"White folks, who else?"

"But for what?"

"You really don't know, huh?"

"Naw, I just got here."

"Well, it seems that some of your folks—C.C.O . . . " and with that he stared hard at me, " . . . have killed a correctional sergeant in San Quentin. So they want all you C.C.O.s locked up."

"Oh, is that right?"

"That's right. But I think the B.G.F.s did it, to tell you the truth."

"Can I go now?"

"Yeah, Kody, you can go. But there's one thing I want to ask you. Did Suma hook you up?"

"No, man, I ain't no C.C.O."

"But—"

I turned and walked out the door before he could finish. I was told that the only way they could classify you as a member of a prison gang is if you admitted to it or they found a constitution on you. Later I learned that this was wrong.

I went back to my block feeling pretty good about what

I'd heard from Ballard. Comrades had put in some work on a pig. Fuck the pigs. I was so full of hatred that I could have been ordered to kill a pig—or anybody—and not thought twice about it.

Back in the unit the homies were playing around, just grabbing each other and stuff, when a pig hollered out the warning.

"STOP! FIGHT!"

Everyone froze and looked to see where the fight was, not realizing that he was referring to them. The pig came running down the tier like a madman, and when he got to the homies he began to cuff Li'l Man up. Everyone was dumbfounded, but no one said a thing. So I did.

"They was just playin', they wasn't fightin', man."

"Don't you tell me, I know what they were doing. Fighting, that's what."

"You stupid pig, if I had a gun I'd blow yo' brains all over that silly-ass uniform you wearin'."

I constructed my hand like a weapon and aimed it right in his face.

"Boom," I said.

He continued cuffing Li'l Man and another homie from Hoover and told everyone else to lock it up, which we did. Ten minutes later the pig came back with a sergeant and two other pigs.

"That's him, sir, the one with the gun."

"What?" I said.

"Roll your shit up. You going to the Hole," the sergeant told me.

"For what?"

"Threatening staff."

When I got to Palm Hall—the Hole—Lieutenant Ballard wanted to see me. His office was actually located in the Hole, so he called me in to see him.

"They gotcha, I see."

"Yeah, but that's bullshit, man."

"Listen to me, Kody. These folks is scared to death of y'all in the first place. And now that you have organized y'all selves, that makes it worse. Anything you do they gonna be on you, man. Anything. You young, black, and strong. That's why they can't see you out in the street. In here, you organized, unified, and uncontrollable, so you gotta be put in the Hole. Be cool, man, or you'll be in the Hole for your whole seven years."

"I'll try, man."

I wanted to say more but couldn't articulate it. I wanted to know why "white folks" hated us so much, were so afraid of us. I had a thousand questions, but Ballard was still a pig, New Afrikan or not.

I was put on the first tier in the last cell. My neighbor was Chocolate from Four Tray Hoover. He was also a C.C.O. member, as well as one of the Hoovers who had stabbed the East Coasts in 4800. He had two knives. I told him what they had me for and we talked about other things. I asked if he felt that he'd be in trouble with the organization for participating in tribalism. He said that he didn't know, but that he had been worried about it. He had a pretty good grasp on Kiswahili and said he'd help me with mine.

Not an hour later, after Ballard had gone home, an American pig with an enormous belly came to my cell.

"Scott?"

"Yeah."

"We made a mistake by putting you over here, you belong in Cypress Deep Seg, so—"

"Deep Seg?" I said in a what-the-fuck-is-that voice.

"Aw, cuz, it's fucked up in Deep Seg," Chocolate said. "Man, why y'all doin' him like that, he don't belong in no damn Deep Seg," he said to the pig.

"Get your shit together, Scott," the pig ordered, ignoring Chocolate. "We'll be back in five minutes to get you."

He walked away.

"Eh, comrade, what is Deep Seg?" I asked, perplexed.

"It's only four little tiny cells way in the back of Cypress on the first tier. It's fucked up back there. It's for total fuck-ups."

"Damn! I don't know why they trippin' on me like this. Talkin' 'bout a mistake. That's bullshit!"

"Scott, you 'bout ready?" said the pig, who had returned and was standing in front of my cage. He'd been gone for forty seconds.

I didn't say a thing, just backed up to the bars so he could chain me up for the escort across the hall to Deep Segregation. The pig tried to make small talk, but I didn't respond. How could he make conversation, and expect a response, with a man he was putting in a Hole inside a Hole?

I was marched through so many gates and doors that I felt like Maxwell Smart. It was depressing. When we finally got to the small cage—and I couldn't believe how small—I was made to strip and go through the degrading motions. One last stab at my humanity. I was locked behind a series of bars, then a door with a heavy plate of steel that, when closed, could isolate me from any light whatsoever. There was no light in the cell. There was an opening in the upper left corner, and from the back of the cell an outside floodlight stuck through, protected by wire mesh. The bed was a hard, concrete slab no wider than a child's little red wagon. The sink and toilet were attached together and both reeked with atrocious fumes of bile, defecation, urine, and God knows what else.

Before he left I asked the pig if I could have some cleaning material for the cell, and he replied that I wouldn't be able to see anything no way and that I'd get used to the smell in a few days. And with that he closed the big door and let down the heavy metal covering over my window, leaving me in total darkness.

"Hey," I hollered, reaching for the bars in front of me. "Hey, turn on the lights. Hey! I know you hear me!"

But I got no response.

I felt my way over to the bed and sat down. I thought long and hard about what Muhammad had called repression, about what Elimu had taught me about resistance, and what Ballard had said about the white folks' fear of us. I thought that I hadn't even resisted yet, but still I was being treated like this. Little did I know that I had been resisting all my life. By not being a good black American I was resisting. But my resistance was retarded because it had no political objective. I was an unconscious resister.

Repression is funny. It can breed resistance, though it doesn't mean that the resistance will be political, positive, or revolutionary.

So I sat there in total darkness, in total silence, repressed to the max. I had nothing to feed on that could explain this level of action to me. There was no mattress on the concrete, so I lay back on the hard slab and went over the words in my head that, while unconnected, didn't have any meaning to me whatsoever. As I lay there I remembered my mother coming to Y.T.S. to see me, crying and shaking her head.

"Baby, I got something to tell you. Something you are old enough to know now."

"What is it, Mom?"

"Scott is not your father. Baby, your last name isn't supposed to be Scott. Oh, Kody, I . . . listen, do you remember seeing this book?"

In her hands she was holding a blue-and-white book with a football player in uniform on the cover.

"Yeah, I've seen that book around the house."

"Well, this is your father, baby. His name is Dick Bass. He played football for the Rams."

"Wait a minute, Mom, I'm confused here. Who is Scott, then? I mean whose father is he?"

"He's Shaun, Kerwin, and Kendis's father. Kevin and Kim have the same father, but he's not Scott."

"But . . ."

"Wait, let me explain. When I was pregnant with you, Scott and I were not getting along. Dick and I had met through your godparents, Ray and Della."

My godfather was Ray Charles, the famous musician.

"Dick was there when I needed him," she went on. "Scott knew you were not his child and asked me to get an abortion, but I refused. I wanted you, Kody. This is why he and I would fight all the time. He hated you, baby."

"That's why he never took me anywhere like he did Kerwin and Shaun?"

"Yes, baby."

"So, where is . . . Dick?"

"I don't know. He . . ."

"Mom, I'm not even gonna worry about it 'cause I'm a man now. I don't *need* no daddy. For what?"

"Kody, I have tried my hardest to raise you guys up right. But I had to work hard every day just to feed you by myself. You know Scott and I got a divorce in 1969 and there has not been a man in your lives since. I wonder if that's how I lost you and Shaun to the streets. You guys have turned from my darling little ones into savage little animals and I just don't know what to do no more. I really don't."

"But Mom, it's not your fault, it's not your fault," I said over and over.

As I lay on that slab I now said it over and over to myself. "It's not your fault." And I hated that muthafucka Scott and Dick Bass. What could Mom do? She could only be our father for so long. I do remember not being taken on any trips like the others and being treated differently by Scott. When the others were on trips, I would be alone and sad. Sometimes Della would come and take me to different places, or I'd spend the weekend at Ray and Della's house. My only consolation for not being treated like the others was that Ray Charles was my godfather, so I'd always have new toys, new bicycles, and Hot Wheels.

Mom would pretend that the reason I couldn't go on the trips was that she wanted me with her because I was her favorite. She tried very hard to keep my spirits up, even when hers were down. Scott would take the others to Houston to visit his mother, their grandmother. But I was an illegitimate child and he was ashamed of me, hated me, Mom said. I never met my grandmother.

I fell into a rough sleep and don't know how long I'd been

out when someone started beating on the steel covering over the window in my door.

"Get up," said the voice, distinctively American. "Get up!"

Irritated by being awakened, and generally mad, I shouted back. "What, muthafucka, what?"

"Hey, I got some paperwork for you to sign, Scott."

"I ain't signin' shit, and my name ain't no fuckin' Scott!"

"Are you refusing to sign?"

Not only did I refuse to sign, I refused to talk anymore. Why? What else could they do to me if I didn't? I stretched my sheets out as best I could and tried to go back to sleep, but I couldn't. My eyes had adjusted to the darkness and I could at least see my hand in front of my face, though barely. As I lay there I could hear rats scurrying across the cell floor. It sounded like there were a lot of them. I cursed the pigs under my breath.

The next night I was given a mattress. When the lights came on, ten rats darted for cover. The only reason I knew a whole day had passed when they brought the mattress was that they'd brought me three meals before that. The pigs expected me to beg or snivel about the conditions, but when they opened the door, I walked to the bars to receive the paper plate of food they slid under the door and took it without saying a word. Can't stop, won't stop.

I fed myself on the strength of the C-Nation, on seeing and knowing of the existence of a unified, organized Crip Nation. I tried to feed on what Muhammad had taught me, but it was too complicated. The words were too political, so I went with what I knew best and had seen for most of my life. And I endured.

I was kept in that cell, in the dark—except when they

brought meals—for a week. One morning an American pig came to feed me and when he turned the light on I gave an involuntary moan.

Since I was always in the dark, the bright light hurt my eyes. It hurt so much that I couldn't open them to get my meals. After three days of ice-pick pain through my brain from the stabbing light, I'd decided it was better not to try to adjust to it. I knew that to stand straight up, turn ninety degrees to my left, and take three steps would put me at the bars. I'd feel my way down the bars until I'd find the paper plate, and then I'd retrace my steps to the bed. Most of the time they'd turn the light off immediately after they'd closed the door. I'd eat with my eyes closed till they doused it. They wouldn't say anything to me and I wouldn't say anything to them.

But on this day, I had been caught with my eyes open, and the light blasted my brain into little pieces. The pain was overwhelming, and I moaned in response to it.

"Hey, Scott, you all right? How long you been back here?"

I didn't say anything. I just walked blindly to the bars, retrieved my paper plate, and ate with my eyes tightly closed. He stood there and watched me. I knew he was there, I felt him in my space, looking, thinking. But there was no room in my space for him. He was an intruder, a violator. He had to be expelled.

"What you lookin' at, man?"

Startled, he stammered and said, "How'd you know I was here if your eyes were closed?"

"I feel you. Will you leave now?"

"I'm gonna get you outta here, Scott."

I gave no reply and waited for him to leave before I continued to eat.

I finished my meal and took my morning walk—three

steps to the front, turn, four steps to the back. I'd repeat this for a few hundred steps, then sit back down for an hour or so and listen to the rats eat the remains of my food. We had come to an overstanding, the rats and I. When I was on the floor the rats yielded. Like in Congress: the rats yield the floor and recognize Monster Kody from the Crips. And when I got on my red-wagon slab bed, I recognized the rats from Deep Seg. I like it like that—mutual respect.

Suddenly the rats stopped abruptly and darted for cover. This told me someone was coming. Sure enough, the spear of light shot out like some damn lightning bolt, but I'd prepared for it and it missed me.

"Scott," said the voice of my earlier invader, "gather your things, bud, you're outta here."

"Can you turn the light out when you leave?"

"Leave? No, Scott, we are letting you out of Deep Seg and putting you in Palm Hall."

I sat there and waited for the door to close, a cruel joke played on a repressed man. But it didn't. He was still standing there.

"Who is that with you?"

"It's me," said a female voice, "the M.T.A., Scott."

This was the prison nurse.

"Am I really leaving here?"

"Yes, Scott, you been back here too long."

I gathered my things: two sheets and a worn blanket. I rolled them, sleeping-bag style, and backed to the bars to be chained up. I was escorted slowly across the hall to the normal Hole. The nurse examined me, telling me to open my eyes to let them adjust to the light. When I did, the pain was not as intense as it had been in Deep Seg. The floodlight in that tiny space was one thousand watts—deliberately so. I hadn't been in prison two weeks and was already subjected to this type of treatment. From the start there was perfect hate. I was grateful for a shower and a change of clothes.

From Chino I was sent to the prison at Soledad. I was taken off the bus and put directly in the Hole. I was put in the cell with my li'l homie, Li'l Rat. I taught him the small amount of Kiswahili that I knew. He asked if I was hooked up and I told him I was. He was curious and wanted to be in the organization, but I told him to be certain that it was what he wanted to do. Just because I was in didn't mean he should be in. I told him to think about it.

That day I was let out to the general population. Li'l Spike, C-Dog, and Rattone from the set were out on the mainline and greeted me cordially. We talked and kicked it about old times, but they sensed something wasn't right when they found me reluctant to speak on the war between the Sixties and us. I told them I wasn't into the set tripping–tribalism thing anymore. I told them that it was now all about the unification of the C-Nation under the government of the C.C.O. They freaked.

"Cuz, you hooked up?" Rattone asked. He'd been down since he and my brother had been captured in 1981 for the payback killings in response to my shooting.

"Yeah, I'm in. You?"

"Naw, never was my style. I know all of them, though. Where they hook you up at?"

"The County."

"Damn, cuz," said Li'l Spike, "why you go out like that?"

"What you mean out like that?"

It was the first time I'd heard someone say anything remotely against the C.C.O.

"I mean, the set is the only organization you need," he continued. "It held you fine till you came to prison. So why it won't hold you now?"

"I ain't left the set, I just think that we could be stronger combined as a nation than as a little set. After all, we all Crips."

"I kill Crips," Li'l Spike declared. "I'm a gangsta."

"He's right, Monster," added Rattone. "Remember what Rayside used to tell us 'bout that—"

"Fuck Rayside!" I exploded. "Where is he now, huh? That shit was cool out there as long as we had guns in our hands and dope in our systems. But that Sixty, Nine-O killa shit ain't gonna work for us here, cuz. It ain't gonna work! We got too many other enemies to be trippin' on one another. Too many! Until Rayside come to prison and walk on the yard and see what we gotta deal wit' daily, monthly, *yearly,* cuz can't tell me shit!"

"I don't know, homie," C-Dog said. He was the youngest of us all.

"How many Sixties here?" I asked them.

"Three."

"How many Nine-O's?"

"None."

"How many Mexicans from the south, and how many Nazis?"

"Shit, 'bout three hundred or so, but—"

"You see?" I said.

"But they ain't killed no Eight Trays," Rattone countered.

"They've killed black people . . . they've killed Crips. It's just a matter of time, Ratt. You been down five years. You know!"

"Yeah, you right."

"I'll always be from Eight Tray, that's my neighborhood. But I was born black."

"Monster, you trippin'," Li'l Spike said.

"Naw, Spike, *you* trippin'! I ain't ashamed of being black, I know I come from Afrika. I am a soldier for my people, all citizens of the C-Nation."

"Yeah, all right, Monster. We gonna see how long you think like that," Li'l Spike said, looking over the top of his Locs at the others.

"Yeah," I said, standing to walk away. "You'll see."

My commanding officer was Kidogo—Whiskey from Santana Block—who I had known from the county jail back in the early eighties. But the line was being run by Drack from Six-Deuce East Coast. He had been there two or three years. There were thirteen of us—C.C.O.—in Soledad. I was in charge of C-wing. It was my duty to make sure that no Crips came out on the tiers with shower thongs on, because this was a security risk. One couldn't very well defend himself in shower shoes. I had to make sure that there were at least two knives out on the tier and available whenever we were out in the wing or the dayroom. I designated two people to carry the weapons. Any time one of us took a shower, the area was cordoned off and secured. A quiet period was designated from eleven P.M. till seven A.M. Every Saturday was mass exercise day. All two hundred and twelve Crips would form three huge circles on the yard and go through the routine.

Kidogo was dissatisfied with Drack and petitioned the

Central Committee to remove him. He had to go to Folsom for court in a stabbing incident and said he'd handle it down there. I was left second in command. When Kidogo returned, Drack was removed for ineptitude and poor leadership. Kidogo and I forged ties with the other new Afrikan groups there—U.B.N., Vanguards, B.G.F.s and 415s. We networked with communication, military intelligence, and in some cases, weaponry. We got our hacksaw blades from the 415s who worked as plumbers. I had Crips in C-wing cutting steel off of everything to make weapons. There was never a shortage of knives or people to make them.

One afternoon I came into the wing from the yard and found Red from Shotgun showering with no cover. I went in the dayroom, and there was Shark from Harlem watching soap operas! I asked him who had security and he said he did. I told him to go and cover Red in the shower. But Doc from West Covina, who was on the disciplinary crew—those who were used to stab and beat law breakers—said he'd supply cover for Red. Well, that wasn't his job. So I again told Shark to go handle it. When he left I called over Zacc from Hoover and began discussing the lax atmosphere. Unexpectedly, Shark came stomping back into the dayroom saying how tired he was of being a security guard and how he wanted some action. I asked him where Red was. He said he had left him in the shower.

I exploded and slapped him hard across the face. He responded by reaching for his waistband, where he kept the knife. But before he could draw it, Doc stepped up and put his knife to Shark's throat. I disarmed Shark and slapped him again.

"If you would have pulled the kisu out I would have killed you! Now get yo' sorry ass outta my face!"

He staggered out of the dayroom, holding his face.

I gave the kisu to Zacc and he took up the slack at the shower. Doc stayed by me.

That evening I held a meeting in the back of the unit to explain the importance of security.

"Today we had a problem with our security," I began, looking disgustedly at Shark, "that we shouldn't have had. Don't y'all know what's going on in Folsom and San Quentin? War, that's what. And it's just a matter of time before the Surrats try to strike at us here. We gotta be ready! They ain't gonna walk up to our face and stab us. They gonna bring they sneaky asses up from behind and stab us in the back! So we have to watch out for each another. Secure one another, dig? And another thing, I want to apologize to the community for disciplining Shark in public when I should have taken it to a discreet area. It won't happen again."

A few others spoke and the meeting was adjourned.

The next day I was given orders by Kidogo to plant one in a renegade from Folsom. The following week G-wing erupted in an all-out knife fight. The Southern Mexicans attacked the Northern Mexicans and the pigs started blasting away. The Americans were herded into the dayroom. Since the Southern Mexicans and the Americans were allies and the New Afrikans and Northerners were allies, the New Afrikans attacked the Americans, stabbing seven of them. One prisoner was shot and killed.

It was during this time that the New Afrikan community at Soledad began to get flack from one particular pig. That one particularly racist guard was attacked. I was implicated in the accident and three days later, Buck, Zaire, and I were locked in solitary confinement for the incident and given forty-eight months in Security Housing Unit (S.H.U.). Buck and I were sent to San Quentin and Zaire was sent to Folsom. We appealed the decision to put us in the Hole based on confidential information, but the appeal was denied. They did, however, reduce our sentence to twenty-eight months.

I cannot begin to describe how I felt as the prison bus rolled through the massive gates at San Quentin. An incredible sense of destiny seemed to overtake me. And with each successive foot the bus moved forward, additional layers of the "old me" seemed to peel away. When the bus swung around the lower yard and I saw the Native Nation—American Indian—tepees and sweat lodges enclosed by a chainlink fence, I sat upright in my seat.

"This is the house that George Jackson built," Buck said. He had been here several times. "You'll feel the comrade strong here. Bro, you'll read books here, see things here that are gonna change the way you walk, talk, and think. This is the best place for an aspiring young revolutionary. This is repression at its best."

We filed off the bus under the watchful eye of gunmen with mini-14s. The shotgun had been phased out because it failed to disable attacking prisoners. The mini-14 is an assault weapon. It shoots a .223 round, as does the M-16 and the AR-15. We moved from the bus to R & R, guards on the huge industrial wall's catwalk watching us from above.

San Quentin is one hundred years older than Chino, and it shows. As soon as we got inside of R & R, the pigs took Buck to the Adjustment Center, which is like the triple-max unit. I would be spared this time and only put in double-max. I was being sent to East block, and two others—a Chicano and a Native brother—were being taken to North block. They were escorted out first. Ten minutes later I was taken out of R & R in leg and wrist chains, marched up across the upper yard and into East block.

When I stepped in I was astounded. I was dwarfed by the unit. It looked like a huge slave ship. There were five tiers, and they were so long that if you were at one end it would be impossible for you to recognize someone at the other end. I was put in a holding cage and stripped. The chains were removed, and I was handcuffed. The awesome size of the block continued to blow me away. I was apprehensive, as well. Damn, this was the major league, the big house, the *real* penitentiary. It was the ultimate test of faith, courage, and strength.

I was taken up two flights of stairs to the second tier and walked down. I got mad-dog stares from every occupant in the tiny cells along the way. New Afrikans, Chicanos, and Americans, all in single-man cells. I was put in 2-East-26. My neighbor in 25 was an American, and to my right in number 27 was a Chicano.

Once I got in my cell the handcuffs were removed. There was a bed—with bedsprings that could be used to make ice-pick knives—a sink, and a toilet. There were two circular vents, one above the sink and another below it.

The American and the Chicano were talking to each other, seemingly about nothing in particular. But just by hearing them talk I knew that the Chicano was a Southern Mexican and the American was a Nazi (the Unholy Alliance). I began to feel around under the bed for loose metal, something I could pull or yank out that I could fashion into a weapon for spearing.

Might as well start my time here off right. One of these cats is going to get speared.

I found a piece of metal loose enough to get my hand under, so I slid halfway beneath the bed, braced my foot against the wall, and began to pull violently. Heave-ho, heave-ho. Back and forth I pulled until it moved with ease under pressure. Just a few . . . more . . . *plink!* And I had it—a piece of bed railing eleven inches long. Now I had to sharpen it, get some newspaper, and roll me up a spear. I'd attach the blade and then just wait for either the Surrat or the Mzungu (European) to come out.

"Hey, twenty-six?"

The American and Chicano went silent.

"Hey, twenty-six?"

Twenty-six . . . that was me. Someone was calling my cell number.

"Hey, twenty-six?!"

"Yeah."

"Get that line in front of your cell."

I looked out on the tier and a clear medicine bag with a white, thin line attached to it was in front of my cell, so I retrieved it.

"Pull it," said the sender.

Attached to the line was a kite. I opened it and read.

Salamu Ndugu,
Where did you come from? I am Li'l Bit from Bounty Hunter. Next to you is an A.B. and on the other side is an E.M.E. Stay up, stay alert.

Blood Love,
Li'l Bit

"Hey, Li'l Bit."

"Yeah?"

"I need a pen to get back."

"All right, pull the line."

I retrieved the pen and wrote back telling him that I was Sanyika from C.C.O. and that I came from Soledad. I told him of his people from Bounty Hunter who were down there and I added that I planned to bust on my neighbors at the first opportunity. He wrote back telling me to hold on that, he had to get to his tier captain. He withdrew his line from my cell and flung it down the tier toward the front with an ease that came from experience. When he pulled his line back, there was another line attached to it. He told me to grab it. I was now plugged into the tier captain. He told me to pull, and I reeled in his line. There was another kite attached to the end. It read:

> Hujambo Sanyika,
> I am Italo from the Black Guerrilla Family. Perhaps you know some of my tribesmen? All your people are in the back. We, B.G.F. and B.L., have a peace treaty with the A.B. and E.M.E. on this tier. I suggest that you get at your folks about a cell move.
>
> In struggle,
> Italo

Peace treaty? What was that? I wrote him and said that I overstood about their agreement with the Brands and the Flies, but C.C.O. ain't got no treaty with them. But out of respect for the brothas on the tier, I wouldn't jeopardize them. He then sent me *Wretched of the Earth* by Frantz Fanon, which was no good to me because I couldn't read that well. And at that time, Franz seemed very, very heavy to me. I tried, nevertheless, and continued to fashion my weapon.

Three days later I was moved to the back bar, where my comrades were. I was put in cell 2-East-54. All around me were comrades and allies. My neighbor in 53 was Lunatic Frank from Rollin' Sixties. Lunatic and I were in the Boy Scouts together in '73. He and I were friends. We had saved each other's lives during our participation in the war.

He and his homies, Pie Face and Ronnie Pace, had caught China and me on Denker and Seventy-fourth Street one night when I was not strapped. We had been at my house making love and she wanted to go home. I was walking her there, pushing Li'l Monster's bike as we went, when they rolled up on us in Pie's Monte Carlo.

"Damn, Sixties," I whispered to China. "Just be cool." They jumped out of the car.

"Well I'll be damned," said Pie Face. "If it ain't the Bonnie and Clyde of Eight Tray—Monster Kody and China."

"What's up, Pie?" I said. I knew all of them.

"Monster, you packin'?" asked Lunatic.

"You know I am," I shot back, lying.

"Cuz, that nigga ain't got no gun. Let's smoke these tramps and get outta here," Ronnie Pace said vehemently.

"No, wait, hold it. I got a better idea," added Pie. "Let's take China from Monster."

"Let her go, man, she ain't got nuttin' to do wit' what we got goin' on," I said.

"Fuck that—" began China, but was cut off by Lunatic.

"Man, this bitch been puttin' mo' work in than a li'l bit. If we take her we can't leave Monsta."

"So what's up?" asked Pie.

"Let's do 'em, man," said Ronnie Pace, looking around nervously.

"Naw, I'll tell you what. You and Monsta go head up, Ronnie."

"What?" said Ronnie, as if not hearing right. "Head up? This nigga didn't go head up wit' our homies he caught slippin'. Ain't no head up in war," he shouted and drew his weapon. "And he ain't got no gun, 'cause he would have already shot us."

Ronnie was scared to fight me, and I zeroed in on that and used it.

"Yeah, I'll go head up wit' cuz," I said.

"I'm a killa, not a fighter," he shot back. "Now either we kill these two—"

"Let's go," said Lunatic, interrupting Ronnie. "You owe me one, Monsta . . . you too, China," he said over his shoulder. And they got in the car and drove off.

China and I did an about-face, went back to my mom's house, and constructed a plan of attack.

Not three weeks later, Tray Stone came around the corner on Eightieth and Halldale with Lunatic on the barrel of his gun—a prisoner of war. Tray Stone was the happiest I had ever seen him. He wanted everyone to see his prisoner.

"Let him go, Stone," I said grudgingly.

"What?!" said Stone, not believing he'd heard correctly.

"I owe cuz one. Turn him loose."

"Damn, cuz, but this Lunatic Frank."

"I know who he is. Let him go."

"Can I just shoot him in the leg, or knock his teeth out?"

"Naw, he let me and China pass one night, so I owe him."

"Shit!" exclaimed Stone. And that was that.

Now, six years later, he was my neighbor. He went by the name Akili Simba and was C.C.O. On the other side of me was a Northern Chicano named Curly.

That first night Akili and I talked all night long on the "telephone," which was made out of a television cable. He had pulled all the wiring out of the black rubber skin, and we used it for private conversations between cells.

The next day I had to turn my paperwork over to the intelligence officer of C.C.O. so he could make sure I wasn't a rat. To those I didn't know I introduced myself as Sanyika, and I instructed those who knew me as Monster to call me by my Kiswahili name. The transformation had begun, and I made a conscious effort to make attachments, connections.

Akili and Kubwa Simba—Leebo from Front Hood, and my closest comrade—helped me sharpen my Kiswahili to a fine point. Within nine months I had a small class of my own. My education at San Quentin was made easy because there were New Afrikans who cared. Asinia taught me the necessity of mathematics, Taliba taught me to recognize our culture as being distinct from Americans, and Zaire (not the same man as my co-defendant) taught me to be scientific. These brothas were Crips—C.C.O., scholars, and theoreticians.

No English was spoken over the tier after six P.M. No foul language was permitted or used in reference to New Afrikan women or men. We had a mandatory study period from seven A.M. to twelve noon. The study period was also a quiet period where no talking was allowed. Seven A.M. also heralded the "alert" period, when every soldier was to be up and out of his kitanda (bed) and dressed. At nine P.M. the alert period ended.

Around this time, Tamu had somehow tracked down Dick Bass, and he'd given her his address to pass on to me. I tried to write to him, but found the pain too great. I began the first page with the normal greeting, but then, naturally, the questions started to surface: *Where have you been?* and *Why did you abandon me?* Eventually it came to *I needed you, man, and you weren't there for me* and *It's people like you who contribute to the destruction of people like me.* As the questions flowed, so did the pain, heart-wrenching pain that made me feel emotionally unstable. I didn't know how to write things down at the time, to communicate my feelings.

I wasn't able to finish the letter, just mailed it half-finished, like his fatherhood had been to me. He never wrote back, which didn't surprise me at all. Through this I learned that I had to be a real father to my own children, no matter what. The pain I was experiencing because of my parents' promiscuity and father's lack of responsibility was not something I wanted my children to feel.

Blue June was slated as a month to remember the fallen soldiers and citizens of the C-Nation. We went to the small S.H.U. yard three times a week—mandatory for all soldiers—and ran while doing the Universal Crip cadence. Then we'd exercise and fall into our classes. Only after this could we play basketball or lift weights. After ten months I began to lead the exercises. I quickly made the transition from soldier to sergeant of arms to intelligence officer.

I believed in what we were doing. I was introduced to Fidel Castro, Mao Tse-tung, Amilcar Cabral, Ho Chi Minh, Kim Il Sung, and George Jackson. My reading picked up, and so did my writing skills. We were given a test on the contents of each book we read and were expected to write a book report about it. The reviewers were stern, and there was no favoritism. I failed so many times that it's not even funny. I kept at it, though, and in time became one of the sharpest in the cadre.

Muhammad kept writing and sending me literature, which helped a lot. He sent one pamphlet called *Were Marx and Engels White Racists?*, which I thought was outstanding. Here were Marx and Engels, blowing about internationalism while neglecting to include the majority of the world's people, who were of color.

We all considered ourselves communists in the C.C.O. Once, when I asked the unit if communism wasn't actually a Eurocentric philosophy, they jumped all over me as if I had committed blasphemy. As I learned, communism as practiced in the Soviet Union was Eurocentric, and Soviet internationalist duty was looking more and more like imperialist conquests.

But I still wanted to know what movement we were attached to, and I complained to the cadre commanders about it. What was our goal as an organization, and who were we trying to liberate? This is where their knowledge fell short. No one was thinking that far ahead. No one realized that the future was three minutes ahead of us, not light years away. As Tamu says, with everything I do I try to do my best, and rightfully so. I am an extremist, so I took our revolutionary premise seriously.

As I grew and my consciousness expanded I began to see cracks and faults in our structure. We were making the same mistakes that the Black Panthers had made. We were importing revolutionary ideals, trying to apply them to our setting. In this light, those who could quote Marx, Mao, or Comrade George the most were the sharpest. It began to irritate the hell out of me. Nothing was corresponding with concrete conditions, and we had no mass appeal. On top of this, our troops sent back out into Babylon were falling prey to parochialism and tribalism.

One such case that caused a problem was that of Mumbles

from the Sixties. He was supposed to try to get his homies to stop clockin' our 'hood, in an attempt to slow down the war. But Mumbles fell back into bangin' and was clocked on Florence and Normandie. The homies stepped to him and he dissed the 'hood. He was executed.

In response, my young homie Joker's door was kicked in, and his innocent sixty-five-year-old mother and fourteen-year-old brother were deliberately murdered. Because Mumbles was C.C.O., they put a blue light on Joker, who had supposedly executed Mumbles. I argued that C.C.O. couldn't blue-light any uncultured Crip for killing a comrade who was in the wrong. Joker was involved in the war and had no idea of what C.C.O. was at that time. He was not responsible to us, but Mumbles was. Mumbles was out of bounds, clocked and tagged in a free-fire zone. If anyone should have been blue-lighted it was the cowards who murdered Joker's people.

It was things like this that caused me to question the leadership of the organization. Also, we had to contend with the new Crip organization—the Blue Notes. They saw themselves as traditionalists and saviors of the Crip culture. The organization was started on death row by Treacherous and Evil from Raymond Avenue Crips, and was supposedly headed by Tookie. B.N.C.O. (Blue Note Crip Organization) gave uncultured Crips an alternative to the rigid, more disciplined organization of C.C.O., which they accused of being too much like the B.G.F.'s. They further accused the C.C.O. leadership of abandoning the protocols of Crip terrorism for some unattainable revolutionary utopia. The B.N.C.O. blossomed quickly, because it appealed to the patriotic sense of Cripping. They also had such stalwart generals as Tookie, Treach, and Evil, who are all extremely smart and courageous.

Other maladies befell the leadership at Folsom, where the Mexican mafia was winning the war. Two Hoovers were stabbed for bringing unsanctioned weapons to the yard. Tony Stacy charged the Central Committee with tribalism and called for all Hoovers in the state to resign from C.C.O. That was a big blow to the organization. Imagine all the Americans pulling out of the Democratic party. The fatal blow came when the Central Committee agreed to a peace treaty with the Mexican mafia, then turned around and declared war on the Blue Notes. The Hoovers sided with the B.N.C.O. and shit began to fall apart.

San Quentin was exempt from none of this. The B.N.C.O. took off and stabbed Kidogo, Rabbit, and Roho. The Hoovers stabbed Notchie and Taliba. The C.C.O. struck back and stabbed Glen, Kencade, and Spark. Shit got crazy, fast. I cut my bed up for weapons with a hacksaw blade but was caught by a snooping pig. They charged me with destruction of state property and billed me $180 for the bed.

I went to my hearing the same day the pigs killed Weusi, a Blood from Pasadena, for defending himself against a Southern Mexican, who was also shot and killed. I refused to sign the trust withdrawal to pay for the bed by saying, "I don't make deals with terrorists who shoot and kill Afrikan people." The pig turned dark red and told the escort pigs to lock me up.

The most important connection I made was through Muhammad, with the New Afrikan Independence Movement. I received the New Afrikan ideological formulation material and it redeemed me. It gave me answers to all the questions I had about myself in relation to this society. I learned about how our situation in this country was that of an oppressed nation, colonized by capitalist-imperialists. The science was strong and precise. I saw then that all the talk of the C-Nation was actually an aspiration of our nationalistic reality. Once I overstood the New Afrikan ideology and pledged my allegiance to the Republic of New Afrika's independence, I began to see Cripping in a different light. There was a faction in C.C.O. at the time claiming to be revolutionary Crips, but this was contradictory and could not be attained without transforming the criminal ideology of Crip and its relation to the masses of people. So the debate was on.

In 1987 we disbanded the C.C.O. in San Quentin. It had failed to evolve because the leadership had failed to realize that real revolution is futuristic, not static. Muhammad came to see me and we had a good visit. I believe he was seeing my growth. My test would come in the real world of society.

In 1987 I met a sister named Akiba Dhoruba Shakur, whom I affectionately called Adimu. She was a student at Cal State, Long Beach, and an aspiring revolutionary. Muhammad had introduced us through the mail, and she and I began to write and discuss politics and the future. All of my influences were positive. Those that were not, I excluded.

That same year I was let out of the Hole and sent to Folsom. All the generals and Central Committee members were there: Askari, Suma, Imara, Tabari, Sunni, and Talib. The Crip population was totally antagonistic toward them, with the exception of Talib, who became my confidant. He saw things as I did, so I turned him on to the New Afrikan Independence Movement.

After six months of ideological struggle with the others, trying to get them to make the leap with us, Talib and I left the Crips and threw our lot in with the Independence Movement.

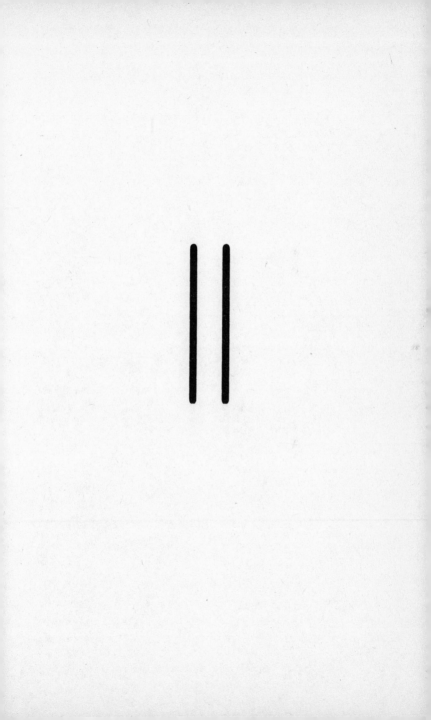

NATION TIME

It's not enough to say that I had transcended the mind-set of being a banger by this time. After having spent thirteen years of my young life inside what had initially seemed like an extended family but had turned into a war machine, I was tired and disgusted with its insatiable appetite for destruction. Destruction no longer fed my narcissism. It was not an expression of my thoughts. I wanted to construct something, which in banging is tantamount to treason.

It took me a full three years to get out of the Crips. I could not just go to the administration building and put in for a transfer to civilian life. I had to practice what I wanted to express, expression eventually to come through the practice of my new beliefs. Getting out turned out to be much like getting in, in the sense of building one's name and deeds in conjunction with what you believe. Many fail in trying to make this break. Some attempt to make the change to civilian life through working, going to school or church, or moving out of the neighborhood. But many find themselves drawn back in by the strong gravitational pull of the safe familiarity of the set and the 'hood.

It was hard for me to truly substantiate my break because the opposition was quite strong and I had no support whatsoever. I knew that my enemies of old would never believe that I had actually stopped, so they would not cease trying to destroy me. My homies would feel let down, disappointed, and perhaps betrayed. And I would be locked in a defensive posture for goodness knows how long.

During my time in Folsom prison I distanced myself as much as possible from the madness of the Crips and the Bloods. Unless it was a racial conflict, I didn't have time to walk, talk, and gather in the realm of negativity. My everyday actions demonstrated my seriousness in respect to my new direction. I got some flak from a few individuals, but overall the initial stages of my transition went smoothly. My daily routine was simple. In the morning I'd go to my electronics class and stay until midafternoon. Once the class let out, I'd do my exercise, which consisted of running and calisthenics. I had long since given up on weights in exchange for a sleek, defined, limber body. I had a job as a clerk in the evenings and would go there after my exercise routine. I used my clerk job to help make others aware of the New Afrikan Independence Movement. I began to write, and in 1988 I completed a piece called "Where Does Correct Terminology Come From?" for one of our publications. It was my first writing, and it was printed. It was so exciting to see my thoughts in print, and was a tremendous help in my revolutionary development. Talib and I were cellmates for most of my two years there.

Surprisingly, the gang community accepted my break and some even began to support my efforts, but this came after an entire year of my steadfast practice. I still talked with all the bangers, and they still talked with me. Some asked questions and others said nothing about my change from banger to revolutionary. I didn't go around trying to persuade the bangers that their line was wrong. But it was wrong to me, though I did not reach that conclusion overnight. Once I recognized it, however, I had to stick with it.

I had faced the realization of who would ultimately be betrayed if I did not stop, which put banging in its proper perspective. While it did and still does supply wayward youth with an idea of collective being and responsibility, in the end it wrecks the lives of its participants and the innocents who live anywhere near its "silo," or base of operations. It is, unfortunately, the extreme expression of hopelessness in New Afrikan communities: misdirected rage in the form of retarded resistance.

To continue banging would be a betrayal first of my children, who now depend on me for guidance, morals, and strength. What type of guidance or morals could I possibly offer from inside the ranks of a group that had no morals, where Monsters and Fat Rats ran around like heroes for wanton acts of mindless aggression? While I take full responsibility for all the wickedness I have done, I do not take pride in it. To me, now, there is no beauty in destruction for destruction's sake.

The second betrayal is that of all those who have been killed in our past, who fought so hard for our freedom only to have us follow in their wake with massive destruction, rolling back most of the community unity they had constructed. What about our obligation to them?

These things are what held me against the all-powerful suction of the set. It was by no means easy, and I wasn't always sure that I had chosen the right path. I got no pats on the back or congratulations from anyone. For a long time it was just Talib and me amidst a sea of antagonists, skeptics, and obdurate onlookers waiting in the wings for me to stumble and fall. I took it one day at a time.

In November of 1988 I was paroled. I had served four years and nine months on a seven-year sentence. I was met in Sacramento by a Muslim that Muhammad had sent to take me to the airport. Akiba had bought the plane ticket. Once I got to the Los Angeles airport I felt much better.

When I entered the terminal I didn't see anybody familiar. Not ten steps later I heard a voice.

"*Freeze!* Put your hands slowly on your head and interlock your fingers."

I didn't even bother to turn around. I went through the motions without a word.

"Where you come in from?" the voice asked. "And what's in the pouch?"

"I am coming from Sacramento."

"Oh yeah? Who were you with up there, huh?"

"A friend of mine from Sacramento City College. He and I were discussing the atmosphere."

"You ain't got no drugs in that pouch, do you?"

"Naw, just some things from school."

"You a student, too?"

"Yeah, I'm a student."

I had learned to tell the pigs, and anyone else for that matter, only what they needed to know. The pig asked where I'd come from and I told him. He asked who I was with and I told him. And yes, I was a student. A student of revolutionary science.

"Motherfucker," whispered a second pig, who'd been searching my pouch, "you just got released from state prison."

"Yeah, it's in Sacramento."

He threw my pouch to the ground, the contents spilling to the floor around my feet. Then the other pig came to my left ear and whispered.

"Welcome home, nigger."

And with that they faded back into the flow of terminal traffic. In my younger years that wouldn't have bothered me much. But with my new direction and expanded consciousness, it struck me hard.

I was picked up by my brotha, Kerwin, and we went straight to my mother's job. She was a bartender. She didn't see us enter the darkened club and before she could spot us we were standing there before her.

"Oh," said Mom, "my baby!"

"Hey, Mom," I said with genuine love and affection as I leaned over the bar to hug her.

"Honey, I've missed you so much."

"Me too, Mom, I've missed you, too." My eyes were shut tight over Mom's shoulder to hold back the rising tide of tears. After all our disagreements, our fights, and my total disregard for her feelings, she still loved me, still supported me. I knew then what she had gone through in trying to raise us, especially

Kershaun and me, who seemingly lived in juvenile hall, court, or some other detention center. Despite this hardship, Mom would faithfully be there every time to plead for our release. Because of us, she took more abuse from the authorities than we ever knew.

"I get off at ten, but I know you have a lot to do, so let's get together tomorrow, all right?"

"Yeah, Mom," I said, wiping my eyes with the back of my hand. "For sure, huh?"

"Yeah, for sure."

"All right, Mom. I love you."

"And I love you, too, baby."

Kerwin and I left and made our way through the South Central streets toward Mom's house, where everyone had gathered for my arrival. I couldn't believe the drabness of the city. Burned-out buildings and vacant houses took up whole blocks. Gas stations and liquor stores owned by Koreans were on every corner. Mexican merchants hung on corners, hawking oranges like dope. The obvious things that had been there all along I now saw differently. Washington Boulevard was wrecked, rife with empty lots and homeless people pushing grocery carts commandeered from supermarkets. They used to seem like lazy bums. Now they seemed to manifest the cruel irresponsibility of society. Graffiti-sprayed walls that I once was able to read and overstand were now scrawled with some illegible markings—a new age in banging, the preppie gangs making their debut.

We got to the house in twenty minutes. When I walked inside it seemed smaller than I had remembered. Everyone was sitting around the table staring at me. They all wanted to know, and no doubt hoped, that Sanyika was real and had finally put to rest the old beast, Monster. No one spoke. They just looked at me, hoping that the first word out of my mouth wouldn't be "cuz."

"Habari za jioni," I said, which is Kiswahili for Good evening, and the whole room seemed to exhale with relief.

No one knew what I had said, but they did know that it was not Crip talk. They all broke into smiles—Tamu, Kendis, Kershaun, and Kerwin.

I tried to explain to them the new path I was taking but it was hard to communicate it all because I was still learning myself.

Kendis seemed the most disturbed by the changes I had made, and I knew it was up to me to better articulate them. My siblings had always paired off in twos: Kevin and Kim got along best and usually stuck together; Kerwin and Kendis were co-conspirators; and Shaun and I were comrades. Never had the six of us gone anywhere together or all gotten along at the same time. Kim went on to join the Air Force and Kevin moved away, seldom to be seen. Kerwin got a job and spied on us for Mom, and Kendis, while trying to remain neutral, leaned hard toward Kerwin and really didn't get along too well with anyone. And Shaun and I were looked upon with dismay by all. Now, here I was, back in the ruins of my family, trying to explain my new path, but somehow not getting it across. Kendis kept cutting her eyes to Kerwin and he kept sighing. Tamu just looked at me and Shaun seemed to be thinking about something else. It was clear that Tamu and Shaun were my brightest prospects for conversion.

Over the next hour, the homies started arriving. First came Red and Eric.

What up, nigga?!" said Red ecstatically.

"Don't call me nigga, Red. I'm cool, you know. Glad to be out and all."

"Right, yeah. Me and E got somethin' for you, Monsta."

"Red, I changed my name. It's Sanyika now."

"Right," said Red like he hadn't even heard my corrections. "Here you go, homie. If you need anything else let us know. We gone."

He handed me a bunch of bills folded neatly. I didn't count them, just put them in my pocket and walked Red and Eric to the door.

"Thanks, homie."

"Righteous. But if you need somethin' else just page me."

"All right, brotha."

When I finally did count the money, I found it was a thousand bucks.

Next came J-Dog, the financier of the 'hood and a stomp-down loyalist, though not much of a talker. He called the house from his Blazer out on the street.

"Yo, cuz, I heard you was out. Is it cool if I come on in?"

"Yeah, Dog, come on in."

Dog was the only New Afrikan I knew with a press and curl. I admired him, though, because he never put nuclear waste in his hair. Dog was cool. Shit, he still wore pork-chop sideburns! He has never denied anyone anything. Like "The Rebirth of Slick" by the comrades from Digable Planets, he was "cool like dat."

"Eh, yo, what up, Monster?" Dog said in his smooth, cool style. As usual, he had blue rollers in his hair and a sweatsuit on.

"Ain't nothin', just coolin' wit' my fam 'bam, kickin' blackness. Oh, and you know I changed my name while I was a prisoner."

"Oh yeah?"

"Yeah, my name is Sanyika now."

"What is that, Muslim?" asked Dog, genuinely curious.

"No, there is no 'Muslim' language. But there is Arabic, that Muslims speak. But my name is Kiswahili."

"Where is Kiswahili? In Afrika, I know."

"There is no place called Kiswahili. Kiswahili is a language spoken in East Afrika."

"That's deep. And how you say it again?"

"San-yi-ka," I said slowly, sounding out the syllables.

"What does that mean? I heard all Afrikan names have meanings, you know, say somethin' 'bout people."

"Pretty much, which shows the depth of our culture. Sanyika means 'unifier, gatherer of his people.' "

"Cool. How you say Dog?"

"Mbwa."

"Naw, that's too hard. People might not never call me," he said and grinned bashfully. "Hey, homie, here you go. And if you need somethin' else, get at me."

"Oh, wait, wait. Yo, what is this, crack?"

"Yeah, it's two zones there for you."

"Dog, I ain't no drug dealer no mo', man. I can't feed my family wit' this. They can't wear this or live in this. How much these zones go for now?"

"Oh," said Dog, looking rather disappointed, "they go fo' five hundred apiece, but I be givin' them to the homies for three hundred."

"Well here," I said, giving Dog back the two ounces, "let

me have six hundred bucks then, 'cause I can't deal no dope. That's treason."

"It's what?"

"Long story, homie." I was getting bored and stir-crazy in the house.

"All right, homie, you drive a hard bargain, but I hear what you sayin'. I can respect that. Here you go." He handed me six hundred dollars.

"Righteous, Dog."

"Only fo' you though, cuz. Oh, and Li'l Monster, too. Cuz' name still Li'l Monster, ain't it?"

"Yeah," I said, getting up to show Dog out, "for right now it is."

When I went back into the living room, Whiteboy Eric was there.

"Get yo' coat on," said Whiteboy.

"Fo' what?"

"So I can take you shoppin' fo' some new clothes and shit. Come on."

"He ain't goin' nowhere, he just got here," complained Tamu.

"Yeah, bro, she's right," I said, happy that Tamu had saved me.

"Well," said Whiteboy, digging into his pocket, "here, then. But I'll be back tomorrow to get you, nigg—"

"Don't call me that," I said with my head down, eyes closed, and hands raised.

"What, nigga?"

"Yeah, that's disrespectin' me, brotha."

"Oh, well excuse me," Whiteboy said with a feigned look of dismay.

"It's all right *this* time."

Everyone looked at one another. They knew that although I had changed my name and reconnected to reality, the 'Monster' still lay dormant.

"Here you go, homes." He handed me the crumpled bills.

"Thank you, E, and I'll be here tomorrow when you swing by, huh?"

"All right then. Watch yourself, too."

"I will."

I closed the door and leaned on it in an exaggeration of exhaustion and told Tamu I'd be ready to go in a minute. I now had $2,100. I gave Shaun $900 of that as he tried to explain what was happening in the 'hood. We had gotten off to ourselves in the back room.

"It's the dope, man, it has tore the 'hood up. Check this out, there are some homies who got a grip from slangin', but they don't come around 'cause they think the homies who ain't got nothin' gonna jack 'em. And the homies who ain't got nothin' feel like those who do got a grip have left them behind. So there is a lot of backbiting, snitchin', and animosity around here now."

"What happened with Crazy De?"

"Poor De, you know he was having big money, right?"

"Yeah, I heard that."

"He tried to wait for you, bro. Said he was gonna make it right for you when you came home. Had a car and everything for you. But De wasn't like the others. He cared about the homies and put a lot of the li'l homies down with crack and straps. He got caught up in some bullshit and was gaffled for two hot ones. I miss cuz, too."

"Yeah, I heard about the murders. Two girls, wasn't it?"

"Yeah, but I don't believe De did it. Cuz is a killa, but he ain't stupid, you know?"

"Yeah, that's right."

"He's in L.A. County. We should swing down there and check him out."

"Yeah," I said, now thinking about something else. "What's up with the Sixties?"

"Same ol' thing, back and forth. They hit us and we hit them. But the dope has slowed down the war too, in a way. While there ain't that many riders on either side willing to put constant work in, everybody got fullies, so one ride usually is enough now to drop several bodies at once."

"Have there been any negotiations with anybody over there?"

"Negotiations? Bro, you ain't hearin' me. *Nothing* has changed, man. The shooting war is in full gear. Negotiations are conducted over the barrels of fullies. Those left standing have won the debate."

"Still like that, huh? You know who was my neighbor in San Quentin?"

"Who?"

"Lunatic Frank. He taught me Kiswahili. We got along good, too."

"Yeah, but Lunatic Frank didn't have no fullie in there, either."

"No, but I doubt that if he had he would have shot me. He has changed."

"*Shot* you? No, let me explain what fullies do. They don't blow you up, they don't shoot you, they *spray* you. Remember when you were shot back in eighty-one, you were hit six times? Bro, Chino just got sprayed with a fullie and he was hit seventeen times! Sprays are permanent. They ain't no joke. We got shit that shoots seventy-five times. I heard that the Santanas got LAWS rockets. The latest things out here are fullies, body armor, and pagers. Offense, defense, and communication. This shit is as real as steel."

"Damn, that's heavy. And you, what you got?"

"I got a Glock model seventeen that shoots eighteen times. It's a hand strap. Bro, this is the real world."

The real world. How ever could I have expected anything else. Although prison had been where I'd acquired knowledge of self and kind, it also was a very simple place. Slow and methodic, almost predictable. This new, highly explosive atmosphere was a bit frightening. It's almost as if I had contributed to a structure here, but then had somehow slept through years of its development, and now was awakening to find a more advanced, horrifying form of the reality I had known. It was shocking. Homeboys who were once without money like the rest of us now had expensive cars, homes, cellular phones, and what seemed to be an endless cash flow. All this talk of fullies and body armor made me feel old. I was like Rip Van Winkle—or, more aptly, Crip Van Winkle.

"So, where does the set stand now, I mean in respect to the larger gang world?" I asked Li'l Bro.

"Well, you see, it's difficult to explain, 'cause nothin' is stable—you can't ever make a statement that can sum up what may happen tomorrow. Everything is fragile, more so than ever before, 'cause it's all about profit. Muhammad says that capitalism has hit the gang world."

"Do you have a job?"

"Naw," he said, his head hanging down, "I slang dope."

And so did everyone else who had no marketable skills or

who was not already on drugs. So little money in the community came from employment that some elderly people had even gotten into the drug trade just to make ends meet. Before I'd do it, though, I might as well put my combat black back on and go out shooting people, the destruction, in the end, being equal.

I found a job as a file clerk and, from that position, rose to assistant loan advisor. Working was not as bad as I had thought it would be. Through my teachings and new consciousness I knew that in order to really feel the actual weight of the state I had to be a part of the working class. This was no easy decision to come to, as most of the brothas in the pen have this I-ain't-workin'-for-whitey attitude. That goes over well in prison, but it didn't seem to hold up out in society, where I was faced with the very real responsibility of taking care of home, bills, and two children, as in addition to Keonda we now had a son, Justin. Initially my job didn't pay much, but I was managing my responsibilities for those who relied on me. It was by no means easy for Tamu and me. We only had one car, and it was old and had problems. And Tamu had moved to Rialto, which is sixty miles outside the city of Los Angeles, while I was a prisoner. So I had to stay in the city on weekdays while I worked and go home to Tamu and the children only on weekends. This gave me the opportunity to be in the community and talk to folks, while maintaining a refuge for weekends with my family.

Tamu and I had grown very close because she had chosen to come into the Movement with me, which firmly cemented our relationship. She appreciated my change and surmised that any organization that could retrieve me from the almost certain clutches of doom couldn't be that bad. We weathered the week-long separations with nightly phone conversations and did things as a family on the weekends.

One particular weekend, while we were driving along in our little raggedy car, we were pulled over by the Rialto police, who proceeded to write Tamu a ticket. I was sitting in the passenger seat and Keonda was in the back. Suddenly, out of nowhere, another police officer came up and began knocking on my window. I ignored him, didn't even look over. I was not driving and he had no need to talk to me. But his knocks became so hard that I feared he'd break the window, so I rolled it down.

"Yeah, what's up?" I asked, still looking forward, not giving the officer the time of day.

"Let me see your I.D.," he said.

"For what? I'm not driving. Why do you need to see my identification?"

"Look, we can do this the hard way or the easy way."

Now Tamu was bending over and craning her neck, trying to see the officer who was talking to me.

"Hey, Miss," said the officer who was writing her the ticket, "over here. You got a problem or something?"

"No," she said, "I haven't got a problem. I just want to see who is talking to my husband."

"He's an officer, and that's all you need to know."

I still hadn't looked over at the one who was talking to me.

"I don't see what my I.D. has to do with any of this," I said, feeling my anger rise.

"If I have to ask you again there's going to be a problem. Now let me see your I.D.!"

And for the first time I looked at him, though I'd already pictured him in my mind. He was a young American male, cocky, full of adrenaline and perhaps an unfocused hatred for me, even though we'd never met. I knew his next move would be to draw his weapon and, with shouts and threats, order me out of the car and onto the ground. Naturally, I didn't want to subject Tamu and Keonda to such treatment, so I handed him my I.D. He took it and went back to his car to run a make on my name. In minutes he returned, clearly agitated.

"What's your real name?"

"Sanyika Shakur," I replied matter-of-factly, knowing that Sanyika Shakur had no record whatsoever. When I was first released I'd had my name changed to Sanyika Shakur, so I could now honestly answer that that was my name.

"No," said the officer, "your real name before you changed it."

"Sanyika Shakur," I said, holding fast, knowing that the only way he could find out that I was once Kody Scott would be to fingerprint me, and he had no cause to take me to the station.

"What was your name before you changed it?" he asked again.

"Sanyika Shakur," I answered once again.

And then from the back seat Keonda said, "No, Daddy," thinking she was offering a helpful tip. "Your real name, that Mommy used to call you."

I turned a few shades darker. I couldn't believe it: Keonda had given me up. Although I wasn't a fugitive, it was the principle of the thing. Simply because Sanyika Shakur was not in the police computer the officer had become suspicious—after all, *every* young New Afrikan male *had* to be in the computer! When I looked up at the officer he had a expression on his face that said, Now was that so hard? I was boiling mad.

"Kody Scott," I said grudgingly, knowing what they'd find under that name. It didn't take long.

"Well, Kody Scott, you are on state prison parole and you are fifty miles from your parole office, which means that I can run you in for violating your parole. But since you have your family with you I won't, this time. But if I stop you again in this town you're going to jail. Do I make myself clear?"

I didn't answer.

"Here you go, *Kody Scott.*" And he threw my I.D. in my lap and slapped the roof of the old car. I was furious.

When we got home I had a father-daughter talk with Keonda. She certainly didn't know any better, but would have to learn. After all, this was the real world.

Kershaun and I were given AK-47s for Christmas by a homeboy who had somehow secured a truckload of them. He had gone around the entire neighborhood passing them out—brand-new, still in the boxes—to O.G.s. When he asked Li'l Bro if there was anyone he thought he shouldn't give one to, Bro replied, "Yeah, Darryl Gates."

Shaun and I began to frequent the firing range weekly, practicing the use of our AKs. Eventually we were able to organize a small shooting club. Meanwhile, I began looking for a job closer to my family, one that afforded me the opportunity to spend more time with the children. It didn't take too long to find employment out in Rialto. And although my parole officer had forbidden me to live there and the police had threatened to jail me if they stopped me again, I had a responsibility to my family. I'd just have to risk it.

I was driven to take risks with my freedom by the frightening thought of being the type of father mine had been to me. Absentee fatherhood was despicable, and I vowed to get to my family when and wherever I could. Being a prisoner for great lengths of time helped in one very real sense: it had prevented me from having multiple children by different women. All of my children are by Tamu. I can't imagine having children and not being able to raise them, to live with them.

The job I found was directly behind our house. I worked for a security firm owned by a New Afrikan man. My job was to simply watch the construction equipment and building materials so that they weren't stolen. My hours were from 11 P.M. till 7 A.M., which gave me most of the day to do things around the house.

My motivation was grounded in being an upright father to my children, a proper husband to Tamu—though we weren't yet married in the traditional sense—and a revolutionary symbol for my people. I went from college campus to college campus passing out pamphlets I had written on Tamu's typewriter. I still held small backyard lectures for the young Eight Trays at my mom's house. But the hardest thing I had to do was go to the Los Angeles County Jail and see Crazy De. I tried everything to avoid going. I made excuses and appointments and outright lied to myself several times in useless attempts to avoid what I knew would be perhaps the most painful thing I'd had to face in some time. Crazy De and I had talked on the phone a few times, and I could almost hear the certainty of the future for him in his words. He'd urge me to come see him and I'd tell him I was busy that particular day or say something else to change the subject. But I believe he knew all along what I was going through. My phone number had gotten out, and soon every one of the homies with murder cases were calling me. I began to function like sort of a counselor to some of them. Others wanted me to neutralize their witnesses. But De, all he wanted was for me to come and see him. I resisted right up until he sent his mother to get me and bring me down to the county jail. When Alma, De's mother, came over, I couldn't refuse. I had to go and face my road dog in jail, where perhaps he'd be trapped for the rest of his life.

Alma and I made most of the trip in silence. I had to gear up psychologically to deal with the police-state atmosphere of the L.A. County Jail visiting room, where some of the officers would take liberties with hassling those visitors they felt were coming to see gang members. Sympathizers, girlfriends, supporters, and especially affiliates were discouraged from being regular visitors. One's dress code often brought down the wrath of the deputies. I no longer dressed like a gang member, but I didn't dress "normal" either. I usually wore a red, black, and green fez, a black t-shirt, and black fatigues bloused over my combat boots. This was my standard attire in 1988 and 1989, long before hip-hop made it fashionable.

Alma and I waited in line for our chance to sign up to see De. I scanned the waiting room, focusing on the women, mostly young New Afrikans and Chicanos, with their children running happily about the filthy room. I began to recall memories of times past I had experienced with Crazy De, my loyal companion. It was De who taught me how to persevere under police interrogation. It was he who'd advised me to stick with Tamu over China because, as he'd explained it, Tamu would teach me things that we could only dream about from where we were then. It was De who'd accompanied me when I visited my godparents' home in Windsor Hills. I'd left him in the van, high on PCP, only to come out with my godmother and find that the van had rolled backward down the hill and onto someone's front lawn. When we got down the hill and opened the van door, De stepped out like an embalmed zombie, in full Crip gear, never having realized that the van had moved. He'd smiled and said, "Nice to meet you, godmama," and Della had damn near fainted. My "dog." I remembered seeing his electric smile through muzzle flashes on many missions. I recalled hearing his hardy laughter echoing off the shack walls in reaction to a good joke. I've seen him in tears of joy, pain, and rage. He taught me how to cry with dignity, with strength, and with pride. That I had learned to express emotions was attributable to De. If I was the epitome of the militarist in the 'hood, then De symbolized the most multifaceted gang member. De was one you wished to have around you at all times, under any circumstances. He was a leader of leaders, with the potential to be a king of kings. But I couldn't get to him in time enough to show him a new path of expression, a meaningful way of achieving realistic goals. A path that emphasized knowledge of self and of kind, while not requiring the dehumanization of anyone else. De would have liked that.

"Visitors for Denard," said a metallic voice over the P.A. system, and Alma and I moved through the crowded visiting room toward the area sectioned off for visitors. De was already there waiting. When he saw us he lit up like a thousand-watt bulb. He talked with Alma first, but kept looking up at me and smiling, his whole face beaming. Knowing that each visit is limited to twenty minutes, Alma spoke quickly and handed me the telephone.

"Hey, you, what's up, De?"

"You," he replied, and then added, "I'm glad you came, Sanyika."

"Yeah, well, you know, I didn't want to have to see you like this."

"I know, but you know what, this may be the only way you will ever see me again. Sanyika, I'm stuck. They caught us dead-bang with a kidnapped hostage. That alone carries a life sentence. On top of that I got two murders. They gonna gas me, homie."

He was staring hard into my face, waiting for a response, a sign that would signal that I could actually feel the weight of what he was expressing. Sitting there with his mother, I didn't know how to respond. What, I wondered, could I say to make him see and feel that I knew what he was going through? And did I really know?

"Damn, De, how you get stuck like that, man? I mean, what . . . " But I couldn't even talk, I was so choked up.

"Dope," he said simply. "One word. You hear me, Sanyika? I've fucked my life up for a kilo of cocaine. Don't get involved in that shit, homie, I'm telling you."

"Naw, naw, I'm not. But, De, I want you to know, man, that I'm here for you. I love you."

"Check this out. You have chosen another path now, some other way to make your mark. And although I'm not what you are and haven't been through some of the things which contributed to your decision to be a revolutionary, I respect what you're doing, and no love is lost from me to you. But you gotta understand that I'm still in this to the fullest. This is all I know. It's Gangsta for life, homie." And then, to get his point fully across he said solemnly, "Gangsterism continues."

This was not a challenge or a smite, just the facts as they were at that moment. De felt perfectly comfortable inside of the chaotic confines of the set and the larger subculture of banging.

To break with the set, I'd had to draw on my well of strength and sum up the courage to step out of myself, my set, my learned ways and take an objective look at what was going on in the world around me. This had been neither easy nor comfortable. The process was slow, often obscured, and always painful. I'd had to look back beyond the good times and happy days to the tears and grief-stricken faces of mothers who had lost their children. I've found that unless you have children you'll never know what it's like to lose a child. I'd had to open my eyes and ears to hear the sounds of clips being pushed in and weapons being cocked, screeching car tires, running feet, the hunted and the hunters, the sudden blasts of gunfire; to see the twisted, lifeless bodies, the wounded still trying to run or crawl, the yellow homicide tape being strung, the tears over a family's lack of funds for a proper burial, the drugs, the alcohol, the angry faces—this process, the way of life for so many, repeated itself over and over. Two sides, each violently throwing itself against the other. These are the scenes that contributed to my awareness: a firsthand knowledge of life and death on the front lines of all-out war.

Although I didn't agree with De's continued participation in the cycle of violence, I did overstand how he could still feel content. I had been fortunate in my capacity to get a perspective and make a break. And now, sitting here with De, I felt fortunate once again.

"De, what I have chosen to do with my life is, I think, the answer to the question of why we bang in the first place. You see, it comes down to—"

But the phone abruptly clicked off, signaling the end of the visit. De heard it, too. We sat there for a moment, just staring at each other, separated from a handshake, a hug, and now conversation by a thick Plexiglas window. When the deputies came to retrieve De and we both stood to go our separate ways, we simultaneously saluted each other—my salute was a clenched fist and his was the Eight Tray sign. The final chain had been broken.

Gangsterism continues. But more importantly, the struggle to eradicate the causes of gangsterism continues. And it is this struggle to which I am dedicated.

EPILOGUE

In January of 1991 I was captured by the L.A.P.D. for assault and grand theft auto. These charges stemmed from a healthy beating I had given a stubborn crack dealer who had refused to stop selling his product on my corner. His van was confiscated because of his stubborn insistence, which led to the GTA charge. I make no excuses for this, and I have no regrets. When the police and other government agencies don't seem to care about what is going on in our communities, then those of us who live in them must take responsibility for their protection and maintenance. As it turned out, this specific dealer was also a paid police informant.

Because of my terrible record, I faced a sentence of seventeen years. I eventually pleaded guilty and received seven years.

When I arrived back at prison, I was immediately put in solitary confinement for an indefinite stay. Charged with being a threat to institutional security, I am now into my third year of solitary confinement.

I admit that I am responsible for deeds that have caused irreparable damage, such as the taking of life, but I did so in a setting that seemed to dictate such action. I do not mean to place total blame on outside forces, though they do play a prominent role in my behavior and that of many others. But I feel I've done nothing to warrant the treatment I've received since returning to prison. I am held here in isolation because of my political views and for assertions I've made.

Many developments have taken place since my capture and incarceration. Kershaun has given up dealing drugs and has come into the New Afrikan Independence Movement. He and his wife have had a child, which I think has contributed greatly to his awareness. He now travels throughout the country giving lectures on the all-powerful trappings of gang activity and the gang life. He and I are still the closest in my family. Tamu and I got married just months before my incarceration and we had another child: Sanyika Kashif Shakur. Crazy De escaped the gas chamber and was given a life sentence without the possibility of parole. He's still dedicated to gangsterism.

One of the most important things to occur was the Rodney King beating, which is not unusual given the current relations between the New Afrikan community and the police. The unique thing about the incident, though, was that it was filmed by someone from the community and shown by the media, which says a lot in itself. For me, it was not so much the beating itself that hit home, but the repeated sight of it actually happening in all of its ugliness. The obvious helplessness of Rodney King as he was pummeled continuously by the robot-like gunslingers, despite the fact that he was clearly submitting: This summed up for me the condition of the New Afrikan man in this country. Rodney King could have been any New Afrikan male in America. He could have been my son.

This incident also brought the realization of my powerlessness crashing down upon me, and with it, my rage and appetite for destruction rose. It was while in this mind-set that I clearly overstood the agitated rage meted out during the 1992 rebellion in Los Angeles, which was truly surprising to me. I wasn't surprised that it occurred—that was inevitable. But I was surprised by the swiftness with which it unfolded. Some people say that the participants burned their own neighborhoods, which seems as crazy as saying that the Vietnamese destroyed their land to route out the Americans. The point I'm trying to make is that the businesses that were destroyed were not owned by the people who lived in those communities. They were owned and operated by folks who live in the suburban areas. The services that they were supplying were provided at astronomical prices, and the products were often inferior. No matter how many Toms try to paint a different scenario, there was a collective consciousness among the oppressed that is evidenced in their selection of targets and items taken. As a victim of exploitation I know the mind-set of the average rebel who took part in the burning and expropriation of goods.

What it boils down to is an overwhelming sense of inadequacy: the invisible man syndrome. The contributing factors are complex and many, and no singular person or group has the absolute solution. From what I've studied and seen it would seem that this country's 130-year-old experiment of multiculturalism has failed. Perhaps it was never designed to work. My fear is that an atmosphere is developing here similar to that in Bosnia and Herzegovina, due to the failure of positive multicultural existence. My personal belief is that separation is the solution.

The majority of Crips and Bloods have come together under the banner of a cease-fire, an effort which I applaud. But realistically, it hasn't accomplished the objective, which I believe was sidetracked by the open media coverage. Before there can ever be Crip and Blood peace there must be Crip and Crip peace. As evidenced by the accounts in this book, the number-one enemy of Crips is other Crips. This fact must be addressed before any one Crip set can come forth with an offer of peace to the Bloods. Although the cease-fire is still holding in Watts, where C.J. from Bounty Hunter and Tony Bogart from PJ Watts first organized it, other parts of South Central are still conducting their "talks" with fullies, body armor, and pagers. During the writing of this Epilogue, two Eight Trays have been killed, reportedly by Rollin' Sixties, bringing the Eight Tray death toll to thirty-two.

And what about the children? What do we tell them, or our wives? How do we come to grips with the fact that this thing has gotten way too real, out of control like some huge snowball rolling down a hill, threatening to smash and kill all in its path, including those who originally fashioned it? Time is of the essence, and every thinking person with a stake in life—especially those involved in the fighting—should put forth an effort, something more concrete than a "media truce," to deal with this tragedy. The children deserve to have a decent childhood where they live. They shouldn't have to be uprooted to the suburbs to experience peace. We cannot contaminate them with our feuds of madness, which are predicated on factors over which we have no control.